Contents

Introduction

Published statistical series and marketing data play an important role in the provision of information for business, industry, economic analysis, academic and other research. In the United Kingdom as in most major economies, Central Government and its departments are the main suppliers of statistical information. These statistics are usually referred to as 'official statistics' and details of the range of official statistics available can be obtained from National Statistics (www.statistics.gov.uk). As well as Central Government, there are many other organizations involved in compiling and disseminating statistics and these include: trade associations, professional bodies, market research organizations, banks, other financial services companies, chambers of commerce, economic research and forecasting organizations, consultants, academic institutions, commercial publishers, and some manufacturing companies. Sources from these publishers form the basis of the entries in this directory, and these resources are usually referred to as 'non-official statistics' to differentiate them from data published by government. They may also be referred to as 'non-governmental statistics'.

Traditionally, the two areas of statistical publishing – official and non-official – have been largely separate from each other, although some trade association data has been used in selected official series, and various non-governmental bodies often lobby and advise government statisticians on statistical series and issues. In recent years, however, the line between official and non-official sources has become increasingly blurred with more official data being distributed and sold through private sector sources, and more data from non-governmental sources being incorporated in government series and services.

This fifth edition of *Sources of Non-official UK Statistics* provides details of almost 900 non-official titles and services, and is a unique and well-established source of information on an important area of business information.

Non-official Statistics

Although Central Government is the major producer of statistics, there are various reasons why these statistics do not always provide sufficient detail on specific markets, sectors, and products. Non-official sources can cover product areas and sectors excluded from Central Government data, and they may also cover different types of data not usually included in official sources. Examples of the latter include end-user statistics covering the consumption of specific products and services rather than just total sales, salary surveys, opinion surveys, product price information, and forecasts. In some cases, non-official sources simply repackage and comment on official data but these commentaries often provide a useful analysis of the major trends in official series. New markets, such as the Internet and mobile technologies, are often covered in more detail by non-official sources. Many of the private sector companies now selling detailed time series from Central Government sources are also adding value to the data with commentaries, ratios, and further analysis based on the original figures.

Prices of non-official statistics can vary from a few pounds to thousands of pounds for detailed research, but a considerable proportion of the UK titles are still available free of charge. More publishers are beginning to put some or all of their statistical output on their web sites and are offering the data as a freely accessible feature.

One disadvantage of non-official statistics is that, in some cases, the material is not available generally. Many trade associations and professional bodies, for example, only circulate material to members while other organizations limit access to clients, survey participants, or others specific groups. However, the percentage of the total non-official output restricted to only a limited group of users is relatively small and, even where detailed statistics are confidential, an executive summary or synopsis of data may be available generally. Another problem is that the reliability and accuracy of the data can vary considerably from one non-official source to the next. The amount of resources devoted to statistical activity, and the level of statistical expertise can vary from one organization to another and this is likely to have an effect on the statistics produced. Only a few sources give details on how the figures have been compiled and the specific methodologies used.

Most of the items included in the directory are clearly statistical publications but non-statistical sources, such as trade journals and yearbooks, are included if they contain a regular statistical series or feature. This edition of the directory also has a separate section in each entry for Web-based sources of statistics where these are available.

Sources included in the Directory

This edition contains information on 879 titles and services produced by over 430 organizations. The entries are based largely on information supplied by the publishers in Spring/Summer 2001, supported by desk research by IRN Services. The compilers would like to thank all those publishing organizations responding to our request for information.

Statistics of interest to business and industry, and which are produced regularly, are included. For a source to be considered as regular, it must be produced at least once every six years. Most publications and services included are either continuous or annual, twice-yearly, quarterly, or monthly. One-off surveys or market reports do not qualify but market reports updated regularly are included.

Only sources issued in, and concerning, the United Kingdom or Great Britain are covered. Material with international coverage has been excluded unless it has a strong element of UK coverage. Some regional sources, relating to Scotland, Wales, Northern Ireland and other regions have been included as well as material covering the capital city, London. Other local statistics on very specific local areas have been excluded.

Most sources included are available generally but there are some titles and services which have a restricted circulation. These have been included as summaries or older editions which may be made available to others. In some cases, publishers have asked to be excluded from the directory and we have agreed to this request.

As well as standard time series statistics, forecasts, trend surveys, and opinion surveys are also included but data dealing with only one corporate body, such as company annual reports, has generally been excluded.

Finally, the sources listed cover a range of delivery formats including the standard book form, those which are produced on one or two sheets of paper such as press releases and pamphlets, through to electronic data available on the Web, or via proprietary databases, CD-ROM, discs, or magnetic tape. Details of statistics available on publisher web sites have been included for the first time.

Structure of the Directory

The directory is divided into the three parts.

Part I The Statistics

The entries are arranged alphabetically by publishing organization, and numbered consecutively. The entries have been based on responses from the publishing bodies themselves supplemented, where possible, by a scanning of the source document. Usually, if an organization publishes more than one title, each title has a separate entry. The exceptions are regular market research surveys produced by one publisher on various topics. As most of these latter surveys follow the same format, they are included in one general entry rather than listed separately.

All of the categories below may be included in an individual entry although some entries may have no information in certain categories if these are not relevant, or if the information is not available:

- **Name** of the publishing body

- **Title** of source

- **Coverage,** including details of any text/analysis supporting the data, and sources of statistics

- **Frequency** of source

- **Web Site,** with details of any data free on site, paid-for access to data, online ordering facilities, or general details of sources

- **Cost,** usually refers to cost per year unless otherwise stated

- **Comments,** about the publication, including any restrictions on availability

- **Address** of publisher

- **Telephone and Fax** numbers

- **Web site and email** URL and address.

Part II Title Index

All the specific titles and services covered in the directory are listed alphabetically here. Titles beginning with numbers are listed at the beginning of the sequence. Annual reports are listed individually under Annual Reports followed by the name of the organization publishing a particular annual report. The numbers given for each title are entry numbers not page numbers.

Part III Subject Index

A detailed subject index containing references to the relevant entry number in Part 1.

Part I

The Statistics

1

	3I PLC
Title	**Enterprise Barometer**
Coverage	Based on an opinion survey of its companies, 3I produces a regular report on likely trends in turnover, profit, investment, employment etc. A commentary supports the statistics.
Frequency	Regular
Web Facilities	
Cost	On request
Comments	Published by Bannock Consulting at the address below.
Address	47 Marylebone Road, London W1M 6LD
Tel./e-mail	0207 535 0200
Fax / Web site	0207 535 0201

2

	ABACUS DATA SERVICES (UK) LTD
Title	**UK Import and Export Statistics**
Coverage	Import and export data, from 1987 onwards, for any traded product with basic data available by value, volume, month or year to date, country of origin, country of destination, port of entry or departure, flag or carrier used. Abacus is an officially appointed agent of HM Customs and Excise.
Frequency	Monthly and Annual
Web Facilities	General details of statistics, and ordering facilities, on Web site.
Cost	Depends on information required
Comments	Data available in various machine readable formats including CD-ROM, diskette.
Address	Waterloo House, 59 New Street, Chelmsford CM1 1NE
Tel./e-mail	01245 252222 info@abacusuk.co.uk
Fax / Web site	01245 252244 www.abacusuk.co.uk

3

	ABSA
Title	**Business Support for the Arts**
Coverage	An annual review of business sponsorship of the arts broken down by type of sponsorship, type of art form, regions. Based on data collected by the association.
Frequency	Annual
Web Facilities	Free key findings section on site, plus news.
Cost	£40, £20 to members
Comments	ABSA is the Association for Business Sponsorship of the Arts. Basic statistics from the annual survey freely available on the web site.
Address	Nutmeg House, 60 Gainsford Street, Butlers Wharf, London SE1 2NY
Tel./e-mail	0207 378 8143 info@absa.org.uk
Fax / Web site	0207 378 7527 www.absa.org.uk

4

Title
Coverage

AC NIELSEN MMS
Digest of UK Advertising Expenditure
Total advertising expenditure for brands spending over £75,000 per annum. 550 product groups are included. Data covers the latest quarter, a monthly breakdown within the quarter, and a moving annual total. Based on a monitoring of advertising in the press, television, satellite TV, radio, outdoor, and the cinema.

Frequency
Quarterly

Web Facilities

Cost
On request

Comments

Address
Madison House, High Street, Sunninghill, Ascot SL5 9NP

Tel./e-mail
01344 627583   mms@mediamonitoring.co.uk

Fax / Web site
01344 621037

5

Title
Coverage

ADECCO
Adecco Salary Survey
A survey of salaries based on 11 job categories and covering over 6,000 specific jobs in industrial and service sectors. Based on data collected by the company.

Frequency
Annual

Web Facilities
Summary details on site.

Cost
Free to clients, price to others on request

Comments

Address
Adecco House, Elstree Way, Borehamwood WD6 1HY

Tel./e-mail
0208 307 6336

Fax / Web site
0208 236 0253   www.adecco.co.uk

6

Title
Coverage

ADMAP
Adstats
Statistics on various aspects of advertising and the media including total expenditure, expenditure by media, expenditure in selected product categories. Most of the data is from Advertising Association surveys.

Frequency
Monthly in a monthly journal

Web Facilities

Cost
£220

Comments

Address
NTC Publications Ltd, Farm Road, Henley-on-Thames RG9 1EJ

Tel./e-mail
01491 411000   info@warc.com

Fax / Web site
01491 418000   www.warc.com

7

Title — ADVERTISING ASSOCIATION
Quarterly Survey of Advertising Expenditure

Coverage — Summary tables on advertising trends by main media followed by specific sections on the total press, national newspapers, regional newspapers, consumer magazines, business and professional magazines, and all magazines. A final section looks at trends in specific industry sectors.

Frequency — Quarterly

Web Facilities — Some free statistics available on the site.

Cost — £595, £395 for members of the Advertising Association

Comments

Address — NTC Publications Ltd, Farm Road, Henley-on-Thames RG9 1EJ

Tel./e-mail — 01491 411000   info@ntc.co.uk

Fax / Web site — 01491 418600   www.adassoc.org.uk

8

Title — ADVERTISING ASSOCIATION
Advertising Forecast

Coverage — Forecasts for the main media categories - TV, radio, newspapers, colour supplements, magazines, classifieds, display advertising and posters. Also forecasts of expenditure in the main product sectors, eg retail, industrial, financial, government, services, durables, and consumables. Historical data is also included.

Frequency — Quarterly

Web Facilities — Some free statistics on the site.

Cost — £825, £495 for members

Comments

Address — NTC Publications Ltd, Farm Road, Henley-on-Thames RG9 1EJ

Tel./e-mail — 01491 411000   info@ntc.co.uk

Fax / Web site — 01491 418600   www.adassoc.org.uk

9

	ADVERTISING ASSOCIATION
Title	**Advertising Statistics Yearbook**
Coverage	General trends in advertising and the annual Advertising Association survey. Statistics by type of advertising, eg cinema, direct mail, poster, newspapers, magazines, directories, radio, TV. Also statistics on prices, expenditure by product sector, top advertisers, agencies, complaints, attitudes, and international trends. Data for earlier years and based on various sources.
Frequency	Annual
Web Facilities	Some free statistics available on the site.
Cost	£125
Comments	
Address	NTC Publications Ltd, Farm Road, Henley-on-Thames RG9 1EJ
Tel./e-mail	01491 411000 info@ntc.co.uk
Fax / Web site	01491 418600 www.adassoc.org.uk

10

	ADVERTISING ASSOCIATION
Title	**Long Term UK Advertising Expenditure Forecasts**
Coverage	Tables and commentary on advertising expenditure expectations for the next 10 years.
Frequency	Annual
Web Facilities	Some free statistics available on the site.
Cost	£950
Comments	
Address	NTC Publications Ltd, Farm Road, Henley-on-Thames RG9 1EJ
Tel./e-mail	01491 411000 info@ntc.co.uk
Fax / Web site	01491 418600 www.adassoc.org.uk

11

	ADVERTISING STANDARDS AUTHORITY
Title	**ASA Annual Report**
Coverage	Gives a summary of complaints received by media and by type. Based on complaints received by the ASA.
Frequency	Annual
Web Facilities	Full free access to all statistics on site (including historical data).
Cost	Free
Comments	Also publishes summary monthly complaints figures in ASA Monthly Report.
Address	2 Torrington Place, London WC1E 7HW
Tel./e-mail	0207 580 5555
Fax / Web site	0207 631 3051 www.asa.org.uk

12	
	AGRICULTURAL ENGINEERS' ASSOCIATION
Title	**Trade Statistics**
Coverage	Import and export data for agricultural products and machinery based on Central Government trade statistics.
Frequency	Quarterly
Web Facilities	
Cost	On request
Comments	Also produces price guides for agricultural products and machinery.
Address	Samuelson House, Orton Centre, Peterborough PE2 0LT
Tel./e-mail	01733 371381
Fax / Web site	01733 370664 www.aea-farm-machinery.co.uk

13	
	ALAN JONES & ASSOCIATES
Title	**Maternity & Childcare Policy Survey Report**
Coverage	A survey of UK trends regarding maternity and childcare trends, based on original research by the company.
Frequency	Twice yearly
Web Facilities	General details of all surveys on site.
Cost	£140
Comments	Various other surveys and reports published.
Address	Apex House, Wonastow Road, Monmouth NP25 5JB
Tel./e-mail	01600 716916 apexhouse@easynet.co.uk
Fax / Web site	01600 715521 www.alan-jones.co.uk

14	
	ALAN JONES & ASSOCIATES
Title	**Company Car Survey Report**
Coverage	A survey of the UK company car market based on research by the company.
Frequency	Annual
Web Facilities	General details of all surveys on site.
Cost	£165
Comments	Various other surveys and reports published.
Address	Apex House, Wonastow Road, Monmouth NP25 5JB
Tel./e-mail	01600 716916 apexhouse@easynet.co.uk
Fax / Web site	01600 715521 www.alan-jones.co.uk

15	ALAN JONES & ASSOCIATES
Title	**Shift and Overtime Survey Report**
Coverage	A survey of UK trends in shift and overtime work based on original research by the company.
Frequency	Twice yearly
Web Facilities	General details of all surveys on site.
Cost	£140
Comments	Various other surveys and reports published.
Address	Apex House, Wonastow Road, Monmouth NP25 5JB
Tel./e-mail	01600 716916 apexhouse@easynet.co.uk
Fax / Web site	01600 715521 www.alan-jones.co.uk
16	ALAN JONES & ASSOCIATES
Title	**Benefits Summary**
Coverage	An annual review of trends in benefits with data taken from the various salary surveys undertaken by the company.
Frequency	Annual
Web Facilities	General details of all publications on site.
Cost	On request
Comments	Various other surveys published.
Address	Apex House, Wonastow Road, Monmouth NP25 5JB
Tel./e-mail	01600 716916 apexhouse@easynet.co.uk
Fax / Web site	01600 715521 www.alan-jones.co.uk
17	ALAN JONES & ASSOCIATES
Title	**Salary Surveys**
Coverage	The company publishes over 50 salary surveys including general, geographical, industry, job function, and specialist surveys.
Frequency	Regular
Web Facilities	General details of all publications on site.
Cost	On request
Comments	
Address	Apex House, Wonastow Road, Monmouth NP25 5JB
Tel./e-mail	01600 716916 apexhouse@easynet.co.uk
Fax / Web site	01600 715521 www.alan-jones.co.uk

18	**ALUMINIUM FEDERATION LTD**
Title	**Aluminium Federation Annual Report**
Coverage	Contains some basic statistics covering production, overseas trade etc.
Frequency	Annual
Web Facilities	
Cost	£1
Comments	More detailed statistics available to members.
Address	Broadway House, Calthorpe Road, Five Ways, Birmingham B15 1TN
Tel./e-mail	0121 456 1103 alfed@alfed.org.uk
Fax / Web site	0121 456 2274 www.alfed.org.uk

19	**APPAREL KNITTING AND TEXTILES ALLIANCE**
Title	**Trends in Textile and Clothing Trade**
Coverage	Detailed import and export statistics for textiles and clothing based on Central Government trade data.
Frequency	Quarterly
Web Facilities	
Cost	£85, free to members
Comments	
Address	5 Portland Place, London W1N 3AA
Tel./e-mail	0207 636 7788
Fax / Web site	0207 636 7515

20	**APPLIED MARKET INFORMATION LTD**
Title	**20-- UK Plastic Industry Handbook**
Coverage	An analysis of trends in the polymer industry and key polymer markets with statistics on production, consumption, capacity, and end user markets.
Frequency	Annual
Web Facilities	General details of publications on site.
Cost	£130
Comments	
Address	45-47 Stokes Croft, Bristol BS1 3QP
Tel./e-mail	0117 9249442
Fax / Web site	0117 9241598 www.amiplastics.co.uk

21	ARCHITECTS' JOURNAL
Title	**Workload Survey**
Coverage	Workload trends for the latest quarter compared to the previous quarter and the corresponding quarter in the previous year. Includes data on the value of new commissions, staffing levels, and sector trends. Based on a survey by the journal.
Frequency	Quarterly in a weekly journal
Web Facilities	
Cost	£75, £2 per issue
Comments	
Address	EMAP Construct, 151 Rosebery Avenue, London EC1R 4QX
Tel./e-mail	0207 505 6600
Fax / Web site	0207 505 6701 www.emapconstruct.co.uk/aj/aj.htm
22	ARCHITECTS' JOURNAL
Title	**Industry Forecast**
Coverage	Commentary and statistics on likely trends in the architecture sector in the coming 12 months.
Frequency	Annual
Web Facilities	
Cost	£75, £1.80 per issue
Comments	
Address	EMAP Construct, 151 Rosebery Avenue, London EC1R 4QX
Tel./e-mail	0207 505 6600
Fax / Web site	0207 505 6701 www.emapconstruct.co.uk/aj/aj.htm
23	ASSOCIATION FOR PAYMENT CLEARING SERVICES
Title	**Plastic Card Review**
Coverage	A review of trends in the credit card market.
Frequency	Annual
Web Facilities	General details and free summary data on site
Cost	£50
Comments	
Address	Mercury House, Triton Court, 14 Finsbury Square, London EC2A 1LQ
Tel./e-mail	0207 7116 359 publicaffairs@apacs.org.uk
Fax / Web site	0207 7116 276 www.apacs.org.uk

24

	ASSOCIATION FOR PAYMENT CLEARING SERVICES
Title	**Annual Review**
Coverage	A review of bank clearings and payment trends based mainly on data from members.
Frequency	Annual
Web Facilities	General details and free summary data on site
Cost	Free
Comments	
Address	Mercury House, Triton Court, 14 Finsbury Square, London EC2A 1LQ
Tel./e-mail	0207 7116 359 publicaffairs@apacs.org.uk
Fax / Web site	0207 7116 276 www.apacs.org.uk

25

	ASSOCIATION FOR PAYMENT CLEARING SERVICES
Title	**Yearbook of Payment Statistics**
Coverage	Statistics on the turnover of inter-bank clearings, automated clearings, inter-branch clearings, Scottish clearings, and London currency dealings. Based on figures collected by APACS from its members.
Frequency	Annual
Web Facilities	General details and free summary data on site
Cost	£100
Comments	
Address	Mercury House, Triton Court, 14 Finsbury Square, London EC2A 1LQ
Tel./e-mail	0207 7116 359 publicaffairs@apacs.org.uk
Fax / Web site	0207 7116 276 www.apacs.org.uk

26

	ASSOCIATION FOR PAYMENT CLEARING SERVICES
Title	**In Brief - Payments Market Briefing**
Coverage	A general review of trends in the payments market based mainly on data from members. Included are forecasts up to ten years ahead.
Frequency	Annual
Web Facilities	General details and free summary data on site
Cost	Free
Comments	
Address	Mercury House, Triton Court, 14 Finsbury Square, London EC2A 1LQ
Tel./e-mail	0207 7116 359 publicaffairs@apacs.org.uk
Fax / Web site	0207 7116 276 www.apacs.org.uk

27	**ASSOCIATION FOR PAYMENT CLEARING SERVICES**
Title	**Clearing Statistics**
Coverage	Statistics on the turnover of inter-bank clearings through the clearing house and automated clearings. Based on figures collected by APACS from its members.
Frequency	Monthly and Annual
Web Facilities	Free access to the latest Clearing Statistics on the site.
Cost	Free
Comments	
Address	Mercury House, Triton Court, 14 Finsbury Square, London EC2A 1LQ
Tel./e-mail	0207 7116 359 publicaffairs@apacs.org.uk
Fax / Web site	0207 7116 276 www.apacs.org.uk
28	**ASSOCIATION OF BRITISH INSURERS**
Title	**Insurance Trends**
Coverage	Includes articles on current trends and issues plus 27 statistical tables based mainly on the association's own surveys. Produced in January, April, July, and October.
Frequency	Quarterly
Web Facilities	General details of statistics, some free summary data, and paid-for access to all data on site. Annual online subscription for data - £2,000
Cost	£25
Comments	
Address	51 Gresham Street, London EC2V 7HQ
Tel./e-mail	0207 600 3333 info@abi.org.uk
Fax / Web site	0207 696 8996 www.abi.org.uk
29	**ASSOCIATION OF BRITISH INSURERS**
Title	**Facts, Figures and Trends**
Coverage	
Frequency	Quarterly
Web Facilities	General details of statistics, some free summary data and paid-for access to all data on site. An online subscription for data - £2,000
Cost £25	
Comments	
Address	51 Gresham Street, London EC2V 7HQ
Tel./e-mail	0207 600 3333 info@abi.org.uk
Fax / Web site	0207 696 8996 www.abi.org.uk

30 ASSOCIATION OF BRITISH INSURERS

Title	**Insurance Statistics Yearbook**
Coverage	Detailed figures on all classes of long-term and general insurance and most statistics cover a 10 year period. For long-term business, the information includes sources of new business, long-term business revenue accounts, and investment of funds. For general business, the data given includes revenue account figures by class and for UK and overseas business. Based on the association's own survey and usually published in October.
Frequency	Annual
Web Facilities	General details of statistics, some free summary data and paid-for access to all data on site. Annual online subscription for data - £2,000
Cost	£55
Comments	
Address	51 Gresham Street, London EC2V 7HQ
Tel./e-mail	0207 600 3333 info@abi.org.uk
Fax / Web site	0207 696 8996 www.abi.org.uk

31 ASSOCIATION OF BUSINESS RECOVERY PROFESSIONALS (R3)

Title	**Survey of Personal Insolvency**
Coverage	An analysis of personal insolvency trends over the last year based on returns from members. The latest issue is based on over 1,200 individual cases.
Frequency	Annual
Web Facilities	Free access to report on the site.
Cost	Free
Comments	Previously known as the Society of Practitioners in Insolvency.
Address	Halton House, 2-23 Holborn, London EC1N 2DE
Tel./e-mail	0207 831 6563 association@r3.org.uk
Fax / Web site	0207 405 7047 www.r3.org.uk

32

ASSOCIATION OF BUSINESS RECOVERY PROFESSIONALS (R3)

Title	**Survey of Business Recovery in the UK**
Coverage	Based on returns from members, this report shows the trends in company insolvencies over the last 12 months. The report analyses the reasons for failure and the characteristics of failed companies. Based on almost 3,000 individual cases.
Frequency	Annual
Web Facilities	Free access to report on site.
Cost	Free
Comments	Previously known as the Society of Practitioners in Insolvency
Address	Halton House, 2-23 Holborn, London EC1N 2DE
Tel./e-mail	0207 831 6563 association@r3.org.uk
Fax / Web site	0207 405 7047 www.r3.org.uk

33

ASSOCIATION OF CATERING EQUIPMENT MANUFACTURERS AND IMPORTERS (CESA)

Title	**UK Catering Equipment Market**
Coverage	Based on returns from member companies, and estimates of sales by non-members, the association produces statistics for sales, imports, and exports broken down by type of catering equipment.
Frequency	Annual
Web Facilities	
Cost	Free
Comments	Usually only available to members but requests considered.
Address	Carlyle House, 235 Vauxhall Bridge Road, London SW1V 1EJ
Tel./e-mail	0207 233 7724 enquiries@cesa.org.uk
Fax / Web site	0207 828 0667 www.cesa.org.uk

34

ASSOCIATION OF CONTACT LENS MANUFACTURERS

Title	**Annual Statistics**
Coverage	Annual statistics relating to the sales of contact lenses and contact lens solutions. Based on a survey of members' sales by the association.
Frequency	Annual
Web Facilities	News items about new research with some data on site.
Cost	
Comments	Published in the association's journal.
Address	PO Box 735, Devizes, Wiltshire SN10 3TQ
Tel./e-mail	01380 860418
Fax / Web site	01380 860121 www.aclm.org.uk

35	**ASSOCIATION OF FRANCHISED DISTRIBUTORS OF ELECTRONIC COMPONENTS**
Title	**AFDEC Statistical Forecasts**
Coverage	Forecasts of market trends for electronic components based on research by the association.
Frequency	Regular
Web Facilities	
Cost	On request
Comments	
Address	Owles Hall, Owles Lane, Buntingford SG9 9PL
Tel./e-mail	01763 271209 afdic@owles.co.uk
Fax / Web site	01763 273255

36	**ASSOCIATION OF INSURERS AND RISK MANAGERS**
Title	**Status and Salaries Report**
Coverage	A twice-yearly survey covering salary and trends in working conditions for insurers and risk managers. Based on a survey by the association.
Frequency	Twice yearly
Web Facilities	
Cost	£25, free to members
Comments	Also publishes various research reports.
Address	6 Lloyds Avenue, London EC3N 3AX
Tel./e-mail	0207 480 7610 enquiries@airimic.com
Fax / Web site	0207 702 3752 www.airmic.com

37	**ASSOCIATION OF MANUFACTURERS OF DOMESTIC ELECTRICAL APPLIANCES (AMDEA)**
Title	**AMDEA Survey Yearbook**
Coverage	Deliveries by UK manufacturers and imports by country of origin for various appliances including fridges, freezers, dryers, washing machines, cookers, vacuum cleaners, heaters, electric blankets etc. Additional data on prices and employment. Based primarily on AMDEA data supported by some official statistics.
Frequency	Annual
Web Facilities	Web site under development at time of compilation.
Cost	£600, or £750 combined subscription with AMDEA Quarterly Statistics (see next entry)
Comments	
Address	Rapier House, 40-46 Lambs Conduit Street, London WC1N 3NW
Tel./e-mail	0207 405 0666 info@amdea.org.uk
Fax / Web site	0207 405 6609

38

ASSOCIATION OF MANUFACTURERS OF DOMESTIC ELECTRICAL APPLIANCES (AMDEA)

Title **AMDEA Quarterly Statistics**

Coverage Deliveries and imports of various electrical appliances covering over 25 product headings. Similar data to that contained in the AMDEA Statistical Yearbook (see entry above) with statistics for the latest quarter and summary data for the earlier quarter. Based primarily on AMDEA data supported by some official statistics.

Frequency Quarterly

Web Facilities Web site under development at time of compilation.

Cost £750, combined subscription with AMDEA Statistical Yearbook

Comments

Address Rapier House, 40-46 Lambs Conduit Street, London WC1N 3NW

Tel./e-mail 0207 405 0666   info@amdea.org.uk

Fax / Web site 0207 405 6609

39

ASSOCIATION OF MANUFACTURERS OF DOMESTIC ELECTRICAL APPLIANCES (AMDEA)

Title **AMDEA Monthly Statistics**

Coverage Monthly data in 16 separate reports each covering a specific product sector. There is also a summary volume. Based on data collected by the association.

Frequency Monthly

Web Facilities Web site under construction at time of compilation.

Cost Prices range from £250 to £1,000 (summary) per report.

Comments

Address Rapier House, 40-46 Lambs Conduit Street, London WC1N 3NW

Tel./e-mail 0207 405 0666

Fax / Web site 0207 405 6609

40

ASSOCIATION OF UNIT TRUSTS AND INVESTMENT TRUSTS

Title **Quarterly Chart Pack**

Coverage Quarterly summary of average UK equity income.

Frequency Quarterly

Web Facilities Freely available on site.

Cost Free

Comments

Address 65 Kingsway, London   WC2B 6TD

Tel./e-mail 0207 831 0898   Autif@investmentfunds.org.uk

Fax / Web site 0207 831 9975   www.investmentfunds.org.uk

41

ASSOCIATION OF UNIT TRUSTS AND INVESTMENT TRUSTS

Title **Investment Funds Statistics**

Coverage Sales of units trusts, ISAs, OEICs, and PEPs in the previous month, comparisons with earlier months, and cumulative data. Based on the association's own survey and accompanied by a commentary.

Frequency Monthly

Web Facilities Freely available on site.

Cost Free

Comments

Address 65 Kingsway, London   WC2B 6TD

Tel./e-mail 0207 831 0898   autif@investmentfunds.org.uk

Fax / Web site 0207 831 9975   www.investmentfunds.org.uk

42

AUDIENCE SELECTION

Title **Key Directors Omnibus**

Coverage 200 managing directors and 200 finance directors from the top 10% of UK companies are interviewed each quarter. Results cover purchasing trends, brand awareness, advertising awareness, readership trends etc.

Frequency Quarterly

Web Facilities

Cost Varies according to amount and nature of data required

Comments Results available on disc. Other packages and special analysis available.

Address 14-17 St John's Square, London   EC1M 4HE

Tel./e-mail 0207 608 3618   info@audsel.com

Fax / Web site 0207 608 3286   www.audsel.com

43

AUDIENCE SELECTION

Title **Phonebus**

Coverage A general omnibus survey carried out every weekend with a sample size of around 1,000. Questions can be agreed up to the Friday and results are available on the Monday.

Frequency Weekly

Web Facilities

Cost Varies according to amount and nature of data required

Comments Results available on disc. Other packages and special analysis available.

Address 14-17 St John's Square, London   EC1M 4HE

Tel./e-mail 0207 608 3618   info@audsel.com

Fax / Web site 0207 608 3286   www.audsel.com

44	**AUDIT BUREAU OF CIRCULATIONS LTD (ABC)**
Title	**ABC Review**
Coverage	A well-established report on audited certified net sales, circulation, and distribution data for over 2,000 publications. Covers journals, magazines, and newspapers. Based on a survey by the company.
Frequency	Twice yearly
Web Facilities	Free access to circulation data for 3,500 magazines, newspapers, directories, exhibitions on site. Also link to ABC Electronic.
Cost	£150, £15 to members
Comments	The data is held on a computerised database and various packages and searches are available. Also publishes monthly National Newspaper Figures (annual subscription - £495).
Address	Black Prince Yard, 207-209 High Street, Berkhamstead HP4 1AD
Tel./e-mail	01442 870800 rayh@abc.org.uk
Fax / Web site	01422 877407 www.abc.org.uk
45	**AUTOMATIC VENDING ASSOCIATION**
Title	**AVA Census**
Coverage	In 1994, the association carried out its first detailed census of the beverage and snack foods vending sector. The survey, now produced annually, has details of machines in use, types of machines, products vended.
Frequency	Annual
Web Facilities	Some free summary data on the site
Cost	£175
Comments	Now AVA but previously AVAB - the Automatic Vending Association of Great Britain.
Address	1 Villiers Court, Upper Mulgrave Road, Cheam SM2 7AJ
Tel./e-mail	0208 661 1112 info@ava-vending.org
Fax / Web site	0208 661 2224 www.ava-vending.org

46	BAA PLC
Title	**BAA Airport Traffic Data**
Coverage	Based on an ongoing survey of passenger, freight and aircraft movements at BAA airports, this regular publication has statistics on UK traffic.
Frequency	Regular
Web Facilities	
Cost	Varies according to the amount of data required
Comments	
Address	Jubilee House, Furlong Way, North Terminal, Gatwick Airport RH6 0JN
Tel./e-mail	0870 000 2468
Fax / Web site	www.baa.co.uk

47	BAA PLC
Title	**BAA Monthly Traffic Summary**
Coverage	Based on traffic counts of freight, passengers and aircraft at BAA airports, this monthly report is a traffic summary for the UK.
Frequency	Monthly
Web Facilities	
Cost	On request
Comments	
Address	Jubilee House, Furlong Way, North Terminal, Gatwick Airport RH6 0JN
Tel./e-mail	0870 000 2468
Fax / Web site	www.baa.co.uk

48	BAA PLC
Title	**Patterns of Traffic**
Coverage	Based on traffic counts at BAA airports, an annual report on passenger movements in the United Kingdom.
Frequency	Annual
Web Facilities	
Cost	£10
Comments	More detailed statistics available to members who participate in the survey.
Address	Jubilee House, Furlong Way, North Terminal, Gatwick Airport RH6 0JN
Tel./e-mail	0870 000 2468
Fax / Web site	www.baa.co.uk

49	BANK OF ENGLAND
Title	**Bank of England Monetary & Financial Statistics**
Coverage	Statistical data covering UK and international banking, money stock, official market operations, government finance, reserves and official borrowing, exchange rates, interest rates and national financial accounts. Mainly the bank's own figures.
Frequency	Monthly and Quarterly
Web Facilities	The whole publication is available free on the Web site. Monthly data on the Web site and quarterly in hard copy.
Cost	£60 subscription for hard copy
Comments	
Address	Monetary and Financial Statistics Division, Threadneedle Street, London EC2R 8AH
Tel./e-mail	0207 601 5353
Fax / Web site	0207 601 3208 www.bankofengland.co.uk

50	BANK OF ENGLAND
Title	**Bank of England Statistical Abstract**
Coverage	Annual statistics, with historical data, on monetary and financial trends based largely on the bank's own figures.
Frequency	Annual
Web Facilities	The whole publication is available free on the Web site.
Cost	£25 for hard copy
Comments	
Address	Monetary and Financial Statistics Division, Threadneedle Street, London EC2R 8AH
Tel./e-mail	0207 601 5353
Fax / Web site	0207 601 3208 www.bankofengland.co.uk

51	BANK OF ENGLAND
Title	**Inflation Report**
Coverage	A review of current price trends in the economy and the outlook for prices in the short term.
Frequency	Monthly
Web Facilities	The whole publication is available free on the Web site
Cost	£12, or £40 with a combined subscription to Bank of England Quarterly Bulletin
Comments	
Address	Monetary and Financial Statistics Division, Threadneedle Street, London EC2R 8AH
Tel./e-mail	0207 601 4353
Fax / Web site	0207 601 3208 www.bankofengland.co.uk

52	BARCLAYS BANK
Title	**Annual Importers Survey**
Coverage	A survey covering importing and re-exporting in the UK market. Highlights the impact that the downturn in the global economy is having on importers.
Frequency	Annual
Web Facilities	Free access to reports on site.
Cost	On request
Comments	
Address	6th Floor St Swithin's House, 11-12 St Swithins Lane, London EC4N 8AS
Tel./e-mail	0207 621 5408
Fax / Web site	0207 621 5409 www.barclays.co.uk/economic reports/

53	BARCLAYS BANK
Title	**Small Business Bulletin**
Coverage	Analysis and data on forthcoming trends in the small business sector and developments over the previous few months.
Frequency	Regular
Web Facilities	Free access to reports on site.
Cost	On request
Comments	Also publishes various short pamphlets on specific UK markets and sectors.
Address	1 Wimborne Road, Poole BH15 2BB
Tel./e-mail	01202 671212
Fax / Web site	01202 402303 www.barclays.co.uk/economic reports/

54	BARCLAYS BANK
Title	**UK Construction Survey**
Coverage	Commentary, graphs, and statistical tables covering trends in the UK construction industry. Based on various official and non-official sources.
Frequency	Regular
Web Facilities	Free access to reports on site.
Cost	Free
Comments	Also publishes various short pamphlets on specific UK markets and sectors.
Address	1 Wimborne Road, Poole BH15 2BB
Tel./e-mail	01202 671212
Fax / Web site	01202 402303 www.barclays.co.uk/economic reports/

55 BARCLAYS BANK

Title	**UK Economic Review**
Coverage	A general commentary on the UK and international economy and a statistical appendix with data on exchange rates, interest rates, money market. Text covers 50% of the report.
Frequency	Quarterly
Web Facilities	Free access to reports on site.
Cost	Free
Comments	Also publishes various short pamphlets on specific UK markets and sectors.
Address	1 Wimborne Road, Poole BH15 2BB
Tel./e-mail	01202 671212
Fax / Web site	01202 402303 www.barclays.co.uk/economicreports/

56 BEAUFORT RESEARCH LTD

Title	**Welsh Omnibus Survey**
Coverage	A quarterly survey of a sample of 1,000 adults resident in Wales. Data on opinions, attitudes, advertising and product recall and awareness, purchase and usage, image and perception. Analysis available by sex, age, gender, social class, region, Welsh speaking.
Frequency	Quarterly
Web Facilities	
Cost	On request
Comments	Also carries out a regular omnibus survey of Welsh speakers.
Address	2 Museum Place, Cardiff CF1 3BG
Tel./e-mail	01222 378565 beaufortr@aol.com
Fax / Web site	01222 382872

57 BIRDS EYE WALL'S LTD

Title	**Children's Pocket Money Monitor**
Coverage	A commissioned research survey of pocket money given to 5 to 16 year-olds in the UK. Covers average weekly pocket money by age, region, and sex plus earnings from jobs and friends and relatives.
Frequency	Annual
Web Facilities	
Cost	Free
Comments	
Address	Station Avenue, Walton-on-Thames KT12 1NT
Tel./e-mail	01932 263 000
Fax / Web site	01932 263 788

58

BISCUIT, CAKE, CHOCOLATE & CONFECTIONERY ALLIANCE (BCCCA)

Title **Statistical Yearbook**

Coverage Statistics on the deliveries to the home and export markets of biscuits, cakes, and confectionery. Historical trends and data on specific product areas. Based largely on surveys of members with supporting data from other sources.

Frequency Annual

Web Facilities Industry facts and figures freely available on site.

Cost Free to members, £395 to others

Comments

Address 37-41 Bedford Row, London WC1R 4JH

Tel./e-mail 0207 404 9111   office@bccca.org.uk

Fax / Web site 0207 404 9110   www.bccca.org.uk

59

BISCUIT, CAKE, CHOCOLATE & CONFECTIONERY ALLIANCE (BCCCA)

Title **Four-Weekly Summaries Services**

Coverage Monthly data on the deliveries of products with individual reports on biscuits, chocolate confectionery, and sugar confectionery. Detailed breakdowns in each report by type of product. Based on returns from members.

Frequency Monthly

Web Facilities Industry facts and figures freely available on site.

Cost Free to members, £300 (biscuits), £350 (chocolate confectionery), £250 (sugar confectionery)

Comments

Address 37-41 Bedford Row, London WC1R 4JH

Tel./e-mail 0207 404 9111   office@bccca.org.uk

Fax / Web site 0207 404 9110   www.bccca.org.uk

60

Title	**Books and the Consumer**
Coverage	Based on research using a panel of 7,000 households, a report on the book market covering buying, book types purchased, reading habits, prices, retailing of books, postal buying of books, library usage.
Frequency	Annual
Web Facilities	A summary report from the research is available to anyone. Full survey results and tabulations are only available to survey subscribers
Cost	On request
Comments	
Address	7a Bedford Square, London WC1B 3RA
Tel./e-mail	0207 580 7282 bookmark@londonweb.net
Fax / Web site	0207 580 7236 www.londonweb.net/users/bookmark

BOOK MARKETING LTD

61

BOOKSELLER

Title	**Book Prices/Publishers' Output/Libraries**
Coverage	Various surveys appear throughout the year including surveys of book prices, number of titles published, public and academic library expenditure, salary surveys.
Frequency	Regular in a weekly journal
Web Facilities	News and some data on site.
Cost	£149
Comments	
Address	Bookseller Publications, 12 Dyott Street, London WC1A 1DF
Tel./e-mail	0207 420 6000
Fax / Web site	0207 420 6103 www.thebookseller.com

62

BOOKSELLER PUBLICATIONS

Title	**20-- Book Sales Yearbook**
Coverage	Comprehensive analysis of actual sales data in the UK's general retail market.
Frequency	Annual
Web Facilities	News and some data on site.
Cost	£250
Comments	
Address	12 Dyott Street, FREEPOST WC4593, London WC1A 1BR
Tel./e-mail	0207 420 6080
Fax / Web site	0207 420 6177 www.thebookseller.com

63	
Title	**Booktrack**
Coverage	A continuous survey of retail sales of books based on a panel of over 4600 retail outlets.
Frequency	Continuous
Web Facilities	
Cost	On request
Comments	
Address	Woolmead House, West Bear Lane, Farnham GU9 7LG
Tel./e-mail	01252 742555 booktrack-info@teleord.co.uk
Fax / Web site	01252 742556 www.the bookseller.com/booktrak.htm

BOOKTRACK

64	
Title	**Flavours Reports**
Coverage	A series of reports on the flavoured food and drink market with reports on adult food and drink and children's food and drink markets. The reports include data on flavourings, market factors, changing lifestyles, manufacturers, retailers, and future prospects.
Frequency	Regular
Web Facilities	
Cost	On request
Comments	
Address	Deningham Road, Wellingborough NN8 2QJ
Tel./e-mail	01933 440022
Fax / Web site	01933 440053

BORTHWICK FLAVOURS LTD

65	
Title	**BBPA Statistical Handbook**
Coverage	Production and consumption of beer and other alcoholic drinks, brewing materials, prices, incomes, duties, licensing data, structure of the industry, and drunkenness. Based largely on Central Government data with additional data from the association and other sources. A small amount of supporting text.
Frequency	Annual
Web Facilities	General details of statistics plus free access to some basic industry data.
Cost	£45, £27 to members
Comments	Organisation changed its name from the Brewers' and Licensed Retailers' Association at the end of September 2001
Address	Market Towers, 1 Nine Elms Lane, London SW8 5NQ
Tel./e-mail	0207 627 9191 prmail@beerandpub.com
Fax / Web site	0207 627 9123 www.beerandpub.com

BRITISH BEER AND PUB ASSOCIATION

66	BREWING AND DISTILLING INTERNATIONAL
Title	**Crop Commentary**
Coverage	Details of the UK barley crop and hop output based on BDI's European Malting Barley Survey.
Frequency	Regular in a weekly journal
Web Facilities	
Cost	£48
Comments	UK beer production figures and surveys of specific areas of the brewing trade are also included in the journal at regular intervals.
Address	52 Glenhouse Road, Eltham, London SE9 1JQ
Tel./e-mail	0208 859 4300
Fax / Web site	0208 859 5813

67	BRITISH ADHESIVES AND SEALANTS ASSOCIATION
Title	**UK Adhesives Market / UK Sealants Market**
Coverage	Sales in value terms of various types of sealant plus value and volume sales split by chemical type. Based on a survey of members.
Frequency	Twice yearly
Web Facilities	
Cost	Free
Comments	Available to participating members only.
Address	33 Fellowes Way, Stevenage SG2 8BW
Tel./e-mail	01438 358514 secretary@basa.uk.com
Fax / Web site	www.basa.uk.com

68	BRITISH AEROSOL MANUFACTURERS' ASSOCIATION
Title	**BAMA Annual Report - UK Aerosol Production**
Coverage	Gives details of aerosol filling statistics by various product categories. Based on a survey of members.
Frequency	Annual
Web Facilities	General details and free access to all statistics. Online ordering of publications.
Cost	Free
Comments	
Address	King's Building, Smith Square, London SW1P 3JJ
Tel./e-mail	0207 828 5111 enquiries@bama.co.uk
Fax / Web site	0207 834 8436 www.bama.co.uk

69

BRITISH AGRICULTURAL AND GARDEN MACHINERY ASSOCIATION

Title	**Market Guide**
Coverage	A guide to the used tractors and farm machinery market based on a survey by the association.
Frequency	Regular
Web Facilities	
Cost	£114, £90 to members
Comments	
Address	14-16 Church Street, Rickmansworth WD3 1RQ
Tel./e-mail	01923 720241 info@bagma.com
Fax / Web site	01923 896063 www.bagma.com

70

BRITISH APPAREL AND TEXTILE CONFEDERATION

Title	**Trendata**
Coverage	Statistics covering production, exports, imports, balance of trade, consumer expenditure, employment for the UK apparel and textile industry. Based on both official and non-official sources.
Frequency	Quarterly
Web Facilities	Web site under re-development at time of compilation.
Cost	£95 (members), £195 for non-members
Comments	Available in loose-leaf format.
Address	5 Portland Place, London W1N 3AA
Tel./e-mail	0207 636 7788 batc@dial.pipex.com
Fax / Web site	0207 636 7515 www.batc.co.uk

71

BRITISH APPAREL AND TEXTILE CONFEDERATION

Title	**Quarterly Export Data - All Textiles and Made-up Items**
Coverage	Export statistics by product category.
Frequency	Quarterly
Web Facilities	Web site under re-development at time of compilation.
Cost	£50
Comments	
Address	5 Portland Place, London W1N 3AA
Tel./e-mail	0207 636 7788 batc@dial.pipex.com
Fax / Web site	0207 636 7515 www.batc.co.uk

72	**BRITISH APPAREL AND TEXTILE CONFEDERATION**
Title	**Quarterly Import Data - All Textiles and Made-up Items**
Coverage	Import statistics by product category.
Frequency	Quarterly
Web Facilities	Web site under re-development at time of compilation.
Cost	£70
Comments	
Address	5 Portland Place, London W1N 3AA
Tel./e-mail	0207 636 7788 batc@dial.pipex.com
Fax / Web site	0207 636 7515 www.batc.co.uk

73	**BRITISH APPAREL AND TEXTILE CONFEDERATION**
Title	**Quarterly Production Data - Cotton and Allied Textiles**
Coverage	Production trends for cotton and textiles.
Frequency	Quarterly
Web Facilities	Web site under re-development at time of compilation.
Cost	£70
Comments	
Address	5 Portland Place, London W1N 3AA
Tel./e-mail	0207 636 7788 batc@dial.pipex.com
Fax / Web site	0207 636 7515 www.batc.co.uk

74	**BRITISH APPAREL AND TEXTILE CONFEDERATION**
Title	**Industry Statistical Overview**
Coverage	Statistics covering production, consumption, overseas trade, employment etc.
Frequency	Annual
Web Facilities	Web site under re-development at time of compilation.
Cost	£35
Comments	Latest published volume - 1997.
Address	5 Portland Place, London W1N 3AA
Tel./e-mail	0207 636 7788 batc@dial.pipex.com
Fax / Web site	0207 636 7515 www.batc.co.uk

75	**BRITISH APPAREL AND TEXTILE CONFEDERATION**
Title	**Quarterly Statistical Review - Cotton & Allied Textiles**
Coverage	Statistics on production, imports, exports, and apparent consumption particularly for cotton and allied fibres. Based on a mixture of official and non-official sources.
Frequency	Quarterly
Web Facilities	Web site under re-development at time of compilation.
Cost	£135
Comments	
Address	5 Portland Place, London W1N 3AA
Tel./e-mail	0207 636 7788 batc@dial.pipex.com
Fax / Web site	0207 636 7515 www.batc.co.uk

76	**BRITISH BANKERS' ASSOCIATION**
Title	**Sterling Lending**
Coverage	Trends in sterling lending with data for the latest available month and cumulative statistics. Based on data supplied by members.
Frequency	Monthly
Web Facilities	Monthly statistics, some other data, and online ordering facilities on site.
Cost	On request
Comments	
Address	10 Lombard Street, London EC3V 9AP
Tel./e-mail	0207 623 4001
Fax / Web site	0207 283 7037 www.bba.org.uk

77	**BRITISH BANKERS' ASSOCIATION**
Title	**Monthly Statement**
Coverage	General statistics covering the activities of the major UK banks. Based largely on data from members.
Frequency	Monthly
Web Facilities	Monthly statistics, some other data, and online ordering facilities on site.
Cost	On request
Comments	
Address	10 Lombard Street, London EC3V 9AP
Tel./e-mail	0207 623 4001
Fax / Web site	0207 283 7037 www.bba.org.uk

78	BRITISH BANKERS' ASSOCIATION
Title	**Abstract of Banking Statistics**
Coverage	Detailed statistics on the banks and banking with sections on bank groups, clearing statistics, credit card statistics, branches, and financial data. Based on various sources, including data from the association. Many tables have ten-year statistical series.
Frequency	Annual
Web Facilities	Monthly statistics on site, some other data, and online ordering facilities.
Cost	On request
Comments	
Address	10 Lombard Street, London EC3V 9AP
Tel./e-mail	0207 623 4001
Fax / Web site	0207 283 7037 www.bba.org.uk

79	BRITISH BANKERS' ASSOCIATION
Title	**Major British Banking Groups' Mortgage Lending**
Coverage	Trends in mortgage advances by UK banks with figures for the latest month and cumulative data. Based on returns from members.
Frequency	Monthly
Web Facilities	Monthly statistics, some other data, and online ordering facilities on site.
Cost	On request
Comments	
Address	10 Lombard Street, London EC3V 9AP
Tel./e-mail	0207 623 4001
Fax / Web site	0207 283 7037 www.bba.org.uk

80	BRITISH CARPET MANUFACTURERS' ASSOCIATION
Title	**Annual Report**
Coverage	A statistical section concentrates on carpet imports and exports. Based mainly on Central Government data.
Frequency	Annual
Web Facilities	
Cost	Free
Comments	
Address	PO Box 1155, Kidderminster DY11 6NP
Tel./e-mail	01562 747351 bcma@clara.net
Fax / Web site	01562 747359

81	BRITISH CERAMIC CONFEDERATION
Title	**Annual Production and Trade Statistics by Sub-Sector**
Coverage	Summary of the total production and sales of the ceramic industry, plus overseas trade data. Based largely on government statistics.
Frequency	Annual
Web Facilities	Access to statistics for members on Web site.
Cost	Free
Comments	Usually only available to members.
Address	Federation House, Station Road, Stoke-on-Trent ST4 2SA
Tel./e-mail	01782 744631 bcc@ceramfed.co.uk
Fax / Web site	01782 744102 www.ceramfed.co.uk

82	BRITISH CERAMIC CONFEDERATION
Title	**Quarterly Trade Statistics**
Coverage	Details of the imports and exports of ceramic products broken down into various industry sub-sectors. Based on government statistics.
Frequency	Quarterly
Web Facilities	Access to statistics for members on Web site.
Cost	Free
Comments	Usually only available to members.
Address	Federation House, Station Road, Stoke-on-Trent ST4 2SA
Tel./e-mail	01782 744631 bcc@ceramfed.co.uk
Fax / Web site	01782 744102 www.ceramfed.co.uk

83	BRITISH CHAMBERS OF COMMERCE
Title	**Quarterly Economic Survey**
Coverage	A quarterly review of business and economic conditions based on returns from a sample of members of a selection of the major regional chambers.
Frequency	Quarterly
Web Facilities	Summary data available free on site plus online ordering facilities.
Cost	£200, £60 each
Comments	
Address	22 Carlisle Place, London SW1P 1JA
Tel./e-mail	0207 565 2000 info@britishchambers.org.uk
Fax / Web site	0207 565 2049 www.britishchambers.org.uk

84	BRITISH CLOTHING INDUSTRY ASSOCIATION
Title	**Report of Activities**
Coverage	Includes a facts and figures section with data on output, trade, production, consumer expenditure, top markets, and EU production.
Frequency	Annual
Web Facilities	
Cost	On request
Comments	
Address	5 Portland Place, London W1N 3AA
Tel./e-mail	0207 636 7788 bcia@dial.pipex.com
Fax / Web site	0207 636 7515

85	BRITISH EDUCATIONAL SUPPLIERS' ASSOCIATION
Title	**UK School Survey on Budget and Resource Provision**
Coverage	Includes data for expenditure by schools on supplies and equipment.
Frequency	Annual
Web Facilities	General details and free summary statistics on site. Access to statistics for members only.
Cost	£250
Comments	Available to members and bone fide researchers
Address	20 Beaufort Court, Admirals Way, London E14 9XL
Tel./e-mail	0207 537 4997 ray@besanet.org.uk
Fax / Web site	0207 537 4846 www.besanet.org.uk

86	BRITISH EDUCATIONAL SUPPLIERS' ASSOCIATION
Title	**Information and Communication Technology in UK State Schools**
Coverage	A review of IT in UK state schools including expenditure data.
Frequency	Annual
Web Facilities	General details and free summary statistics on site. Access to statistics for members only.
Cost	£250
Comments	Available to members and bone fide researchers
Address	20 Beaufort Court, Admirals Way, London E14 9XL
Tel./e-mail	0207 537 4997 ray@besanet.org.uk
Fax / Web site	0207 537 4846 www.besanet.org.uk

87	**BRITISH EGG INFORMATION SERVICE**
Title	**Market Review**
Coverage	Data on value and volume of sales, laying flocks, trade, consumption, regional breakdown of sales, egg production systems.
Frequency	Annual
Web Facilities	General details of statistics and online ordering of publications on site.
Cost	Free
Comments	
Address	126-128 Cromwell Road, London SW7 4ET
Tel./e-mail	0207 370 7411 info@britegg.co.uk
Fax / Web site	0207 373 3926 www.britegg.co.uk

88	**BRITISH EGG PRODUCTS ASSOCIATION**
Title	**Breaking and Production**
Coverage	Includes data on egg production and breakages.
Frequency	Ten issues per annum
Web Facilities	
Cost	On request
Comments	
Address	Suite 101, Albany House, 324-326 Regent Street, London W1R 5AA
Tel./e-mail	0207 580 7172 british.egg.industry@farmline.com
Fax / Web site	0207 580 7082 www.britegg.co.uk

89	**BRITISH EGG PRODUCTS ASSOCIATION**
Title	**Import and Export Statistics**
Coverage	Overseas trade statistics for eggs and egg products based on data obtained from Central Government sources.
Frequency	Ten issues per year
Web Facilities	
Cost	On request
Comments	
Address	Suite 101, Albany House, 324-326 Regent Street, London W1R 5AA
Tel./e-mail	0207 580 7172 british.egg.industry@farmline.com
Fax / Web site	0207 580 7082 www.britegg.co.uk

90	**BRITISH ENERGY ASSOCIATION**
Title	**British Annual Energy Review**
Coverage	A review of trends in the British energy industry, broken down by sector and based on a combination of sources.
Frequency	Annual
Web Facilities	
Cost	On request
Comments	
Address	c/o BNFL 2nd Floor, 65 Buckingham Gate, London SW1E 6AP
Tel./e-mail	0208 767 9744 beawec@aol.com
Fax / Web site	0208 767 9744

91	**BRITISH FLUID POWER ASSOCIATION**
Title	**Statistics Newsletter**
Coverage	Summary data and news on the industry plus details of new statistical developments relevant to the industry.
Frequency	Regular
Web Facilities	General details on site.
Cost	On request
Comments	
Address	Cheriton House, Cromwell Business Park, Banbury Road, Chipping Norton OX7 5SR
Tel./e-mail	01608 647900 bfpa@bfpa.demon.co.uk
Fax / Web site	01608 647919 www.bfpa.co.uk

92	**BRITISH FLUID POWER ASSOCIATION**
Title	**BFPA Annual Hydraulic Equipment Survey**
Coverage	A survey of a sample of member companies providing information on market trends and characteristics. The survey is supplemented by some official statistics and international data.
Frequency	Annual
Web Facilities	General details on site
Cost	On request
Comments	
Address	Cheriton House, Cromwell Business Park, Banbury Road, Chipping Norton OX7 5SR
Tel./e-mail	01608 647900 bfpa@bfpa.demon.co.uk
Fax / Web site	01608 647919 www.bfpa.co.uk

93	BRITISH FLUID POWER ASSOCIATION
Title	**Hydraulic Equipment/Pneumatic Control Equipment: Short Term Trends Survey**
Coverage	Commentary and statistics on short-term trends based on returns from member companies.
Frequency	Quarterly
Web Facilities	General details on site.
Cost	On request
Comments	
Address	Cheriton House, Cromwell Business Park, Banbury Road, Chipping Norton OX7 5SR
Tel./e-mail	01608 647900 bfpa@bfpa.demon.co.uk
Fax / Web site	01608 647919 www.bfpa.co.uk

94	BRITISH FLUID POWER ASSOCIATION
Title	**Hydraulic Equipment Monthly UK Orders and Sales Index**
Coverage	Orders and sales trends based on returns from member companies.
Frequency	Monthly
Web Facilities	General details on site.
Cost	On request
Comments	
Address	Cheriton House, Cromwell Business Park, Banbury Road, Chipping Norton OX7 5SR
Tel./e-mail	01608 647900 bfpa@bfpa.demon.co.uk
Fax / Web site	01608 647919 www.bfpa.co.uk

95	BRITISH FLUID POWER ASSOCIATION
Title	**Distributor Annual Survey**
Coverage	A survey of distributors providing information on sales, market trends, end users, and companies. Also includes salary structure data and some official statistics.
Frequency	Annual
Web Facilities	General details on site.
Cost	On request
Comments	Established in 1994 to replace the Distributor Profiles.
Address	Cheriton House, Cromwell Business Park, Banbury Road, Chipping Norton OX7 5SR
Tel./e-mail	01608 647900 bfpa@bfpa.demon.co.uk
Fax / Web site	01608 647919 www.bfpa.co.uk

96	BRITISH FLUID POWER ASSOCIATION
Title	**Pneumatic Control Equipment Monthly UK Orders and Sales Index**
Coverage	Orders and sales trends based on returns from member companies.
Frequency	Monthly
Web Facilities	General details on site.
Cost	On request
Comments	
Address	Cheriton House, Cromwell Business Park, Banbury Road, Chipping Norton OX7 5SR
Tel./e-mail	01608 647900 bfpa@bfpa.demon.co.uk
Fax / Web site	01608 647919 www.bfpa.co.uk

97	BRITISH FLUID POWER ASSOCIATION
Title	**Annual Salary Survey**
Coverage	Based on a survey of members, it includes data on remuneration, company cars, working hours, holiday entitlements.
Frequency	Annual
Web Facilities	General details on site.
Cost	On request
Comments	
Address	Cheriton House, Cromwell Business Park, Banbury Road, Chipping Norton OX7 5SR
Tel./e-mail	01608 647900 bfpa@bfpa.demon.co.uk
Fax / Web site	01608 647919 www.bfpa.co.uk

98	BRITISH FLUID POWER ASSOCIATION
Title	**BFPA Pneumatic Control Equipment Survey**
Coverage	A survey of a sample of member companies providing information on market trends. Also includes some official statistics and international data.
Frequency	Annual
Web Facilities	General details on site.
Cost	On request
Comments	
Address	Cheriton House, Cromwell Business Park, Banbury Road, Chipping Norton OX7 5SR
Tel./e-mail	01608 647900 bfpa@bfpa.demon.co.uk
Fax / Web site	01608 647919 www.bfpa.co.uk

99	BRITISH FLUID POWER ASSOCIATION
Title	**BFPA Hose and Fittings Survey**
Coverage	A survey of a sample of member and non-member companies (the only BFPA survey to cover non-members), with information on market trends. Supplemented by some official statistics and international data.
Frequency	Annual
Web Facilities	General details on site.
Cost	On request
Comments	
Address	Cheriton House, Cromwell Business Park, Banbury Road, Chipping Norton OX7 5SR
Tel./e-mail	01608 647900 bfpa@bfpa.demon.co.uk
Fax / Web site	01608 647919 www.bfpa.co.uk

100	BRITISH FOOTWEAR ASSOCIATION
Title	**Quarterly Statistics**
Coverage	Detailed production, imports and exports, and consumption data for specific sectors of the footwear industry. Based mainly on Central Government data.
Frequency	Quarterly
Web Facilities	Free facts and figures on site.
Cost	£110 with the monthly publication
Comments	
Address	5 Portland Place, London W1B 1PW
Tel./e-mail	0207 580 8687 bfamarketing@easynet.co.uk
Fax / Web site	0207 580 8696 www.britfoot.com

101	BRITISH FOOTWEAR ASSOCIATION
Title	**Monthly Statistics**
Coverage	Short-term economic indicators for the industry with a brief commentary. Data covers deliveries, employment, prices, retail sales, imports, exports.
Frequency	Monthly
Web Facilities	Free facts and figures on site.
Cost	£110 with quarterly publication
Comments	
Address	5 Portland Place, London W1B 1PW
Tel./e-mail	0207 580 8687 bfamarketing@easynet.co.uk
Fax / Web site	0207 580 8696 www.britfoot.com

102	**BRITISH FOOTWEAR ASSOCIATION**
Title	**Footwear Industry Statistical Review**
Coverage	Statistics on the industry structure, materials, production, profitability, employment and earnings, prices, supplies to the home market, expenditure, retailing, imports and exports. Based mainly on Central Government sources.
Frequency	Annual
Web Facilities	Free facts and figures on site.
Cost	£50
Comments	
Address	5 Portland Place, London W1B 1PW
Tel./e-mail	0207 580 8687 bfamarketing@easynet.co.uk
Fax / Web site	0207 580 8696 www.britfoot.co.uk
103	**BRITISH FRANCHISE ASSOCIATION**
Title	**BFA / NATWEST Franchise Survey**
Coverage	Statistics and commentary on the number of franchisees, types, sectors, sales, employment with the latest year's data compared to the previous year. Based on original research by the association. Commentary supports the text.
Frequency	Annual
Web Facilities	General details and free summary statistics on the site. Online ordering of publications and email alerting services.
Cost	£87.50
Comments	
Address	Thames View, Newtown Road, Henley-on-Thames RG9 1HG
Tel./e-mail	01491 578050 mailroom@british-franchise.org.uk
Fax / Web site	01491 573517 www.british-franchise.org.uk
104	**BRITISH FROZEN FOOD FEDERATION**
Title	**Monthly Bulletin**
Coverage	Includes statistics on the UK frozen food market with data on consumption, expenditure, and markets for specific frozen foods. Based on various sources.
Frequency	Regular
Web Facilities	Some frozen food statistics are freely available on the site.
Cost	£40
Comments	
Address	3rd Floor, Springfield House, Springfield Business Park, Grantham NG31 7BG
Tel./e-mail	01476 515300
Fax / Web site	01476 515309 www.bfff.co.uk

105	BRITISH GLASS MANUFACTURERS' CONFEDERATION
Title	**Recycling Statistics**
Coverage	Statistics on the recycling of glass bottles and other glass products based on data collected by the confederation.
Frequency	Regular
Web Facilities	Some statistics freely available on site.
Cost	On request
Comments	
Address	Northumberland Road, Sheffield S10 2UA
Tel./e-mail	0114 2686201 sales@britglass.co.uk
Fax / Web site	0114 2681073 www.britglass.co.uk

106	BRITISH HARDWARE AND HOUSEWARES MANUFACTURERS' ASSOCIATION
Title	**Business Trends Survey**
Coverage	Based on a survey of members with data on sales, stocks, margins, and business expectations.
Frequency	Quarterly
Web Facilities	
Cost	£50, £25 members, £5 participants
Comments	
Address	Brooke House, 4 The Lakes, Bedford Road, Northampton NN4 7YD
Tel./e-mail	01604 622023
Fax / Web site	01604 631252 www.bhhma.co.uk

107	BRITISH HOSPITALITY ASSOCIATION
Title	**British Hospitality: Trends and Statistics**
Coverage	Commentary and statistics on tourism and hospitality trends. Based on a combination of government data and other data.
Frequency	Annual
Web Facilities	
Cost	£195, free to members
Comments	
Address	Queen's House, 55-56 Lincoln's Inn Fields, London WC2A 3HB
Tel./e-mail	0207 404 7744 bha@bha.org.uk
Fax / Web site	0207 404 7799 www.bha-online.org.uk

108	BRITISH HOSPITALITY ASSOCIATION
Title	**UK Contract Catering Survey**
Coverage	A detailed annual review of the UK contract catering industry with commentary and statistics on the number of businesses, turnover, costs, number of meals served, summary data on the international contract catering industry, and future trends. The report is based on a survey by the association.
Frequency	Annual
Web Facilities	
Cost	£95, free to members
Comments	
Address	Queen's House, 55-56 Lincoln's Inn Fields, London WC2A 3BH
Tel./e-mail	0207 404 7744 bha@bha.org.uk
Fax / Web site	0207 404 7799 www.bha-online.org.uk
109	BRITISH MARINE INDUSTRIES FEDERATION
Title	**UK Marine Industry Annual Statistics**
Coverage	Annual trends in the boating industry and market based on original research.
Frequency	Annual
Web Facilities	Free access to, and downloading of, some statistics on site.
Cost	Free
Comments	
Address	Meadlake Place, Thorpe Lea Road, Egham TW20 8HE
Tel./e-mail	01784 223600 bmif@bmif.co.uk
Fax / Web site	01784 439678 www.bmif.co.uk
110	BRITISH MARINE INDUSTRIES FEDERATION
Title	**National Survey of Boating and Watersports Participation**
Coverage	A review of the percentage of the population participating, expenditure, equipment and services, training, craft ownership by type, frequency of visits to water, attitudes to watersports, and consumer profiles. Based largely on original research.
Frequency	Every 3 or 4 years
Web Facilities	Free access to, and downloading, of some statistics on site.
Cost	£100 members, £195 non members
Comments	The latest issue was published in 1999.
Address	Meadlake Place, Thorpe Lea Road, Egham TW20 8HE
Tel./e-mail	01784 223600 bmif@bmif.co.uk
Fax / Web site	01784 439678 www.bmif.co.uk

111	**BRITISH MARINE INDUSTRIES FEDERATION**
Title	**UK Marine Industry Trends**
Coverage	An opinion survey of member companies producing analysis and data on industry sentiment and confidence.
Frequency	Twice yearly
Web Facilities	Free access to, and downloading of, some statistics on site.
Cost	Free
Comments	
Address	Meadlake Place, Thorpe Lea Road, Egham TW20 8HE
Tel./e-mail	01784 223600 bmif@bmif.co.uk
Fax / Web site	01784 439678 www.bmif.co.uk

112	**BRITISH MARKET RESEARCH ASSOCIATION (BMRA)**
Title	**BMRA Annual Statistics**
Coverage	The BMRA publishes a league table of its member companies by turnover, plus industry-wide data on turnover by type of client (ie, sector), turnover by research method, turnover by survey type. Based on a survey of members.
Frequency	Annual
Web Facilities	Summary statistics on the industry available free on the site.
Cost	On request
Comments	The BMRA was formed in 1998 through a merger of the Association of Market Survey Organisations (AMSO) and the Association of British Market Research Companies (ABMRC).
Address	Devonshire House, 60 Goswell Road, London EC1M 7AD
Tel./e-mail	0207 566 3636 admin@bmra.org.uk
Fax / Web site	0207 689 6220 www.bmra.org.uk

113	**BRITISH MARKET RESEARCH BUREAU (BMRB) INTERNATIONAL**
Title	**Access Omnibus Survey**
Coverage	Includes a weekly omnibus survey of 2,000 adults above the age of 14 with face-to-face interviews carried out in the home. A telephone survey is carried out every weekend and uses a sample of 1,000 adults. Also web-based surveys.
Frequency	Weekly
Web Facilities	Summary data from TGI and other surveys free on site.
Cost	On request
Comments	
Address	Hadley House, 79-81 Uxbridge Road, Ealing W5 5SU
Tel./e-mail	0208 566 5000 web@bmrb.co.uk
Fax / Web site	0208 579 9208 www.bmrb.co.uk

114

BRITISH MARKET RESEARCH BUREAU (BMRB) INTERNATIONAL

Title	**Youth TGI**
Coverage	TGI data specifically for children and youths aged between 7 and 19. Includes data on purchases and consumption of key products.
Frequency	Annual
Web Facilities	Summary data from TGI and other surveys free on site.
Cost	Varies according to the range and nature of the information required. Standard results published in 2 volumes.
Comments	Also available online.
Address	Hadley House, 79-81 Uxbridge Road, Ealing W5 5SU
Tel./e-mail	0208 566 5000 web@bmrb.co.uk
Fax / Web site	0208 579 9208 www.bmrb.co.uk

115

BRITISH MARKET RESEARCH BUREAU (BMRB) INTERNATIONAL

Title	**Target Group Index (TGI)**
Coverage	A national product and media survey based on information from 24,000 adults. The results are published in 34 volumes: volumes 1 and 2 give general demographic information while volumes 3 to 34 cover individual consumer product areas. Detailed consumer profiles and penetration data for each product. A separate volume also provides a general description of the survey.
Frequency	Annual
Web Facilities	Summary data from TGI and other surveys free on site.
Cost	£4,250 per volume
Comments	Specific prices available for reports on individual brands or specific consumer fields. Also available online.
Address	Hadley House, 79-81 Uxbridge Road, Ealing W5 5SU
Tel./e-mail	0208 566 5000 web@bmrb.co.uk
Fax / Web site	0208 579 9208 www.bmrb.co.uk

116	BRITISH MARKET RESEARCH BUREAU (BMRB) INTERNATIONAL
Title	**Premier: The Upmarket TGI**
Coverage	TGI data specifically for consumers in the AB social grades with data covering holidays, leisure, sports, travel, clothing, personal possessions, cosmetics, gifts, household goods, home and car, drinks, and food.
Frequency	Annual
Web Facilities	Summary data from TGI and other surveys free on site.
Cost	Varies according to the range and nature of the information required. Standard results published in 8 volumes.
Comments	Also available online.
Address	Hadley House, 79-81 Uxbridge Road, Ealing W5 5SU
Tel./e-mail	0208 566 5000 web@bmrb.co.uk
Fax / Web site	0208 579 9208 www.bmrb.co.uk
117	BRITISH MARKET RESEARCH BUREAU (BMRB) INTERNATIONAL
Title	**TGI NET**
Coverage	A new TGI survey investigating Internet usage and spending patterns by consumers.
Frequency	Regular
Web Facilities	Summary data from the TGI and other surveys on the site.
Cost	On request
Comments	
Address	Hadley House, 79-81 Uxbridge Road, Ealing W5 5SU
Tel./e-mail	0208 566 5000 web@bmrb.co.uk
Fax / Web site	0208 579 9208 www.bmrb.co.uk

118

BRITISH MEDIA RESEARCH COMMITTEE

Title	**British Business Survey**
Coverage	A survey, sponsored by the media owners, examining readership patterns of business managers and executives. Includes data on readership by key demographic group, by occupation, by industry, and by decision making involvement. Further information on the use of services and profiles of British business.
Frequency	Annual
Web Facilities	Details of various surveys and press releases on site.
Cost	£1,000, £350 for sponsoring organisations
Comments	Produced for the Business Media Research Committee by IPSOS-RSL Ltd at the address below.
Address	Kings House, Kymberley Road, Harrow HA1 1PT
Tel./e-mail	0208 861 8099 information@ipsos-rsl.com
Fax / Web site	0208 863 6647 www.ipsos.rslmedia.co.uk

119

BRITISH METALS FEDERATION

Title	**Annual Report**
Coverage	Includes statistics on scrap consumption, scrap stocks, exports, imports, and scrap prices. Based on a combination of the federation's own data and official statistics.
Frequency	Annual
Web Facilities	
Cost	Free
Comments	In Summer 2001, the federation agreed to merge with the British Secondary Metals Association to form the British Metals Recycling Association.
Address	16 High Street, Brampton, Huntingdon PE18 8TU
Tel./e-mail	01480 455249 admin@britmetfed.org.uk
Fax / Web site	01480 453680 www.britmetfed.org.uk

120	**BRITISH METALS FEDERATION**
Title	**Annual Report**
Coverage	Commentary and statistics on trends in the industry with sections on production, scrap consumption, stocks, exports, imports, and prices. Based on a number of sources.
Frequency	Annual
Web Facilities	
Cost	On request
Comments	In Summer 2001, the federation agreed to merge with the British Secondary Metals Association to form the British Metals Recycling Association.
Address	16 High Street, Brampton, Huntingdon PE18 8TU
Tel./e-mail	01480 455249 admin@britmetfed.org.uk
Fax / Web site	01480 453680 www.britmetfed.org.uk

121	**BRITISH OFFICE SYSTEMS AND STATIONERY FEDERATION (BOSS)**
Title	**Growth of Manufacturers' Turnover**
Coverage	The BOSS Federation survey of manufacturers' turnover gives quarterly data, and comparable data for previous quarters, for three sectors: furniture, machines, office products. The survey is based on returns from companies representing approximately one third of the total market.
Frequency	Quarterly
Web Facilities	
Cost	
Comments	Only available to participating companies.
Address	6 Wimpole Street, London W1G 9SL
Tel./e-mail	0207 637 7692 info@bossfed.co.uk
Fax / Web site	0207 436 3137 www.bossfed.co.uk

122	**BRITISH PHONOGRAPHIC INDUSTRY (BPI)**
Title	**BPI Statistical Handbook**
Coverage	Includes statistics on the production of CDs, tapes and records plus imports and exports, deliveries, sales, prices, advertising expenditure, hardware ownership, video trends, piracy, and leisure market trends.
Frequency	Annual
Web Facilities	General details and free summary statistics
Cost	£30
Comments	
Address	25 Savile Row, London W1X 1AA
Tel./e-mail	0207 851 4000
Fax / Web site	0207 851 4010 www.bpi.co.uk

123

	BRITISH PLASTICS FEDERATION
Title	**BPF Business Trends Survey**
Coverage	A survey of companies in three areas: materials supplies, processing, and machinery manufacturers. Data on sales, orders, stocks, exports, investment, profits, prices, and capacity utilisation. Includes an opinion survey outlining likely future trends and a commentary supports the text.
Frequency	Twice yearly
Web Facilities	General details on site.
Cost	Free to members, £96 non members
Comments	
Address	6 Bath Place, Rivington Street, London EC2A 3JE
Tel./e-mail	0207 457 5000 imcilwee@bpf.co.uk
Fax / Web site	0207 235 5045 www.bpf.co.uk

124

	BRITISH PLASTICS FEDERATION
Title	**BPF Statistics Handbook**
Coverage	Statistics on the UK consumption of plastic materials, material consumption by major end-use, imports, exports, and plastics in packaging, building, and the automotive sectors. Based on BPF and other data with some supporting text. Published in two volumes: 1 - The Bulk Polymers; 2 - The Semi-Commodity Engineering Plastics.
Frequency	Annual
Web Facilities	General details on site.
Cost	£280 per volume
Comments	
Address	6 Bath Place, Rivington Street, London EC2A 3JE
Tel./e-mail	0207 457 5000 imcilwee@bpf.co.uk
Fax / Web site	0207 235 5045 www.bpf.co.uk

125

	BRITISH PLASTICS FEDERATION
Title	**BPF Economic Survey**
Coverage	A review of the economy and business trends and specific trends in the plastics sector.
Frequency	Annual
Web Facilities	General details on site.
Cost	Free to members, £80 non members
Comments	
Address	6 Bath Place, Rivington Street, London EC2A 3JE
Tel./e-mail	0207 457 5000 imcilwee@bpf.co.uk
Fax / Web site	0207 235 5045 www.bpf.co.uk

126	BRITISH POTATO COUNCIL
Title	**Price Weekly**
Coverage	Weekly prices for potatoes in UK and international markets.
Frequency	Weekly
Web Facilities	Free access to data on site, plus weekly news.
Cost	Free
Comments	Also publishes Potato Weekly news service.
Address	4300 Nash Court, John Smith Drive, Oxford OX4 2RT
Tel./e-mail	01865 714455
Fax / Web site	01865 782231 www.potato.org.uk

127	BRITISH PRINTING INDUSTRIES' FEDERATION
Title	**Facts and Figures about the Printing Industry**
Coverage	Basic data on sales, overseas trade, costs, prices, profits, redundancies etc. Based on a mixture of official and non-official sources.
Frequency	Every few years
Web Facilities	Free facts and figures pages on the site
Cost	Free
Comments	
Address	Farringdon Point, 29-35 Farringdon Road, London EC1M 3JF
Tel./e-mail	0207 915 8317 info@bpif.org.uk
Fax / Web site	0207 405 7784 www.bpif.org.uk

128	BRITISH PRINTING INDUSTRIES' FEDERATION
Title	**Directions**
Coverage	A report on the economic state of the printing industry with statistics covering the last 30 months.
Frequency	Quarterly
Web Facilities	Free facts and figures pages on site.
Cost	£25 per issue
Comments	
Address	Farringdon Point, 29-35 Farringdon Road, London EC1M 3JF
Tel./e-mail	0207 915 8317 info@bpif.org.uk
Fax / Web site	0207 405 7784 www.bpif.org.uk

129	BRITISH RADIO AND ELECTRONIC EQUIPMENT MANUFACTURERS' ASSOCIATION (BREEMA)
Title	**Annual Report**
Coverage	The annual report contains some statistics on deliveries of consumer electronic products and a report on the statistical activities of the association.
Frequency	Annual
Web Facilities	Annual report can be viewed on the site and downloaded for free.
Cost	Free
Comments	In Summer 2001, the association announced a merger with the Federation of the Electronics Industry (FEI).
Address	Russell Square House, 10-12 Russell Square, London WC1B 5EE
Tel./e-mail	0207 331 2000 information@brema.org.uk
Fax / Web site	0207 331 2040 www.brema.org.uk

130	BRITISH RETAIL CONSORTIUM
Title	**BRC-KPMG Retail Sales Monitor**
Coverage	Volume and value of UK retail sales based mainly on government statistics supported by data from some non-official sources.
Frequency	Monthly
Web Facilities	Free summary data in press release on site.
Cost	On request
Comments	
Address	5 Grafton Street, London W15 4EG
Tel./e-mail	0207 647 1500 info@brc.org.uk
Fax / Web site	0207 647 1599 www.brc.org.uk

131	BRITISH RETAIL CONSORTIUM
Title	**Retail Crime Survey**
Coverage	Based on a survey of approximately 53,000 outlets, the report analyses retail crime and includes data on the total cost, crime by retailers, type of crime.
Frequency	Annual
Web Facilities	Free summary data in press release on site.
Cost	£25
Comments	
Address	5 Grafton Street, London W15 4EG
Tel./e-mail	0207 647 1500 info@brc.org.uk
Fax / Web site	0207 647 1599 www.brc.org.uk

132	BRITISH RETAIL CONSORTIUM
Title	**Shop Price Index**
Coverage	Information on monthly price movements for 200 goods purchased regularly with general comparisons with the retail price index.
Frequency	Monthly
Web Facilities	Free summary data in press release on site.
Cost	On request
Comments	
Address	5 Grafton Street, London W15 4EG
Tel./e-mail	0207 647 1500 info@brc.org.uk
Fax / Web site	0207 647 1599 www.brc.org.uk

133	BRITISH ROAD FEDERATION
Title	**Basic Road Statistics**
Coverage	Data on roads and road transport including data on traffic, energy, taxation, public expenditure, accidents, and some international comparisons. Mainly based on Central Government sources.
Frequency	Annual
Web Facilities	Free Road Facts 2000 data on site.
Cost	£22
Comments	
Address	194-202 Old Kent Road, London SE1 5TG
Tel./e-mail	0207 703 9769 brf@brf.uk.com
Fax / Web site	0207 701 0029 www.brf.co.uk

134	BRITISH ROAD FEDERATION
Title	**Road Facts 20--**
Coverage	A pocketbook of data and commentary on roads and road transport in the UK.
Frequency	Annual
Web Facilities	Free access to Road Facts 2000 on site.
Cost	Free
Comments	
Address	194-202 Old Kent Road, London SE1 5TG
Tel./e-mail	0207 703 9769 brf@brf.uk.com
Fax / Web site	0207 701 0029 www.brf.co.uk

135 BRITISH ROBOT AND AUTOMATION ASSOCIATION

Title	**Robot Facts**
Coverage	Annual report on UK robot installations within a given year.
Frequency	Annual
Web Facilities	
Cost	Free to members, £50 to non-members
Comments	Also publishes a yearbook.
Address	c/o Dr Ken Young, International Manufacturing Centre, University of Warwick, Coventry CV5 7AL
Tel./e-mail	024 763742 info@bara.org.uk
Fax / Web site	024 763743 www.bara.org.uk

136 BRITISH SECONDARY METALS ASSOCIATION

Title	**Member Survey**
Coverage	A survey of member companies by employment size, number of sites, investment, turnover.
Frequency	Regular
Web Facilities	
Cost	Free
Comments	In Summer 2001, the association agreed to merge with the British Metals Federation to form the British Metals Recycling Association.
Address	Sandford Court, 21 Sandford Street, Lichfield WS13 6QA
Tel./e-mail	01543 255450
Fax / Web site	01543 255325 www.bsma.org.uk

137 BRITISH SOFT DRINKS ASSOCIATION LTD

Title	**Factsheets**
Coverage	Information sheets containing statistics on various aspects of the industry, eg sales, consumption, packaging etc. Each factsheet contains a large amount of text supported by statistics mainly collected by the association.
Frequency	Regular
Web Facilities	Summary information on the industry on site.
Cost	Free
Comments	
Address	20-22 Stukely Street, London WC2B 5LR
Tel./e-mail	0207 430 0356
Fax / Web site	0207 831 6014 www.britishsoftdrinks.com

138	
Title	**Bottled Water - The Facts**
Coverage	Basic data on the bottled water market based largely on original research.
Frequency	Regular
Web Facilities	Summary information on the industry on site.
Cost	Free
Comments	
Address	20-22 Stukely Street, London WC2B 5LR
Tel./e-mail	0207 430 0356
Fax / Web site	0207 831 6014 www.britishsoftdrinks.com

BRITISH SOFT DRINKS ASSOCIATION LTD

139	
Title	**Inbound Tourism Statistics**
Coverage	Tourism facts on volume and value, regional distribution, economic contribution, forecasts.
Frequency	Monthly
Web Facilities	Free access to this data on site.
Cost	Free
Comments	
Address	Research Department, Thames Tower, Black's Road, Hammersmith, London W6 9EL
Tel./e-mail	0208 563 3297 mfisher@bta.org.uk
Fax / Web site	0208 563 3289 www.tourismtrade.org.uk

BRITISH TOURIST AUTHORITY

140	
Title	**Tourism Intelligence Quarterly**
Coverage	Summary and interpretation of up-to-date trends in tourism.
Frequency	Quarterly
Web Facilities	Free access to some statistics on site.
Cost	£95
Comments	
Address	Research Department, Thames Tower, Black's Road, Hammersmith, London W6 9EL
Tel./e-mail	0208 563 3297 mfisher@bta.org.uk
Fax / Web site	0208 563 3289 www.tourismtrade.org.uk

BRITISH TOURIST AUTHORITY

141

	BRITISH TOURIST AUTHORITY
Title	**Digest of Tourist Statistics**
Coverage	Includes extracts and summaries from various travel and tourism surveys including the International Passenger Survey, the UK tourism survey of the residents of Britain, the British National Travel Survey, and many other BTA/ETB and other tourist boards' research results.
Frequency	Annual
Web Facilities	Free access to some statistics on site.
Cost	£75
Comments	
Address	Research Department, Thames Tower, Black's Road, Hammersmith, London W6 9EL
Tel./e-mail	0208 563 3297 mfisher@bta.org.uk
Fax / Web site	0208 563 3289 www.tourismtrade.org.uk

142

	BRITISH TOURIST AUTHORITY
Title	**BTA Annual Report**
Coverage	Includes summary statistics on tourism in the UK with a general review of the short-term outlook for tourism.
Frequency	Annual
Web Facilities	Available free on the site.
Cost	Free
Comments	The web site www.tourismtrade.org.uk has free access to some inbound tourism data.
Address	Research Department, Thames Tower, Black's Road, Hammersmith, London W6 9EL
Tel./e-mail	0208 563 3297 mfisher@bta.org.uk
Fax / Web site	0208 563 3289 www.tourismtrade.org.uk

143

	BRITISH VEHICLE RENTAL AND LEASING ASSOCIATION
Title	**BVRLA Industry Review**
Coverage	Data on the size of the chauffeur drive/private hire, rental, and leasing fleets operated by members of the BVRLA. Usually published around 6 months after the completion of the survey. A large amount of commentary supports the text.
Frequency	Annual
Web Facilities	Free summary data on the Web site plus online ordering of statistics
Cost	£100, £25 to members
Comments	
Address	River Lodge, Badminton Court, Amersham HP7 0DD
Tel./e-mail	01494 434747 info@bvrla.co.uk
Fax / Web site	01494 434499 www.bvrla.co.uk

144	BRITISH VENTURE CAPITAL ASSOCIATION
Title	**Report on Investment Activity**
Coverage	Investment trends and activities of member companies over the previous year. Commentary and statistics based on the association's own survey.
Frequency	Annual
Web Facilities	Free Key Facts summary information free on site.
Cost	£30
Comments	
Address	Essex House, 12-13 Essex Street, London WC2R 3AA
Tel./e-mail	0207 240 3846 bvca@bvca.co.uk
Fax / Web site	0207 240 3849 www.bvca.co.uk

145	BRITISH VENTURE CAPITAL ASSOCIATION
Title	**Performance Measurement Survey**
Coverage	An annual survey offering data on the aggregate net returns to investors from independent venture capitalists and private equity funds. Data by year and by type of fund.
Frequency	Annual
Web Facilities	Free Key Facts summary data on site.
Cost	£30
Comments	Published in association with PriceWaterhouseCoopers.
Address	Essex House, 12-13 Essex Street, London WC2R 3AA
Tel./e-mail	0207 240 3846 bvca@bvca.co.uk
Fax / Web site	0207 240 3849 www.bvca.co.uk

146	BRITISH VENTURE CAPITAL ASSOCIATION
Title	**Economic Impact of Venture Capital in UK**
Coverage	Regular survey of the role of the venture capital sector in the UK economy.
Frequency	Regular
Web Facilities	Free Key Facts summary data on site.
Cost	Free
Comments	Last published for the year 1999 and free report on web site.
Address	Essex House, 12-13 Essex Street, London WC2R 3AA
Tel./e-mail	0207 240 3846 bvca@bvca.co.uk
Fax / Web site	0207 240 3849 www.bvca.co.uk

147

	BRITISH VIDEO ASSOCIATION
Title	**British Video Association Yearbook**
Coverage	Commentary, statistical tables and charts covering sales and rental of video tapes. The sales section includes data on distribution channels, sales by video type, sales by month, region, price group, retailer shares, number of tapes bought, best sellers, and a demographic breakdown. The rental section has data on the market value, seasonality, rentals by video type, source of rentals, frequency of rentals, viewing, and a demographic breakdown. A final section gives statistics on hardware, cinema admissions, employment. and lists BVA members. Many tables give historical data.
Frequency	Annual
Web Facilities	Summary data and top ten rankings on site.
Cost	£35
Comments	First published in 1994.
Address	167 Great Portland Street, London W1N 5FD
Tel./e-mail	0207 436 0041 general@bva.org.uk
Fax / Web site	0207 436 0043 www.bva.org.uk

148

	BRITISH WOODPULP ASSOCIATION
Title	**Annual Report**
Coverage	Includes a statistical section with data on imports of pulp by grade and country of origin, production and consumption of paper and board.
Frequency	Annual
Web Facilities	
Cost	Free to members, a small charge to others
Comments	
Address	9 Glenair Avenue, Lower Parkstone, Poole BH14 5AD
Tel./e-mail	01202 738732
Fax / Web site	01202 738747

149

	BRITISH WOODPULP ASSOCIATION
Title	**Digest of Woodpulp Import Statistics**
Coverage	Tonnage imports of wood pulp for paper making and other purposes based on data supplied by HM Customs and Excise.
Frequency	Monthly
Web Facilities	
Cost	Free to members, annual subscription to others
Comments	
Address	9 Glenair Avenue, Lower Parkstone, Poole BH14 5AD
Tel./e-mail	01202 738732
Fax / Web site	01202 738747

150	BRITISH WOOL MARKETING BOARD
Title	**Annual Report and Accounts 150**
Coverage	Mainly details of the board and its finances, but also contains statistics on wool production by type of wool produced. Based on the board's own figures.
Frequency	Annual
Web Facilities	Some free price information and general data on site.
Cost	Free
Comments	
Address	Oak Mills, Station Road, Bradford BD14 6JD
Tel./e-mail	01274 882091 mail@britishwool.org.uk
Fax / Web site	01274 818277 www.britishwool.org.uk

151	BRITISH WOOL MARKETING BOARD
Title	**Price Schedule**
Coverage	Data on prices sent automatically to producers.
Frequency	Annual
Web Facilities	Some free price information and general data on site.
Cost	Free
Comments	
Address	Oak Mills, Station Road, Bradford BD14 6JD
Tel./e-mail	01274 882091 mail@britishwool.org.uk
Fax / Web site	01274 818277 www.britishwool.org.uk

152	BRITISH WOOL MARKETING BOARD
Title	**Basic Data**
Coverage	Summary information on the sheep population, wool production, prices, registered producers, and the production of mutton and lamb. Based on a board survey.
Frequency	Annual
Web Facilities	Some free price information and general data on site.
Cost	Free
Comments	
Address	Oak Mills, Station Road, Bradford BD14 6JD
Tel./e-mail	01274 882091 mail@britishwool.org.uk
Fax / Web site	01274 818277 www.britishwool.org.uk

153	BROADCASTERS AUDIENCE RESEARCH BOARD (BARB)
Title	**BARB Weekly and Monthly Audience Reports**
Coverage	Television viewing figures produced from a sample survey of 11,000 respondents using electronic TV meters.
Frequency	Weekly and Monthly
Web Facilities	Summary data from weekly and monthly reports plus TV Facts pages on site.
Cost	£3,000 annual registration
Comments	Detailed figures for clients but also general data published in a weekly press release. Other types of analysis available on request.
Address	18 Dering Street, London W1R 9AF
Tel./e-mail	0208 741 9110 enquiries@barb.co.uk
Fax / Web site	0208 741 1943 www.barb.co.uk

154	BUILDER GROUP PLC
Title	**Building Economist**
Coverage	A regular newsletter with a Data File section containing statistics on housebuilding, new orders, contracting, prices, and features on specific market sectors. Based on a combination of official and non-official data.
Frequency	Monthly
Web Facilities	
Cost	£150
Comments	
Address	Exchange Tower, 2 Harbour Exchange Square, London E14 9GE
Tel./e-mail	0207 560 4000
Fax / Web site	0207 560 4009 www.building.co.uk

155	BUILDERS MERCHANTS' FEDERATION
Title	**BMF Sales Indicators**
Coverage	Indexed comparison of turnovers of builders merchants by region and commodity classification. Both adjusted and unadjusted figures are produced. Based on BMF's survey.
Frequency	Monthly
Web Facilities	
Cost	£135
Comments	
Address	15 Soho Square, London W1D 3HL
Tel./e-mail	0870 901 3380 info@bmf.org.uk
Fax / Web site	0207 734 2766 www.bmf.org.uk

156	BUILDING
Title	**Employment Survey**
Coverage	A survey caried out by Gallup examining trends in temporary and permanent employment broken down into two sectors, consultants and contractors.
Frequency	Regular in a weekly journal
Web Facilities	
Cost	£110, £2.40 per issue
Comments	
Address	Exchange Tower, 2 Harbour Exchange Square, London E14 9GE
Tel./e-mail	0207 560 4150
Fax / Web site	0207 560 4404 www.building.co.uk

157	BUILDING
Title	**Procurement Lead Times**
Coverage	Average procurement lead times for specific types of work and for specialist contractors.
Frequency	Six times a year in a weekly journal
Web Facilities	
Cost	£110, £2.40 per issue
Comments	
Address	Exchange Tower, 2 Harbour Exchange Square, London E14 9GE
Tel./e-mail	0207 560 4150
Fax / Web site	0207 560 4404 www.building.co.uk

158	BUILDING
Title	**Tender Cost Forecast**
Coverage	Tender prices for various types of work, and broken down by region. Tender prices are compared with general price trends and forecasts are given for the coming year.
Frequency	Quarterly
Web Facilities	
Cost	£110, £2.40 per issue
Comments	
Address	Exchange Tower, 2 Harbour Exchange Square, London E14 9GE
Tel./e-mail	0207 560 4150
Fax / Web site	0207 560 4404 www.building.co.uk

159	BUILDING
Title	**Datafile**
Coverage	Graphs and commentary on general trends in the building industry, based largely on Central Government data.
Frequency	Monthly in a weekly journal
Web Facilities	
Cost	£110, £2.40 per issue
Comments	
Address	Exchange Tower, 2 Harbour Exchange Square, London E14 9GE
Tel./e-mail	0207 560 4150
Fax / Web site	0207 560 4404 www.building.co.uk

160	BUILDING
Title	**Cost Update**
Coverage	Details of unit rates, material prices, and labour costs.
Frequency	Quarterly in a weekly journal
Web Facilities	
Cost	£110, £2.40 per issue
Comments	
Address	Exchange Tower, 2 Harbour Exchange Square, London E14 9GE
Tel./e-mail	0207 560 4150
Fax / Web site	0207 560 4404 www.building.co.uk

161	BUILDING
Title	**Share Watch**
Coverage	General changes in share prices for the building sector plus specific details of the week's main gainers and losers.
Frequency	Weekly in a weekly journal
Web Facilities	
Cost	£110, £2.40 per issue
Comments	
Address	Exchange Tower, 2 Harbour Exchange Square, London E14 9GE
Tel./e-mail	0207 560 4150
Fax / Web site	0207 560 4404 www.building.co.uk

162	BUILDING COST INFORMATION SERVICE
Title	**BCIS Quarterly Review of Building Prices**
Coverage	Prices by type of building and by region based on a survey of subscribers to BICS.
Frequency	Quarterly
Web Facilities	General details, online ordering, and paid-for access to statistics on site.
Cost	£260
Comments	
Address	12 Great George Street, Parliament Square, London SW1P 3AD
Tel./e-mail	0207 695 1500 bcis@bcis.co.uk
Fax / Web site	0207 695 1501 www.bcis.co.uk
163	BUILDING COST INFORMATION SERVICE
Title	**BMI**
Coverage	Cost information on occupancy and running costs of buildings.
Frequency	Ten issues a year
Web Facilities	General details, online ordering, and paid-for access to statistics on site.
Cost	£395
Comments	
Address	12 Great George Street, Parliament Square, London SW1P 3AD
Tel./e-mail	0207 695 1500 bcis@bcis.co.uk
Fax / Web site	0207 695 1501 www.bcis.co.uk
164	BUILDING COST INFORMATION SERVICE
Title	**Building Cost Information Service**
Coverage	An annual subscription service covering tenders, labour, and materials and based on information supplied by members of BICS.
Frequency	Monthly
Web Facilities	General details, online ordering, and paid-for access to statistics on site.
Cost	£670, Web access - £900
Comments	
Address	12 Great George Street, Parliament Square, London SW1P 3AD
Tel./e-mail	0207 695 1500 bcis@bcis.co.uk
Fax / Web site	0207 695 1501 www.bcis.co.uk

165	BUILDING SOCIETIES ASSOCIATION
Title	**Building Society Yearbook**
Coverage	Key statistics on housing finance and building societies with data on loans, assets, mortgages, commitments etc. Based largely on data collected by the association.
Frequency	Annual
Web Facilities	Press release data and summary statistics free on site.
Cost	£50
Comments	The annual report is available on the web site. Also publishes some titles jointly with the Council of Mortgage Lenders based at the same address (see separate entry).
Address	3 Savile Row, London W15 3PB
Tel./e-mail	0207 437 0655
Fax / Web site	0207 734 6416 www.bsa.org.uk

166	BUILDING SOCIETIES ASSOCIATION
Title	**Building Society Statistics**
Coverage	Monthly data on advances, lending and receipts produced as a press release with supporting data.
Frequency	Monthly
Web Facilities	Press release data and summary statistics available free on site.
Cost	Free
Comments	The annual report is available on the web site. Also publishes some titles jointly with the Council of Mortgage Lenders.
Address	3 Savile Row, London W15 3PB
Tel./e-mail	0207 437 0655
Fax / Web site	0207 734 6416 www.bsa.org.uk

167	BUREAU VAN DIJK
Title	**Lifestyle View**
Coverage	A web-based service offering area profile reports for towns, cities, local areas with data on consumers, product usage, incomes etc.
Frequency	Continuous
Web Facilities	General details and samples on site.
Cost	Price start from £120
Comments	Produced in association with Claritas (see other entry).
Address	Northburgh House, 10 Northburgh Street, London EC1V 0PP
Tel./e-mail	0207 549 5000 marketing@bvd.co.uk
Fax / Web site	0207 549 5010 www.bvd.co.uk

168	**BUSINESS AND TRADE STATISTICS LTD**
Title	**External Trade Statistics**
Coverage	Detailed statistics, from 1979 onwards, on product imports and exports, analysed by trading partners, port of entry and exit. Business and Trade Statistics is an official agent of HM Customs and Excise.
Frequency	Monthly
Web Facilities	
Cost	Depends on the amount and type of data required
Comments	Available in various machine readable formats.
Address	Lancaster House, More Lane, Esher KT10 8AP
Tel./e-mail	01372 63121 BTS@dial.pipex.com
Fax / Web site	01372 69847

169	**BUSINESS GEOGRAPHICS LTD**
Title	**Censys 95**
Coverage	A geodemographic service offering geodemographic profiles, lifestyle profiles, area profiles and geographical information systems. Based on an analysis of 1991 census data plus electoral roll data and market research sources including Target Group Index, BARB, NRS, and RAJAR.
Frequency	Continuous
Web Facilities	General details of services on site.
Cost	On request
Comments	Locate is claimed to be the first web-based source of Census data.
Address	8-10 Dryden Street, London WC2E 9BP
Tel./e-mail	0207 520 5800 info@geoweb.co.uk
Fax / Web site	0207 520 5801 www.geoweb.co.uk

170	**C B HILLIER PARKER**
Title	**Western Corridor Offices**
Coverage	An overview of trends in the office market in the Western corridor (M4/M5).
Frequency	Quarterly
Web Facilities	Access to data on the site and email alerting services.
Cost	Free
Comments	
Address	77 Grosvenor Street, London W1A 2BT
Tel./e-mail	0207 629 7666
Fax / Web site	0207 915 7030 www.cbhillierparker.com

171	**C B HILLIER PARKER**
Title	**UK Econo-Property**
Coverage	Various statistics covering economic and business trends relevant to the property sector. Based on various government and other sources.
Frequency	Quarterly
Web Facilities	Access to data on the site and email alerting services.
Cost	Free
Comments	
Address	77 Grosvenor Street, London W1A 2BT
Tel./e-mail	0207 629 7666
Fax / Web site	0207 915 7030 www.cbhillierparker.com

172	**C B HILLIER PARKER**
Title	**Shopping Centres Investment Activity**
Coverage	Investment trends in the shop property sector. Based on a survey by the company.
Frequency	Annual
Web Facilities	Access to data on the site and email alerting facilities.
Cost	Free
Comments	
Address	77 Grosvenor Street, London W1A 2BT
Tel./e-mail	0207 629 7666
Fax / Web site	0207 915 7030 www.cbhillierparker.com

173	**C B HILLIER PARKER**
Title	**Retail Warehouse Parks in the Pipeline**
Coverage	Details of specific warehouse parks and aggregate data on numbers and floorspace. Based on the company's own data.
Frequency	Twice yearly
Web Facilities	Access to data on the site and email alerting facilities.
Cost	Free
Comments	
Address	77 Grosvenor Street, London W1A 2BT
Tel./e-mail	0207 629 7666
Fax / Web site	0207 915 7030 www.cbhillierparker.com

174	C B HILLIER PARKER
Title	**Property Market Quarterly Review**
Coverage	Investment, rent and other trends for property in various sectors.
Frequency	Quarterly
Web Facilities	Access to data on the site and email alerting facilities.
Cost	Free
Comments	
Address	77 Grosvenor Street, London W1A 2BT
Tel./e-mail	0207 629 7666
Fax / Web site	0207 915 7030 www.cbhillierparker.com

175	C B HILLIER PARKER
Title	**UK Rents and Yields Monitor**
Coverage	Statistics on rents and yields for offices, shops, and industrial premises with data over a 5-year period. Based on the company's own survey.
Frequency	Quarterly
Web Facilities	Access to data on the site and email alerting facilities.
Cost	Free
Comments	
Address	77 Grosvenor Street, London W1A 2BT
Tel./e-mail	0207 629 7666
Fax / Web site	0207 915 7030 www.cbhillierparker.com

176	C B HILLIER PARKER
Title	**Shopping Centres in the Pipeline**
Coverage	Details of specific shopping centres, aggregate data and projected floorspace. Based on the company's own survey.
Frequency	Twice yearly
Web Facilities	Access to data on the site and email alerting facilities.
Cost	Free
Comments	
Address	77 Grosvenor Street, London W1A 2BT
Tel./e-mail	0207 629 7666
Fax / Web site	0207 915 7030 www.cbhillierparker.com

177	**C B HILLIER PARKER**
Title	**Central London Offices**
Coverage	An overview of trends in the central London office market.
Frequency	Quarterly
Web Facilities	Access to data on the site and email alerting facilities.
Cost	£15
Comments	
Address	77 Grosvenor Street, London W1A 2BT
Tel./e-mail	0207 629 7666
Fax / Web site	0207 915 7030 www.cbhillierparker.com
178	**CACI SOLUTIONS**
Title	**Acorn Profiles/Area Reports**
Coverage	Various demographic and area profiles based on an analysis of census data plus postcode address files and electoral roll data. Also uses Target Group Index (TGI) and Financial Research Survey (FRS) data as well as some other market research sources.
Frequency	Continuous
Web Facilities	The site has access to various free sets of data, area reports, and survey summaries.
Cost	On request, and depending on range and nature of information required
Comments	
Address	CACI House, Kensington Village, Avonmore Road, London W14 8TS
Tel./e-mail	0207 602 6000 info@caci.co.uk
Fax / Web site	0207 603 5862 www.caci.co.uk

179	CAMBRIDGE ECONOMETRICS
Title	**Regional Economic Prospects**
Coverage	Detailed analysis and forecasts on economic trends in the UK regions. Long-term forecasts and commentary.
Frequency	Twice yearly
Web Facilities	General details, and free summary statistics, on the site. Paid-for access to all data.
Cost	£1,750
Comments	Published in February and July.
Address	Covent Garden, Cambridge CB1 2HS
Tel./e-mail	01223 460760 info@camecon.com
Fax / Web site	01223 464378 www.camecon.co.uk

180	CAMBRIDGE ECONOMETRICS
Title	**Industry and the British Economy**
Coverage	A detailed forecast of the British economy and industry with forecasts up to ten years ahead. Detailed analysis of over 40 industrial sectors and 19 service sectors.
Frequency	Twice yearly
Web Facilities	General details, and free summary statistics, on the site. Paid-for access to all data.
Cost	£1,750
Comments	Published in January and June.
Address	Covent Garden, Cambridge CB1 2HS
Tel./e-mail	01223 460760 info@camecon.com
Fax / Web site	01223 464378 www.camecon.co.uk

181	CAN MAKERS
Title	**Can Makers Market Review**
Coverage	Details of the beverage can industry and market, broken down by soft drinks and beer. Market data covers the latest four years in some tables and there is also some data on European trends. Based mainly on a mixture of non-official sources including trade association, market research and Gallup data. Detailed commentary supports the tables.
Frequency	Twice yearly
Web Facilities	Free access to data on site and facilities to obtain reports electronically.
Cost	Free
Comments	Also publishes regular press releases and bulletins with statistics.
Address	1 Chelsea Manor Gardens, London SW3 5PN
Tel./e-mail	0207 349 5024 canmakers@gciuk.com
Fax / Web site	0207 352 6244 www.canmakers.co.uk

182

	CAPS INVESTMENT INFORMATION SERVICE
Title	**Quarterly Survey of Pooled Pension Funds**
Coverage	Summarises the returns achieved by different types of pooled pension funds including sector-specific and mixed funds. Based on an analysis of almost 700 funds.
Frequency	Quarterly
Web Facilities	
Cost	£430, £175 per issue
Comments	
Address	11 Albion Street, Leeds LS1 5ES
Tel./e-mail	0113 2460416
Fax / Web site	

183

	CAPSCAN LTD
Title	**Cenario**
Coverage	A CD-ROM providing access to the 1991 Census small area statistics. The Cenario software provides a range of analytical functions including mapping, graphics, customer profiles, postcode sector ranking etc.
Frequency	Annual
Web Facilities	General details of services on site.
Cost	Minimum entry level - £3,000
Comments	
Address	Tranley House, Tranley Mews, Fleet Road, London NW3 2QW
Tel./e-mail	0207 267 7055 sales@capscan.co.uk
Fax / Web site	0207 267 2745 www.capscan.com

184

	CARPET FLOORING RETAIL
Title	**Business Trends**
Coverage	A quarterly survey of trends in the carpet industry based on returns from carpet suppliers and retailers. Includes data on sales by carpet type.
Frequency	Quarterly in a monthly journal
Web Facilities	
Cost	£70
Comments	Also publishes regular surveys on wholesaling, retailing, and specific carpet and floorcoverings markets.
Address	United Business Media International, Sovereign Way, Tonbridge TN9 1RW
Tel./e-mail	01732 377375 tboden@ubminternational.com
Fax / Web site	01732 377203

185		CARRICK JAMES MARKET RESEARCH
	Title	**Parent Omnibus**
	Coverage	Based on a survey of 1,000 parents of children aged between 0 and 14. Parents of 5 to 14 year olds are surveyed every two months while parents of 0 to 14 year olds are surveyed quarterly.
	Frequency	Six times per year
	Web Facilities	General details of services on site.
	Cost	Varies according to the range of questions/information required
	Comments	
	Address	6 Homer Street, London W1H 1HN
	Tel./e-mail	0207 724 3836 cjmr@easynet.co.uk
	Fax / Web site	0207 224 8257 easyweb.easynet.co.uk/cjmr

186		CARRICK JAMES MARKET RESEARCH
	Title	**Youth Omnibus**
	Coverage	Based on a sample of 1,200 young people aged between 11 and 24. Questions cover behaviour, spending, product and advertising awareness etc.
	Frequency	Six times per year
	Web Facilities	General details of services on site.
	Cost	Varies according to the range of questions/information required
	Comments	
	Address	6 Homer Street, London W1H 1HN
	Tel./e-mail	0207 724 3836 cjmr@easynet.co.uk
	Fax / Web site	0207 224 8257 easyweb.easynet.co.uk/cjmr

187		CARRICK JAMES MARKET RESEARCH
	Title	**Child and Teenage Omnibus**
	Coverage	Continuous survey of children from the age of five upwards and teenagers up to the age of 19. Various questions relating to spending, behaviour, opinions, awareness etc.
	Frequency	Monthly
	Web Facilities	General details of services on site.
	Cost	Varies according to the range of questions/information required
	Comments	Also carries out a regular 'European Child Omnibus'.
	Address	6 Homer Street, London W1H 1HN
	Tel./e-mail	0207 724 3836 cjmr@easynet.co.uk
	Fax / Web site	0207 224 8257 easyweb.easynet.co.uk/cjmr

188	CARRICK JAMES MARKET RESEARCH
Title	**All Ages Omnibus**
Coverage	Based on a sample size of 3,000, this regular survey asks questions of adults and children from the age of seven upwards.
Frequency	Monthly
Web Facilities	General details of services on site.
Cost	Varies according to the range of questions/information required
Comments	
Address	6 Homer Street, London W1H 1HN
Tel./e-mail	0207 724 3836 cjmr@easynet.co.uk
Fax / Web site	0207 224 8257 easyweb.easynet.co.uk/cjmr

189	CATERER & HOTELKEEPER
Title	**Market Prices**
Coverage	Based on a survey of 18 specialist catering suppliers, prices are given for various fresh foods. Food categories covered are meat, poultry, game, fresh fish, fruit, vegetables, and salad.
Frequency	Weekly in a weekly journal
Web Facilities	News, email news alerts, and some data on site.
Cost	£89, £1.90 per issue
Comments	The journal also has occasional features on catering and hotel sectors.
Address	Reed Business Publishing Ltd, Windsor Court, East Grinstead House, East Grinstead RH19 1XA
Tel./e-mail	01342 326972
Fax / Web site	01342 335612 www.caterer.com

190	CATERER & HOTELKEEPER
Title	**Industry Trends**
Coverage	Various statistics on the catering and hotel trades including hotel occupancy rates, turnover figures for various catering sectors, share prices. The data available varies from week to week depending on the sources used.
Frequency	Weekly in a weekly journal
Web Facilities	News, email news alerts, and some data on site.
Cost	£89, £1.90 per issue
Comments	The journal also has occasional features on hotel and catering sectors.
Address	Reed Business Publishing Ltd, Windsor Court, East Grinstead House, East Grinstead RH19 1XA
Tel./e-mail	01342 326972
Fax / Web site	01342 335612 www caterer.com

191 CCN SYSTEMS LTD

Title	**Mosaic/Chorus**
Coverage	Geodemographic services based on various sources including census and lifestyle data, electoral roll data, postcode address files, Target Group Index (TGI) and Financial Research Survey (FRS).
Frequency	Continuous
Web Facilities	General details of services on site.
Cost	On request, depending on the range and nature of the information required
Comments	
Address	Abbey House, Abbeyfield Road, Nottingham NG7 2SW
Tel./e-mail	0115 9860801
Fax / Web site	0115 9610888 www.experian.com

192 CEMENT ADMIXTURES ASSOCIATION

Title	**Statistical Return**
Coverage	Sales by weight and value for a variety of admixtures based on a survey of members.
Frequency	Regular
Web Facilities	
Cost	Free
Comments	
Address	36a Tilehouse Green Lane, Knowle B93 9EY
Tel./e-mail	01564 776362
Fax / Web site	01564 776362

193 CENTRE FOR THE STUDY OF REGULATED INDUSTRIES

Title	**UK Airports Industry: Airport Statistics**
Coverage	Operating and financial statistics on UK airports with aggregate data and statistics on specific airports. Based on data collected by CIPFA and the centre.
Frequency	Annual
Web Facilities	General details of all publications and online ordering facilities on site.
Cost	£40
Comments	
Address	School of Management, University of Bath, Bath BA2 7AY
Tel./e-mail	01225 323197 mnsjsm@management.bath.ac.uk
Fax / Web site	01225 323221 www.bath.ac.uk/Departments/Management

194	CENTRE FOR THE STUDY OF REGULATED INDUSTRIES
Title	**Charges for Electricity Services**
Coverage	The first edition of this publication appeared in 1995 following the privatisation of the electricity industry. Based on returns from the companies and CRI research.
Frequency	Annual
Web Facilities	General details of all publications and online ordering facilities on site.
Cost	£10
Comments	Last published issue covers 1998/1999.
Address	School of Management, University of Bath, Bath BA2 7AY
Tel./e-mail	01225 323197 mnsjsm@management.bath.ac.uk
Fax / Web site	01225 323221 www.bath.ac.uk/Departments/Management

195	CENTRE FOR THE STUDY OF REGULATED INDUSTRIES
Title	**The UK Electricity Industry: Financial and Operating Review**
Coverage	Financial and operating data on the UK electricity industry.
Frequency	Annual
Web Facilities	General details of all publications and online ordering facilities on site.
Cost	£40
Comments	
Address	School of Management, University of Bath, Bath BA2 7AY
Tel./e-mail	01225 323197 mnsjsm@management.bath.ac.uk
Fax / Web site	01225 323221 www.bath.ac.uk/Departments/Management

196	CENTRE FOR THE STUDY OF REGULATED INDUSTRIES
Title	**The UK Water Industry: Charges for Water Services**
Coverage	The first edition of this publication appeared in 1994 and gives details of water charges. Based on data supplied by the companies and some CIPFA analysis.
Frequency	Annual
Web Facilities	General details of all publications and online ordering facilities on site.
Cost	£10
Comments	Last published issue covers 1997/1998.
Address	School of Management, University of Bath, Bath BA2 7AY
Tel./e-mail	01225 323197 mnsjsm@management.bath.ac.uk
Fax / Web site	01225 323221 www.bath.ac.uk/Departments/Management

197	**CHAMBER OF SHIPPING**
Title	**Annual Review**
Coverage	Some statistics on fleet, trade, and other market trends.
Frequency	Annual
Web Facilities	General details of statistics, and some free summary data, on the Web site.
Cost	Free
Comments	Usually published end-March. Also publishes quarterly journal - Making Waves.
Address	12 Carthusian Street, London EC1M 6EZ
Tel./e-mail	0207 417 2800 postmaster@british-shipping.org
Fax / Web site	0207 417 2080 www.british-shipping.org

198	**CHARITIES AID FOUNDATION**
Title	**Dimensions 20--**
Coverage	Various reports throughout the year with data and analysis on charity giving and receiving, top charities. Based on CAF research.
Frequency	Regular
Web Facilities	General details of all reports and online ordering facilities on site.
Cost	£32.50
Comments	This new series replaces the annual Dimensions of the Voluntary Sector.
Address	24 Stevenson Way, London NW1 2DP
Tel./e-mail	0207 209 5151 info@cafonline.org
Fax / Web site	0207 209 5049 www.cafonline.org

199	**CHARITY RECRUITMENT**
Title	**Annual Voluntary Sector Salary Survey**
Coverage	Salaries for various job categories and grades in large and small charities. Based on a survey by the company.
Frequency	Annual
Web Facilities	General details of services on site.
Cost	£170 plus VAT, £120 plus VAT for charities with less than 30 staff
Comments	
Address	40 Roseberry Avenue, London EC1R 4RX
Tel./e-mail	0207 833 0770 cr@charityrec.sarce.co.uk
Fax / Web site	0207 833 0188 www.charec.co.uk

200

	CHART ANALYSTS
Title	**UK Point and Figure Library**
Coverage	Comprehensive coverage of the UK Stock Market by market sector. Over 500 charts and tables cover industry group performance, share indices, British funds, money rates, and general indicators. Based on various sources and analysis by the company.
Frequency	Weekly and monthly
Web Facilities	General details of services and samples on site. PDF versions of reports available for purchase.
Cost	£1,315 weekly, £575 monthly
Comments	Name changed from Fullermarkets Ltd.
Address	Plaza 533, Kings Road, London SW10 0SZ
Tel./e-mail	0207 351 5751
Fax / Web site	0207 352 3185 www.chartanalysts.com

201

	CHART ANALYSTS
Title	**Commodities**
Coverage	Trends and prices in UK and USA futures markets. Covers over 30 different commodities in the food, grain, livestock/meat, industrial, metals, and finance sectors. Based on the company's data.
Frequency	Weekly and monthly
Web Facilities	General details of services and samples on site. PDF versions of reports available for purchase.
Cost	£835 weekly, £250 monthly, £33 per issue
Comments	Name changed from Fullermarkets Ltd.
Address	Plaza 533, Kings Road, London SW10 0SZ
Tel./e-mail	0207 351 5751
Fax / Web site	0207 352 3185 www.chartanalysts.com

202

	CHARTERED INSTITUTE OF MANAGEMENT ACCOUNTANTS
Title	**CIMA Survey**
Coverage	Quarterly survey which asks the financial directors of Britain's companies how they perceive their own company's future and what their view is of the economy as a whole.
Frequency	Quarterly
Web Facilities	
Cost	Free
Comments	
Address	63 Portland Place, London W1N 4AB
Tel./e-mail	0207 637 2311
Fax / Web site	0207 631 5309 www.cima.org.uk

203	**CHARTERED INSTITUTE OF MARKETING**
Title	**Marketing Trends Survey**
Coverage	A review of economic and business trends, trends in the marketing sector.
Frequency	Quarterly
Web Facilities	Available free on the Web site along with details of other surveys, including some ad-hoc research
Cost	Free
Comments	
Address	Moor Hall, Cookham, Maidenhead SL6 9QH
Tel./e-mail	01628 427500 marketing@cim.co.uk
Fax / Web site	01628 427329 www.cim.co.uk

204	**CHARTERED INSTITUTE OF PERSONNEL AND DEVELOPMENT**
Title	**IPD Labour Turnover Survey**
Coverage	A survey of employee turnover and job tenure with analysis by type of job, sectors, and manual/non-manual workers. Based on a survey by CIPD.
Frequency	Annual
Web Facilities	
Cost	Free
Comments	
Address	IPD House, Camp Road, Wimbledon, London SW19 4UX
Tel./e-mail	0208 971 9000 ipd@ipd.co.uk
Fax / Web site	0208 263 3333 www.ipd.co.uk

205	**CHARTERED INSTITUTE OF PUBLIC FINANCE AND ACCOUNTANCY (CIPFA)**
Title	**Local Authority Assets Statistics**
Coverage	An analysis of local authority balance sheets with information on operational and non-operational assets, DSOs, other commercial services, Housing Revenue Account, long and short-term borrowing, investments and reserves, capital charges.
Frequency	Annual
Web Facilities	General details and paid-for access to all data via SIS Internet Subscription
Cost	£110
Comments	Data also available on disc.
Address	NLA Tower, 12-16 Addiscombe Road, Croydon CR0 0XT
Tel./e-mail	0208 667 1144 sisinfo@ipf.co.uk
Fax / Web site	0208 681 8058 www.ipf.co.uk/sis

206

CHARTERED INSTITUTE OF PUBLIC FINANCE AND ACCOUNTANCY (CIPFA)

Title	**Cemetries - Actuals**
Coverage	Expenditure, income, fees, and non-financial data on cemetries in local authority areas. Based on data collected by CIPFA.
Frequency	Annual
Web Facilities	General details and paid-for access to all data via the SIS Internet Subscription.
Cost	£60
Comments	Data also available on disc.
Address	NLA Tower, 12-16 Addiscombe Road, Croydon CR0 0XT
Tel./e-mail	0208 667 1144 sisinfo@ipf.co.uk
Fax / Web site	0208 681 8058 www.ipf.co.uk/sis

207

CHARTERED INSTITUTE OF PUBLIC FINANCE AND ACCOUNTANCY (CIPFA)

Title	**Highways and Transportation - Estimates**
Coverage	Data on highways and transportation expenditure by county councils in England and Wales.
Frequency	Annual
Web Facilities	General details and paid-for access to all data via the SIS Internet Subscription.
Cost	£85
Comments	Data also available on disc.
Address	NLA Tower, 12-16 Addiscombe Road, Croydon CR0 0XT
Tel./e-mail	0208 667 1144 sisinfo@ipf.co.uk
Fax / Web site	0208 681 8058 www.ipf.co.uk/sis

208

CHARTERED INSTITUTE OF PUBLIC FINANCE AND ACCOUNTANCY (CIPFA)

Title	**Environmental Health - Actuals**
Coverage	Financial and other data relating to environmental health in specific local authorities. Based on data collected by CIPFA.
Frequency	Annual
Web Facilities	General details and paid-for access to all data via the SIS Internet Subscription.
Cost	£85
Comments	Data also available on disc.
Address	NLA Tower, 12-16 Addiscombe Road, Croydon CR0 0XT
Tel./e-mail	0208 667 1144 sisinfo@ipf.co.uk
Fax / Web site	0208 681 8058 www.ipf.co.uk/sis

209

CHARTERED INSTITUTE OF PUBLIC FINANCE AND ACCOUNTANCY (CIPFA)

Title	**Education (Including Unit Costs) - Actuals**
Coverage	Non-financial data on pupil, school, and teacher numbers and financial data split by types of school and local authority area. The publication now also includes education unit costs, previously published in a separate volume. These costs cover institutional costs, pupil and student support costs, capital costs, salary costs, recurrent expenditure, and university costs. Based largely on Central Government data.
Frequency	Annual
Web Facilities	General details and paid-for access to all data via the SIS Internet Subscription.
Cost	£85
Comments	Data also available on disc.
Address	NLA Tower, 12-16 Addiscombe Road, Croydon CR0 0XT
Tel./e-mail	0208 667 1144 sisinfo@ipf.co.uk
Fax / Web site	0208 681 8058 www.ipf.co.uk/sis

210

CHARTERED INSTITUTE OF PUBLIC FINANCE AND ACCOUNTANCY (CIPFA)

Title	**Planning and Development - Combined Actuals and Estimates**
Coverage	Capital and revenue expenditure on the planning and development functions in summary and by individual local authority. Based on data collected by CIPFA.
Frequency	Annual
Web Facilities	General details and paid-for access to all data via the SIS Internet Subscription.
Cost	£85
Comments	Data also available on disc.
Address	NLA Tower, 12-16 Addiscombe Road, Croydon CR0 0XT
Tel./e-mail	0208 667 1144 sisinfo@ipf.co.uk
Fax / Web site	0208 681 8058 www.ipf.co.uk/sis

211

CHARTERED INSTITUTE OF PUBLIC FINANCE AND
ACCOUNTANCY (CIPFA)

Title	**Capital Expenditure and Treasury Management**
Coverage	An analysis of capital payments and debt statistics for individual local authorities in England, Wales, Scotland, and Northern Ireland. Based on data collected by CIPFA.
Frequency	Annual
Web Facilities	General details and paid-for access to all data via the SIS Internet Subscription.
Cost	£110
Comments	Data also available on disc.
Address	NLA Tower, 12-16 Addiscombe Road, Croydon CR0 0XT
Tel./e-mail	0208 667 1144 sisinfo@ipf.co.uk
Fax / Web site	0208 681 8058 www.ipf.co.uk/sis

212

CHARTERED INSTITUTE OF PUBLIC FINANCE AND
ACCOUNTANCY (CIPFA)

Title	**Council Tax Demands and Precepts - Estimates**
Coverage	Statistics on the level of demands and revenues from council tax based on returns from local authorities collected by CIPFA.
Frequency	Annual
Web Facilities	General details and paid-for access to all data via the SIS Internet Subscription.
Cost	£60
Comments	Data also available on disc.
Address	NLA Tower, 12-16 Addiscombe Road, Croydon CR0 0XT
Tel./e-mail	0208 667 1144 sisinfo@ipf.co.uk
Fax / Web site	0208 681 8058 www.ipf.co.uk/sis

213

CHARTERED INSTITUTE OF PUBLIC FINANCE AND
ACCOUNTANCY (CIPFA)

Title	**County Farms and Rural Estates - Actuals**
Coverage	Financial and other data on county farms and rural estates by local authority area. Based on data collected by CIPFA.
Frequency	Annual
Web Facilities	General details and paid-for access to all data via the SIS Internet Subscription.
Cost	£60
Comments	Data also available on disc.
Address	NLA Tower, 12-16 Addiscombe Road, Croydon CR0 0XT
Tel./e-mail	0208 667 1144 sisinfo@ipf.co.uk
Fax / Web site	0208 681 8058 www.ipf.co.uk/sis

214	CHARTERED INSTITUTE OF PUBLIC FINANCE AND ACCOUNTANCY (CIPFA)
Title	**Crematoria - Actuals**
Coverage	Expenditure, income, fees and non-financial data on crematoria by local authority area. Based on data collected by
Frequency	Annual
Web Facilities	General details and paid-for access to all data via the SIS Internet Subscription.
Cost	£60
Comments	Data also available on disc.
Address	NLA Tower, 12-16 Addiscombe Road, Croydon CR0 0XT
Tel./e-mail	0208 667 1144 sisinfo@ipf.co.uk
Fax / Web site	0208 681 8058 www.ipf.co.uk/sis

215	CHARTERED INSTITUTE OF PUBLIC FINANCE AND ACCOUNTANCY (CIPFA)
Title	**Direct Service Organisations - Actuals**
Coverage	Financial, organisational, and related data on direct service organisations in local authorities. Based on returns to CIPFA from local authorities.
Frequency	Annual
Web Facilities	General details and paid-for access to all data via the SIS Internet Subscription.
Cost	£110
Comments	Data also available on disc.
Address	NLA Tower, 12-16 Addiscombe Road, Croydon CR0 0XT
Tel./e-mail	0208 667 1144 sisinfo@ipf.co.uk
Fax / Web site	0208 681 8058 www.ipf.co.uk/sis

216	CHARTERED INSTITUTE OF PUBLIC FINANCE AND ACCOUNTANCY (CIPFA)
Title	**Archives - Estimates**
Coverage	Statistics on the organisation and financing of archives based on returns from local authorities collected by CIPFA.
Frequency	Annual
Web Facilities	General details and paid-for access to all data via the SIS Internet Subscription.
Cost	£60
Comments	Data also available on disc.
Address	NLA Tower, 12-16 Addiscombe Road, Croydon CR0 0XT
Tel./e-mail	0208 667 1144 sisinfo@ipf.co.uk
Fax / Web site	0208 681 8058 www.ipf.co.uk/sis

217

	CHARTERED INSTITUTE OF PUBLIC FINANCE AND ACCOUNTANCY (CIPFA)
Title	**Housing Rents - Actuals**
Coverage	An analysis of the housing stock by age and type, average weekly rents and rebates, and allowances. Data for individual local authorities and summary tables for individual planning regions. Based on returns to CIPFA from local authorities.
Frequency	Annual
Web Facilities	General details and paid-for access to all data via the SIS Internet Subscription
Cost	£85
Comments	Data also available on disc.
Address	NLA Tower, 12-16 Addiscombe Road, Croydon CR0 0XT
Tel./e-mail	0208 667 1144 sisinfo@ipf.co.uk
Fax / Web site	0208 681 8058 www.ipf.co.uk/sis

218

	CHARTERED INSTITUTE OF PUBLIC FINANCE AND ACCOUNTANCY (CIPFA)
Title	**Local Government Comparative Statistics**
Coverage	Summary statistical indicators covering the range of local authority services. Based on a combination of data collected by CIPFA and other non-official sources.
Frequency	Annual
Web Facilities	General details and paid-for access to all data via the SIS Internet Subscription.
Cost	£110
Comments	Data also available on disc.
Address	NLA Tower, 12-16 Addiscombe Road, Croydon CR0 0XT
Tel./e-mail	0208 667 1144 sisinfo@ipf.co.uk
Fax / Web site	0208 681 8058 www.ipf.co.uk/sis

219

	CHARTERED INSTITUTE OF PUBLIC FINANCE AND ACCOUNTANCY (CIPFA)
Title	**Revenue Collection - Actuals**
Coverage	Revenue collection statistics broken down by local authority area and based on returns to CIPFA from local authorities.
Frequency	Annual
Web Facilities	General details and paid-for access to all data via the SIS Internet Subscription.
Cost	£85
Comments	Data also available on disc.
Address	NLA Tower, 12-16 Addiscombe Road, Croydon CR0 0XT
Tel./e-mail	0208 667 1144 sisinfo@ipf.co.uk
Fax / Web site	0208 681 8058 www.ipf.co.uk/sis

220	CHARTERED INSTITUTE OF PUBLIC FINANCE AND ACCOUNTANCY (CIPFA)
Title	**Education - Estimates**
Coverage	Financial and non-financial estimates for education authorities.
Frequency	Annual
Web Facilities	General details and paid-for access to all data via the SIS Internet Subscription.
Cost	£85
Comments	Data also available on disc.
Address	NLA Tower, 12-16 Addiscombe Road, Croydon CR0 0XT
Tel./e-mail	0208 667 1144 sisinfo@ipf.co.uk
Fax / Web site	0208 681 8058 www.ipf.co.uk/sis

221	CHARTERED INSTITUTE OF PUBLIC FINANCE AND ACCOUNTANCY (CIPFA)
Title	**Superannuation Fund Investment Statistics**
Coverage	A ten-year historical record of superannuation statistics with the first issue, published in 1995, covering the years 1985 to 1995. Based on data supplied by local authorities.
Frequency	Annual
Web Facilities	General details and paid-for access to all data via the SIS Internet Subscription.
Cost	£180
Comments	Data also available on disc.
Address	NLA Tower, 12-16 Addiscombe Road, Croydon CR0 0XT
Tel./e-mail	0208 667 1144 sisinfo@ipf.co.uk
Fax / Web site	0208 681 8058 www.ipf.co.uk/sis

222	CHARTERED INSTITUTE OF PUBLIC FINANCE AND ACCOUNTANCY (CIPFA)
Title	**Leisure Charges - Actuals**
Coverage	Sample survey of charges for leisure centre facilities, swimming pools and outdoor sports. Based on a sample of 150 local authorities.
Frequency	Annual
Web Facilities	General details and paid-for access to all data via the SIS Internet Subscription.
Cost	£60
Comments	Data also available on disc.
Address	NLA Tower, 12-16 Addiscombe Road, Croydon CR0 0XT
Tel./e-mail	0208 667 1144 sisinfo@ipf.co.uk
Fax / Web site	0208 681 8058 www.ipf.co.uk/sis

223

CHARTERED INSTITUTE OF PUBLIC FINANCE AND ACCOUNTANCY (CIPFA)

Title	**Leisure and Recreation - Estimates**
Coverage	Estimated expenditure and income on sports and recreation, cultural and other related facilities by local authory area. Based on data collected by CIPFA from local authorities.
Frequency	Annual
Web Facilities	General details and paid-for access to all data via the SIS Internet Subscription.
Cost	£85
Comments	Data also available on disc.
Address	NLA Tower, 12-16 Addiscombe Road, Croydon CR0 0XT
Tel./e-mail	0208 667 1144 sisinfo@ipf.co.uk
Fax / Web site	0208 681 8058 www.ipf.co.uk/sis

224

CHARTERED INSTITUTE OF PUBLIC FINANCE AND ACCOUNTANCY (CIPFA)

Title	**Housing Revenue Account - Combined Actuals and Estimates**
Coverage	Figures for Housing Revenue Account income in total and for each housing authority in England and Wales. Based on a combination of Central Government statistics and CIPFA data.
Frequency	Annual
Web Facilities	General details and paid-for access to all data via the SIS Internet Subscription.
Cost	£85
Comments	Data also available on disc.
Address	NLA Tower, 12-16 Addiscombe Road, Croydon CR0 0XT
Tel./e-mail	0208 667 1144 sisinfo@ipf.co.uk
Fax / Web site	0208 681 8058 www.ipf.co.uk/sis

225

CHARTERED INSTITUTE OF PUBLIC FINANCE AND ACCOUNTANCY (CIPFA)

Title	**Public Libraries - Estimates**
Coverage	Financial and non-financial estimates of public library operations.
Frequency	Annual
Web Facilities	General details and paid-for access to all data via the SIS Internet Subscription.
Cost	£60
Comments	Data also available on disc.
Address	NLA Tower, 12-16 Addiscombe Road, Croydon CR0 0XT
Tel./e-mail	0208 667 1144 sisinfo@ipf.co.uk
Fax / Web site	0208 681 8058 www.ipf.co.uk/sis

226

CHARTERED INSTITUTE OF PUBLIC FINANCE AND ACCOUNTANCY (CIPFA)

Title **Trading Standards - Actuals and Estimates**

Coverage Financial and non-financial data on trading standards departments with data for individual local authorities. Based on data collected by CIPFA.

Frequency Annual

Web Facilities General details and paid-for access to all data via the SIS Internet Subscription.

Cost £60

Comments Data also available on disc.

Address NLA Tower, 12-16 Addiscombe Road, Croydon   CR0 0XT

Tel./e-mail 0208 667 1144   sisinfo@ipf.co.uk

Fax / Web site 0208 681 8058   www.ipf.co.uk/sis

227

CHARTERED INSTITUTE OF PUBLIC FINANCE AND ACCOUNTANCY (CIPFA)

Title **Police - Estimates**

Coverage Financial and non-financial data on police service operations.

Frequency Annual

Web Facilities General details and paid-for access to all data via the SIS Internet Subscription.

Cost £85

Comments Data also available on disc.

Address NLA Tower, 12-16 Addiscombe Road, Croydon   CR0 0XT

Tel./e-mail 0208 667 1144   sisinfo@ipf.co.uk

Fax / Web site 0208 681 8058   www.ipf.co.uk/sis

228

CHARTERED INSTITUTE OF PUBLIC FINANCE AND ACCOUNTANCY (CIPFA)

Title **Finance and General - Estimates**

Coverage Summary information on local authority income and expenditure with data for each local authority in England and Wales. Based on estimates collected by CIPFA with additional data on estimated income and expenditure per head of the population.

Frequency Annual

Web Facilities General details and paid-for access to all data via the SIS Internet Subscription.

Cost £110

Comments Data also available on disc.

Address NLA Tower, 12-16 Addiscombe Road, Croydon   CR0 0XT

Tel./e-mail 0208 667 1144   sisinfo@ipf.co.uk

Fax / Web site 0208 681 8058   www.ipf.co.uk/sis

229

CHARTERED INSTITUTE OF PUBLIC FINANCE AND ACCOUNTANCY (CIPFA)

Title	**Public Libraries - Actuals**
Coverage	Final out-turn figures for income and expenditure, manpower, agency services, books, and other stocks and service points are given in total and for each library service in Great Britain and Northern Ireland.
Frequency	Annual
Web Facilities	General details and paid-for access to all data via the SIS Internet Subscription.
Cost	£85
Comments	Data also available on disc.
Address	NLA Tower, 12-16 Addiscombe Road, Croydon CR0 0XT
Tel./e-mail	0208 667 1144 sisinfo@ipf.co.uk
Fax / Web site	0208 681 8058 www.ipf.co.uk/sis

230

CHARTERED INSTITUTE OF PUBLIC FINANCE AND ACCOUNTANCY (CIPFA)

Title	**Administration of Justice - Combined Actuals and Estimates**
Coverage	Expenditure and income figures for both magistrates' and coroners' courts per thousand population. Based on returns received by CIPFA.
Frequency	Annual
Web Facilities	General details and paid-for access to all data via the SIS Internet Subscription.
Cost	£60
Comments	Data also available on disc.
Address	NLA Tower, 12-16 Addiscombe Road, Croydon CR0 0XT
Tel./e-mail	0208 667 1144 sisinfo@ipf.co.uk
Fax / Web site	0208 681 8058 www.ipf.co.uk/sis

231

CHARTERED INSTITUTE OF PUBLIC FINANCE AND ACCOUNTANCY (CIPFA)

Title	**Fire - Combined Actuals and Estimates**
Coverage	Summary data on fire service income and expenditure and similar figures for each local authority and per thousand population. Also statistics on fire stations, training, manpower, applications, return of calls, inspections. Based on returns from local authorities received by CIPFA.
Frequency	Annual
Web Facilities	General details and paid-for access to all data via the SIS Internet Subscription.
Cost	£85
Comments	Data also available on disc.
Address	NLA Tower, 12-16 Addiscombe Road, Croydon CR0 0XT
Tel./e-mail	0208 667 1144 sisinfo@ipf.co.uk
Fax / Web site	0208 681 8058 www.ipf.co.uk/sis

232

CHARTERED INSTITUTE OF PUBLIC FINANCE AND ACCOUNTANCY (CIPFA)

Title	**Personal Social Services - Actuals**
Coverage	An analysis of residential, day, and community care provision giving gross and net expenditure and the number of clients by local authority area. Based on data collected by CIPFA.
Frequency	Annual
Web Facilities	General details and paid-for access to all data via the SIS Internet Subscription.
Cost	£85
Comments	Data also available on disc.
Address	NLA Tower, 12-16 Addiscombe Road, Croydon CR0 0XT
Tel./e-mail	0208 667 1144 sisinfo@ipf.co.uk
Fax / Web site	0208 681 8058 www.ipd.co.uk/sis

233

CHARTERED INSTITUTE OF PUBLIC FINANCE AND
ACCOUNTANCY (CIPFA)

Title	**Waste Collection and Disposal - Actuals**
Coverage	Data on revenue income and expenditure, capital expenditure and financing, treatment methods, waste arising and reclaimed waste by tonnage, vehicle disposals, manpower, and unit costs. Summary data and by local authority area. Based on data collected by CIPFA.
Frequency	Annual
Web Facilities	General details and paid-for access to all data via the SIS Internet Subscription.
Cost	£110
Comments	Data also available on disc.
Address	NLA Tower, 12-16 Addiscombe Road, Croydon CR0 0XT
Tel./e-mail	0208 667 1144 sisinfo@ipf.co.uk
Fax / Web site	0208 681 8058 www.ipf.co.uk/sis

234

CHARTERED INSTITUTE OF PUBLIC FINANCE AND
ACCOUNTANCY (CIPFA)

Title	**Personal Social Services - Estimates**
Coverage	Data on revenue, income, and expenditure plus some non-financial data.
Frequency	Annual
Web Facilities	General details and paid-for access to all data via the SIS Internet Subscription.
Cost	£85
Comments	Data also available on disc.
Address	NLA Tower, 12-16 Addiscombe Road, Croydon CR0 0XT
Tel./e-mail	0208 667 1144 sisinfo@ipf.co.uk
Fax / Web site	0208 681 8058 www.ipf.co.uk/sis

235

CHARTERED INSTITUTE OF PUBLIC FINANCE AND ACCOUNTANCY (CIPFA)

Title	**Police - Actuals**
Coverage	Figures are given for income, expenditure and manpower in total and by individual police force and regional crime squad. Based on data collected by CIPFA.
Frequency	Annual
Web Facilities	General details and paid-for access to all data via the SIS Internet Subscription.
Cost	£85
Comments	Data also available on disc.
Address	NLA Tower, 12-16 Addiscombe Road, Croydon CR0 0XT
Tel./e-mail	0208 667 1144 sisinfo@ipf.co.uk
Fax / Web site	0208 681 8058 www.ipf.co.uk/sis

236

CHARTERED INSTITUTE OF PUBLIC FINANCE AND ACCOUNTANCY (CIPFA)

Title	**Highways and Transportation - Actuals**
Coverage	Data on highways and transportation expenditure by county councils in England and Wales. Based on returns received by CIPFA.
Frequency	Annual
Web Facilities	General details and paid-for access to all data via the SIS Internet Subscription.
Cost	£85
Comments	Data also available on disc.
Address	NLA Tower, 12-16 Addiscombe Road, Croydon CR0 0XT
Tel./e-mail	0208 667 1144 sisinfo@ipf.co.uk
Fax / Web site	0208 681 8058 www.ipf.co.uk/sis

237

CHARTERED INSTITUTE OF PUBLIC FINANCE AND ACCOUNTANCY (CIPFA)

Title	**Homelessness - Actuals**
Coverage	A financial survey of the operations of the Housing (Homeless Persons) Act with data for individual local authorities. Based on data collected by CIPFA.
Frequency	Annual
Web Facilities	General details and paid-for access to all data via the SIS Internet Subscription.
Cost	£60
Comments	Data also available on disc.
Address	NLA Tower, 12-16 Addiscombe Road, Croydon CR0 0XT
Tel./e-mail	0208 667 1144 sisinfo@ipf.co.uk
Fax / Web site	0208 681 8058 www.ipf.co.uk/sis

238

CHARTERED INSTITUTE OF PUBLIC FINANCE AND ACCOUNTANCY (CIPFA)

Title	**Housing Rent Arrears and Benefits - Actuals**
Coverage	An analysis of rent arrears and benefits by local authority area. Based on returns to CIPFA from local authorities.
Frequency	Annual
Web Facilities	General details and paid-for access to all data via the SIS Internet Subscription.
Cost	£85
Comments	Data also available on disc.
Address	NLA Tower, 12-16 Addiscombe Road, Croydon CR0 0XT
Tel./e-mail	0208 667 1144 sisinfo@ipf.co.uk
Fax / Web site	0208 681 8058 www.ipf.co.uk/sis

239

CHARTERED INSTITUTE OF PUBLIC FINANCE AND ACCOUNTANCY (CIPFA)

Title	**Probation - Combined Actuals and Estimates**
Coverage	Expenditure and income in the probation service per thousand population aged 15-29 and manpower for the service in England and Wales. Based on data collected by CIPFA.
Frequency	Annual
Web Facilities	General details and paid-for access to all data via the SIS Internet Subscription.
Cost	£60
Comments	Data also available on disc.
Address	NLA Tower, 12-16 Addiscombe Road, Croydon CR0 0XT
Tel./e-mail	0208 667 1144 sisinfo@ipf.co.uk
Fax / Web site	0208 681 8058 www.ipf.co.uk/sis

240

CHARTERED INSTITUTE OF PUBLIC FINANCE AND ACCOUNTANCY (CIPFA)

Title	**Local Government Trends**
Coverage	Provides a set of measures offering trend information by class of authority over a five year period.
Frequency	Annual
Web Facilities	General details and paid-for access to all data via the SIS Internet Subscription.
Cost	£110
Comments	Data also available on disc.
Address	NLA Tower, 12-16 Addiscombe Tower, Croydon CR0 0XT
Tel./e-mail	0208 667 1144 sisinfo@ipf.co.uk
Fax / Web site	0208 681 8058 www.ipf.co.uk/sis

241	CHARTERHOUSE PLC
Title	**UK Economica**
Coverage	A review of UK economic trends with short-term forecasts. Forecasts produced by the company with existing data from Central Government sources.
Frequency	Quarterly
Web Facilities	
Cost	On request
Comments	
Address	1 Paternoster Row, London EC4M 7DH
Tel./e-mail	0207 248 4000
Fax / Web site	0207 246 2033

242	CHEMICAL INDUSTRIES ASSOCIATION
Title	**Graduate Recruitment Survey**
Coverage	Annual survey based on returns from CIA educational contracts and it provides an updated breakdown by discipline of recruitment over the last two years, and a recruitment forecast for the current year.
Frequency	Annual
Web Facilities	General details of publications on the Web site.
Cost	Sample copy free, bulk supply on application.
Comments	Published every October. The association also published international statistics.
Address	Kings Buildings, Smith Square, London SW1P 3JJ
Tel./e-mail	0207 834 3399 commsec@cia.org.uk
Fax / Web site	0207 834 4469 www.cia.org.uk

243	CHEMICAL INDUSTRIES ASSOCIATION
Title	**UK Chemical Industry 20--**
Coverage	Leaflet with basic statistics on the UK chemical industry with historical data over a ten-year period.
Frequency	Annual
Web Facilities	General details of publications on the Web site.
Cost	Free (single copy), £12.50 per 100 copies
Comments	Published in July each year. Also available as a Powerpoint presentation. The association also publishes international statistics.
Address	Kings Building, Smith Square, London SW1P 3JJ
Tel./e-mail	0207 834 3399 commsec@cia.org.uk
Fax / Web site	0207 834 4469 www.cia.org.uk

244

	CHEMICAL INDUSTRIES ASSOCIATION
Title	**Public Image of the Chemical Industry**
Coverage	Results of an opinion survey which considers attitudes to the business, the industry, chemicals, local/national data, and responses to HSE targets and verification.
Frequency	Annual
Web Facilities	General details of publications on the Web site.
Cost	£25 to members, £50 non-members
Comments	The survey is conducted by MORI. The association also publishes international statistics.
Address	Kings Building, Smith Square, London SW1P 3JJ
Tel./e-mail	0207 834 3399 commsec@cia.org.uk
Fax / Web site	0207 834 4469 www.cia.org.uk

245

	CHEMICAL INDUSTRIES ASSOCIATION
Title	**Economics Bulletin**
Coverage	Monitors, analyses and forecasts the economic performance of the UK chemical industry. A main table of chemical industry basic economic indicators is also included. Based on official and non-official sources.
Frequency	Three issues per year
Web Facilities	General details of publications on the Web site.
Cost	Free to members, £75 non-members
Comments	The association also publishes international statistics.
Address	Kings Building, Smith Square, London SW1P 3JJ
Tel./e-mail	0207 834 3399 commsec@cia.org.uk
Fax / Web site	0207 834 4469 www.cia.org.uk

246

	CHEMIST AND DRUGGIST
Title	**Chemist & Druggist Price List**
Coverage	Trade and retail prices for various products sold by chemists. Based on the journal's own survey with prices usually one month old.
Frequency	Weekly
Web Facilities	
Cost	£140
Comments	The journal also has regular features on specific markets and specific products sold via chemists.
Address	United Business Media International Ltd, Sovereign House, Sovereign Way, Tonbridge TN9 1RW
Tel./e-mail	01732 377487 chemdrug@UBMinternenational.com
Fax / Web site	01732 367065 www.dotpharmacy.com

247

	CHESTERTON PLC
Title	**City Centre Office Markets**
Coverage	A review of rents, rates, vacancies, occupancies in the major cities based on data collected by the company.
Frequency	Annual
Web Facilities	Free access to statistics on the Web site.
Cost	£75
Comments	Also publish titles for Central London Office Markets and London Residential Trends.
Address	54 Brook Street, London W1A 2BU
Tel./e-mail	0207 499 0404 tony.burdett@chesterton.co.uk
Fax / Web site	0207 629 7804 www.chesterton.co.uk

248

	CHILLED FOODS ASSOCIATION
Title	**Market Statistics**
Coverage	General data on sales by product category in the chilled foods market.
Frequency	Regular
Web Facilities	Free access to data on site.
Cost	Free
Comments	
Address	PO Box 14811, London NW10 9ZR
Tel./e-mail	0208 451 0503 cfa@chilledfood.org
Fax / Web site	0208 459 8061 www.chilledfood.org

249

	CINEMA ADVERTISING ASSOCIATION
Title	**Caviar - Cinema and Video Industry Audience Research**
Coverage	Provides audience data for cinema and pre-recorded videos from the age of 7 upwards by film, genre, certificate. Based on a survey of almost 3,000 people in various randomly selected sampling points around the country.
Frequency	Annual
Web Facilities	
Cost	£7,150
Comments	The data is also available online, and on disc.
Address	12 Golden Square, London W1R 3AF
Tel./e-mail	0207 534 6363
Fax / Web site	0207 534 6464

	250	CINEMA ADVERTISING ASSOCIATION
Title		**CAA Admissions Monitor**
Coverage		A monthly measure of the attendances at all UK cinemas accepting advertising. Based on the association's own research.
Frequency		Monthly
Web Facilities		
Cost		Free
Comments		The data is also available online and on disc. Conducted by Entertainment Data International for the CAA.
Address		12 Golden Square, London W1R 3AF
Tel./e-mail		0207 534 6363
Fax / Web site		0207 534 6464

	251	CIVIL AVIATION AUTHORITY
Title		**UK Airports**
Coverage		Monthly and annual statements of movements, passengers, and cargo at UK airports, based on data collected by the CAA. Statistics usually cover the previous month.
Frequency		Monthly and Annual
Web Facilities		General details of publications on site.
Cost		On request
Comments		CAA statistics also available on magnetic disc in Word for Windows format or on Excel spreadsheeets. Disc subscription - £118 per annum, £11.80 for individual discs.
Address		Greville House, 37 Gratton Road, Cheltenham GL50 2BN
Tel./e-mail		01242 35151
Fax / Web site		01242 584139 www.caa.co.uk

	252	CIVIL AVIATION AUTHORITY
Title		**UK Airlines**
Coverage		Operating and traffic statistics for UK airlines by domestic and international services, and by types of operation, based on the CAA's own data. Statistics usually cover the previous month.
Frequency		Annual
Web Facilities		General details of publications on site.
Cost		On request
Comments		CAA statistics also available on magnetic discs in Word for Windows format or on Excel spreadsheets. Disc subscription - £118 per annum, £11.80 for individual discs.
Address		Greville House, 37 Gratton Road, Cheltenham GL50 2BN
Tel./e-mail		01242 35151
Fax / Web site		01242 584139 www.caa.co.uk

253	**CLARITAS**
Title	**Claritas**
Coverage	Geodemographic services offering consumer, lifestyle, demographic, and market data for local areas.
Frequency	Continuous
Web Facilities	General details of services on site.
Cost	On request
Comments	
Address	Park House, Station Road, Teddington TW11 9AD
Tel./e-mail	0208 213 5500 info-uk@claritaseu.com
Fax / Web site	0208 213 5588 www.claritas.co.uk

254	**COCA-COLA & SCHWEPPES BEVERAGES LTD**
Title	**Bottled Water Market Profile**
Coverage	A review of the UK bottled water market with sales data for the total market and by type of water. Also includes data on brands, retailing, new products.
Frequency	Regular
Web Facilities	
Cost	On request
Comments	
Address	Charter Place, Uxbridge UB8 1EZ
Tel./e-mail	01895 231313
Fax / Web site	01895 239092

255	**COMPANY CAR**
Title	**Databank**
Coverage	Prices of new cars and the standing, running, and operating costs of car fleets.
Frequency	Monthly in a monthly journal
Web Facilities	
Cost	£91.25
Comments	
Address	DMG World Media Ltd, Queensway House, 2 Queensway, Redhill RH1 1QS
Tel./e-mail	0207 785 5358 companycar@dmgworldmedia.com
Fax / Web site	0207 785 5207 www.dmg.co.uk

256	COMPUTER BUSINESS REVIEW
Title	**Trends and Indicators**
Coverage	Basic data on general economic trends and indicators relevant to the computer sector based on information compiled from various sources.
Frequency	Monthly in a monthly journal
Web Facilities	
Cost	£55
Comments	
Address	12 Sutton Row, London W1V 5FH
Tel./e-mail	0207 208 4245 cbred@computerwire.com
Fax / Web site	0207 439 1105 www.cbronline.com

257	COMPUTER ECONOMICS LTD & REMUNERATION ECONOMICS
Title	**Computer Staff Salary Survey**
Coverage	A survey of 50 job descriptions analysed by location, age, experience, areas of responsibility, fringe benefits etc. Based on a survey by the company. A small commentary supports the text.
Frequency	Twice yearly
Web Facilities	General details of statistics on the Web site.
Cost	£630 minimum
Comments	Only available to subscribing members.
Address	Survey House, 51 Portland Road, Kingston-upon-Thames KT1 2SH
Tel./e-mail	0208 549 8726 cel@celre.co.uk
Fax / Web site	0208 541 5705 www.celre.co.uk

258	COMPUTER ECONOMICS LTD & REMUNERATION ECONOMICS
Title	**Survey of Financial Functions**
Coverage	A salary survey for various levels of responsibility by company size, industry group, location, age, qualifications etc. Additional data on benefits and recruitment. Based on the company's own survey with some supporting text.
Frequency	Annual
Web Facilities	General details of statistics on Web site.
Cost	£340, £185 to participants
Comments	
Address	Survey House, 51 Portland Road, Kingston-upon-Thames KT1 2SH
Tel./e-mail	0208 549 8726 re@celre.co.uk
Fax / Web site	0208 541 5705 www.celre.co.uk

259	COMPUTER ECONOMICS LTD & REMUNERATION ECONOMICS
Title	**Directors' Survey**
Coverage	A survey of salaries and benefits for chief executives, directors, and senior executives.
Frequency	Annual
Web Facilities	General details of statistics on Web site.
Cost	£600
Comments	Produced in association with Bacon & Woodrow.
Address	Survey House, 51 Portland Road, Kingston-upon-Thames KT1 2SH
Tel./e-mail	0208 549 8726 re@celre.co.uk
Fax / Web site	0208 541 5705 www.celre.co.uk

260	COMPUTER ECONOMICS LTD & REMUNERATION ECONOMICS
Title	**Survey of Personnel Functions**
Coverage	A salary survey covering various levels of responsibility by size of company, industry group, location, age, qualifications etc. Additional data on benefits and recruitment. Based on the company's own survey with some supporting text.
Frequency	Annual
Web Facilities	General details of statistics on Web site.
Cost	£340, £185 for participants
Comments	
Address	Survey House, 51 Portland Road, Kingston-upon-Thames KT1 2SH
Tel./e-mail	0208 549 8726 re@celre.co.uk
Fax / Web site	0208 541 5705 www.celre.co.uk

261	COMPUTER ECONOMICS LTD & REMUNERATION ECONOMICS
Title	**Survey of Pensions Managers**
Coverage	A salary survey of pensions managers and related jobs with data by company size, industry group, location, age etc. Based on the company's own survey with some supporting text.
Frequency	Annual
Web Facilities	General details of statistics on Web site.
Cost	£340, £185 for participants
Comments	
Address	Survey House, 51 Portland Road, Kingston-upon-Thames KT1 2SH
Tel./e-mail	0208 549 8726 re@celre.co.uk
Fax / Web site	0208 541 5705 www.celre.co.uk

262	COMPUTER ECONOMICS LTD & REMUNERATION ECONOMICS
Title	**Survey of Actuaries and Actuarial Students**
Coverage	A salary survey of actuaries and students with data by levels of responsibility, company size, age, qualifications etc.
Frequency	Annual
Web Facilities	General details of statistics on Web site.
Cost	£640, £320 to participants
Comments	Produced in association with the Institute of Actuaries.
Address	Survey House, 51 Portland Road, Kingston-upon-Thames KT1 2SH
Tel./e-mail	0208 549 8726 re@celre.co.uk
Fax / Web site	0208 541 5705 www.celre.co.uk

263	COMPUTER ECONOMICS LTD & REMUNERATION ECONOMICS
Title	**A Survey of Sales and Marketing Staff**
Coverage	A salary survey covering nine levels of responsibility and broken down into various sectors. Based on data collected by the company.
Frequency	Annual
Web Facilities	General details of statistics on Web site.
Cost	£370, £185 for participants
Comments	
Address	Survey House, 51 Portland Road, Kingston-upon-Thames KT1 2SH
Tel./e-mail	0208 549 8726 re@celre.co.uk
Fax / Web site	0208 541 5705 www.celre.co.uk

264	COMPUTER ECONOMICS LTD & REMUNERATION ECONOMICS
Title	**National Management Salary Survey**
Coverage	A survey of managers to produce statistics on earnings, fringe benefits, and bonuses. Produced in three volumes: a general review of the survey, a detailed statistics volume, and a small business review.
Frequency	Annual
Web Facilities	General details of statistics on Web site.
Cost	£490, discounts available to participants
Comments	Produced in association with the Institute of Management.
Address	Survey House, 51 Portland Road, Kingston-upon-Thames KT1 2SH
Tel./e-mail	0208 549 8726 cel@celre.co.uk
Fax / Web site	0208 541 5705 www.celre.co.uk

265

COMPUTER ECONOMICS LTD & REMUNERATION
ECONOMICS

Title **Survey of Engineering Functions**

Coverage A survey of engineering salaries covering nine levels of
responsibility, by company size, type of work, qualifications,
location etc. Based on the company's own survey with some
supporting text.

Frequency Annual

Web Facilities General details of statistics on Web site.

Cost £300, £150 for participants

Comments

Address Survey House, 51 Portland Road, Kingston-upon-Thames
KT1 2SH

Tel./e-mail 0208 549 8726   re@celre.co.uk

Fax / Web site 0208 541 5705   www.celre.co.uk

266

COMPUTING SERVICES AND SOFTWARE
ASSOCIATION

Title **Annual Report**

Coverage Includes the association's annual survey based on voluntary
responses from member companies. Data on business activities,
total revenue, revenue by business sector, revenue per
employee, employment trends, profits, and future prospects. A
detailed commentary supports the text.

Frequency Annual

Web Facilities Press releases for trend surveys and detailed data for members
on site.

Cost Free

Comments

Address 20 Red Lion Street, London   WC1R 4QN

Tel./e-mail 0207 395 6700   cssa@cssa.co.uk

Fax / Web site 0107 740 4119   www.cssa.co.uk

267	COMPUTING SERVICES AND SOFTWARE ASSOCIATION
Title	**CEO Trends Survey**
Coverage	A quarterly opinion survey of members assessing trends and likely trends in the sector.
Frequency	Quarterly
Web Facilities	Press releases for trends surveys and access to detailed data for members on site.
Cost	On request
Comments	
Address	20 Red Lion Street, London WC1R 4QN
Tel./e-mail	0207 395 6700 cssa@cssa.co.uk
Fax / Web site	0207 740 4119 www.cssa.co.uk

268	CONFEDERATION OF BRITISH FORGERS
Title	**End of Year Statistics**
Coverage	Annual statistics on the forging industry including market developments, prices, deliveries. Based on the association's own survey.
Frequency	Annual
Web Facilities	
Cost	£10, free to members
Comments	
Address	245 Grove Lane, Handsworth, Birmingham B20 2HB
Tel./e-mail	0121 554 3311
Fax / Web site	0121 523 0761

269	CONFEDERATION OF BRITISH FORGERS
Title	**BFIA Annual Report**
Coverage	Contains some statistics on the economic performance of the forging industry.
Frequency	Annual
Web Facilities	
Cost	On request
Comments	
Address	245 Grove Lane, Handsworth, Birmingham B20 2HB
Tel./e-mail	0121 554 3311
Fax / Web site	0121 523 0761

270	CONFEDERATION OF BRITISH INDUSTRY (CBI)
Title	**Monthly Trends Enquiry**
Coverage	Essentially an abbreviated version of the quarterly 'Industrial Trends Survey' with summary statistics on orders, stocks, output, prices etc. A short commentary supports the statistics. Data is based on a survey of companies with responses varying from around 1,300 to over 1,500.
Frequency	Monthly
Web Facilities	General details of publications and online ordering facilities on site, a joint subscription with Industrial Trends Survey (see entry above)
Cost	£665, £400 to members
Comments	
Address	103 New Oxford Street, London WC1A 1DU
Tel./e-mail	0207 395 8247
Fax / Web site	0207 240 1578 www.cbi.org.uk

271	CONFEDERATION OF BRITISH INDUSTRY (CBI)
Title	**Time Series and Performance Indicators**
Coverage	Monthly trends in pay and pay increases taken from the CBI Pay Databank.
Frequency	Monthly
Web Facilities	General details of publications and online ordering facilities on site.
Cost	£25 per issue, £20 to members
Comments	
Address	103 New Oxford Street, London WC1A 1DU
Tel./e-mail	0207 395 8247
Fax / Web site	0207 240 1578 www.cbi.org.uk

272	CONFEDERATION OF BRITISH INDUSTRY (CBI)
Title	**CBI/Deloitte & Touche Service Sector Survey**
Coverage	A quarterly survey of the services sector based on results from a sample of service industry companies.
Frequency	Quarterly
Web Facilities	General details of publications and online ordering facilities on site.
Cost	£325, £180 for members
Comments	First published in December 1998.
Address	103 New Oxford Street, London WC1A 1DU
Tel./e-mail	0207 379 7400
Fax / Web site	0207 240 1578 www.cbi.org.uk

273	CONFEDERATION OF BRITISH INDUSTRY (CBI)
Title	**Industrial Trends Survey**
Coverage	Trends for over 40 industry groups covering orders, stocks, output, capital expenditure, exports, costs, labour etc for the last four months and the next four months. Based on a CBI survey of around 1,700 companies.
Frequency	Quarterly
Web Facilities	General details of publications and online ordering facilities on site., joint subscription with Monthly Trends Enquiry (see below) £665, £400 to members
Cost	£455, £245 to members
Comments	
Address	103 New Oxford Street, London WC1A 1DU
Tel./e-mail	0207 395 8247
Fax / Web site	0207 240 1578 www.cbi.org.uk

274	CONFEDERATION OF BRITISH INDUSTRY (CBI)
Title	**Economic and Business Outlook**
Coverage	An economic survey plus a forecast up to six months ahead. Also a general survey of industrial and regional trends and some comparative data for other European countries. Based on a combination of CBI data and official statistics.
Frequency	Quarterly
Web Facilities	General details of publications and online ordering facilities on site.
Cost	£366, £208 to members
Comments	
Address	103 New Oxford Street, London WC1A 1DU
Tel./e-mail	0207 395 8247
Fax / Web site	0207 240 1578 www.cbi.org.uk

275	CONFEDERATION OF BRITISH INDUSTRY (CBI)
Title	**CBI/Business Strategies Regional Trends Survey**
Coverage	A survey of economic and business trends in the UK regions based on a survey of a sample of companies in these regions.
Frequency	Annual
Web Facilities	General details of publications and online ordering facilities on site.
Cost	£300, £170 to members
Comments	
Address	103 New Oxford Street, London WC1A 1DU
Tel./e-mail	0207 395 8247
Fax / Web site	0207 240 1578 www.cbi.org.uk

276	CONFEDERATION OF BRITISH INDUSTRY (CBI)
Title	**CBI/GVA Grimley Property Trends Survey**
Coverage	A survey of short-term and long-term property requirements of the private sector.
Frequency	Twice yearly
Web Facilities	General details of publications and online ordering facilities on site.
Cost	On request
Comments	
Address	103 New Oxford Street, London WC1A 1DU
Tel./e-mail	0207 379 7400
Fax / Web site	0207 240 1578 www.cbi.org.uk

277	CONFEDERATION OF BRITISH INDUSTRY (CBI)
Title	**CBI Retail and Wholesale Distributive Trades Survey**
Coverage	A survey of trends in over 20 distributive sectors with data on sales volume, orders, stocks, employment, investment, prices, business expenditure etc. Based on a CBI survey.
Frequency	Monthly
Web Facilities	General details of publications and online ordering facilities on site.
Cost	£425, £255 to members
Comments	
Address	103 New Oxford Street, London WC1A 1DU
Tel./e-mail	0207 395 8247
Fax / Web site	0207 240 1578 www.cbi.org.uk

278	CONFEDERATION OF BRITISH INDUSTRY (CBI)
Title	**CBI/Price Waterhouse Coopers Financial Services Survey**
Coverage	A survey of trends in various financial services sectors with data on income, employment, short-term expectations etc. Based on a CBI survey.
Frequency	Quarterly
Web Facilities	General details of publications and online ordering facilities on site.
Cost	£325, £180 to members
Comments	
Address	103 New Oxford Street, London WC1A 1DU
Tel./e-mail	0207 395 8247
Fax / Web site	0207 240 1578 www.cbi.org.uk

279	CONSENSUS RESEARCH INTERNATIONAL
Title	**Unit Trust Survey**
Coverage	A survey of the awareness of, and attitudes towards, unit trusts amongst unitholders and intermediaries. Based on a company survey. A commentary supports the data.
Frequency	Quarterly
Web Facilities	
Cost	On request
Comments	Also produces an annual Stockbroker Survey, based on the ratings of brokers' analysts by company executives.
Address	1-2 Castle Lane, London SW1E 6DR
Tel./e-mail	0207 592 1700 mail@consensus-research.co.uk
Fax / Web site	0207 738 1271

280	CONSTRUCTION CONFEDERATION
Title	**Construction Trends**
Coverage	Prospects for the building workload, capacity of operations, tender prices and the availability of labour and materials. Based on survey of members with the confederation stating that members account for 75% of all building work. Some commentary supports the survey results.
Frequency	Quarterly
Web Facilities	
Cost	£80
Comments	Subscriptions are handled by CIP Ltd, Federation House, 60 New Coventry Road, Birmingham B26 3AY, telephone 0121 722 8200.
Address	56-64 Leonard Street, London EC2A 4JX
Tel./e-mail	0207 608 5000
Fax / Web site	0207 608 5001

281	CONSTRUCTION FORECASTING AND RESEARCH LTD
Title	**Construction Industry Focus**
Coverage	Data on contractors' activity, order books, tender prices, and short-term prospects for employment and tender prices. Based on a combination of official and non-official data.
Frequency	Monthly
Web Facilities	General details of statistics, and online ordering facilities, on the Web site.
Cost	£110
Comments	Statistics on European construction trends and corporate performance in the construction industry also produced.
Address	Vigilant House, 120 Wilton Road, London SW1V 1JZ
Tel./e-mail	0207 808 7070 cfrjgph@aol.com
Fax / Web site	0207 808 7069 www.construction-forecast.com
282	CONSTRUCTION FORECASTING AND RESEARCH LTD
Title	**Construction Forecasts**
Coverage	Short-term construction forecasts, and current trends, covering housing, industrial, commercial, and infrastructure. Value and volume forecasts are included and a detailed analysis of the forecasts accompanies the tables.
Frequency	Quarterly
Web Facilities	General details of statistics, and online ordering facilities, on Web site.
Cost	£225
Comments	Published on behalf of the Joint Forecasting Committee for the Construction Industries. Statistics on European construction trends and corporate performance in the construction industry also produced.
Address	Vigilant House, 120 Wilton Road, London SW1V 1JZ
Tel./e-mail	0207 808 7070 cfrjgph@aol.com
Fax / Web site	0207 808 7069 www.construction-forecast.com

283

	CONSTRUCTION NEWS
Title	**Annual Contracts Review**
Coverage	An annual review of contracts awarded by type of construction, eg residential, commercial, industrial, and by region. Also statistics on work out to tender.
Frequency	Annual in a weekly journal
Web Facilities	News and general details on site.
Cost	£72.50
Comments	'FT'-Actuaries Indices are also included in each issue.
Address	EMAP Construct, 151 Roseberry Avenue, London EC1R 4GB
Tel./e-mail	0207 505 6868
Fax / Web site	0207 505 6867 www.cnplus.co.uk

284

	CONSTRUCTION NEWS
Title	**Workload Trends**
Coverage	Statistics covering new contracts awarded by construction type updating the data in the annual survey noted in the previous entry.
Frequency	Monthly in a weekly journal
Web Facilities	News and general details on site.
Cost	£72.50
Comments	'FT'-Actuaries Indices are also included in each issue.
Address	EMAP Construct, 151 Roseberry Avenue, London EC1R 4GB
Tel./e-mail	0207 505 6868
Fax / Web site	0207 505 6867 www.cnplus.co.uk

285

	CONSTRUCTION PLANT HIRE ASSOCIATION
Title	**CPA Activity and Hire Rate Studies**
Coverage	Activity percentages and average hire rates for typical machines. Based on a survey of members.
Frequency	Quarterly
Web Facilities	
Cost	Free but only available to members.
Comments	
Address	52 Rochester Row, London SW1P 1JV
Tel./e-mail	0207 630 6868 enquiries@c-p-a.co.uk
Fax / Web site	0207 630 6765 www.c-p-a.co.uk

286

	CONSTRUCTION PLANT HIRE ASSOCIATION
Title	**CPA Machine Cost Studies**
Coverage	Details of the costs to plant hire companies of running typical machines and cost movement indices. Based on data collected by the association.
Frequency	Twice yearly
Web Facilities	
Cost	Free to members but there may be a small charge to others
Comments	
Address	52 Rochester Row, London SW1P 1JV
Tel./e-mail	0207 630 6868 enquiries@c-p-a.co.uk
Fax / Web site	0207 630 6765 www.c-p-a.co.uk

287

	CONSTRUCTION PLANT HIRE ASSOCIATION
Title	**CPA Driver Cost Studies**
Coverage	Details of the costs attached to the employment of drivers under civil engineering or plant hire working rule agreements. Based on a survey by the association.
Frequency	Annual
Web Facilities	
Cost	Free to members but there may be a small charge to others
Comments	
Address	52 Rochester Row, London SW1P 1JV
Tel./e-mail	0207 630 6868 enquiries@c-p-a.co.uk
Fax / Web site	0207 630 6765 www.c-p-a.co.uk

288

	CONSTRUCTION PRODUCTS ASSOCIATION
Title	**Construction Industry Forecast**
Coverage	Forecasts three years ahead for housing starts and completions, other new work and repair, maintenance and improvement. Based on BMP's own forecasts with a large amount of supporting commentary.
Frequency	Twice yearly
Web Facilities	Member access to statistics and online ordering facilities on site.
Cost	£300, £200 per issue
Comments	Published in January and July.
Address	26 Store Street, London WC1E 7BT
Tel./e-mail	0207 323 3770 enquiries@constprod.org.uk
Fax / Web site	0207 323 0307 www.constprod.org.uk

289	CONSTRUCTION PRODUCTS ASSOCIATION
Title	**Construction Market Trends**
Coverage	Covers housebuilding starts and completions, renovations, prices, mortgages, value of new orders and output, capital expenditure, trade, and building materials. Based on a combination of Central Government data and non-official sources.
Frequency	Monthly
Web Facilities	Member access to statistics and online ordering facilities on site.
Cost	£175, £20 per issue
Comments	
Address	26 Store Street, London WC1E 7BT
Tel./e-mail	0207 323 3770 enquiries@constprod.org.uk
Fax / Web site	0207 323 0307 www.constprod.org.uk
290	CONSTRUCTION PRODUCTS ASSOCIATION
Title	**Construction Products Trade Survey**
Coverage	A survey of the UK building materials industry based on an opinion survey of members.
Frequency	Quarterly
Web Facilities	Member access to statistics and online ordering facilities on site.
Cost	£150, £50 per issue
Comments	Published in February, May, August, November.
Address	26 Store Street, London WC1E 7BT
Tel./e-mail	0207 323 3770 enquiries@constprod.org.uk
Fax / Web site	0207 323 0307 www.constprod.org.uk
291	CONSUMER CREDIT TRADE ASSOCIATION
Title	**Consumer Credit**
Coverage	Commentary and statistics on consumer credit trends with comparisons trends in the previous year.
Frequency	Six issues per year
Web Facilities	
Cost	£3.50 to members £5.50 to non-members
Comments	
Address	1st Floor, Tennyson House, 159-163 Great Portland Street, London W1N 5FD
Tel./e-mail	0207 636 7564 cctassoc.demon.co.uk
Fax / Web site	0207 323 0096

292	CONSUMER PROFILE RESEARCH LTD
Title	**Decisions**
Coverage	A regular omnibus survey aimed at researching issues relating to advertising, packaging, new product development etc.
Frequency	Regular
Web Facilities	
Cost	On request
Comments	
Address	18 High Street, Thame, Oxford OX4 2BZ
Tel./e-mail	01844 215672
Fax / Web site	01844 261324

293	CONTINENTAL RESEARCH
Title	**Digital TV, Satellite and Cable Monitor**
Coverage	Quarterly review with statistics on the number of satellite dishes, SMATV, and cable installations in the UK. Also figures on intentions to purchase and viewing levels. Based on original research by the company.
Frequency	Quarterly
Web Facilities	Detailed executive summaries with data free on site.
Cost	£150
Comments	
Address	132-140 Goswell Road, London EC1V 7OP
Tel./e-mail	0207 490 9103 mail@continentalresearch.com
Fax / Web site	0207 490 1174 www.continentalresearch.com

294	CONTINENTAL RESEARCH
Title	**Small Business Omnibus**
Coverage	Monthly survey of 300 small business with various questions asked.
Frequency	Monthly
Web Facilities	Detailed executive summaries with data free on site.
Cost	On request
Comments	
Address	132-140 Goswell Road, London EC1V 7OP
Tel./e-mail	0207 490 9103 mail@continentalresearch.com
Fax / Web site	0207 490 1174 www.continentalresearch.com

295	CONTINENTAL RESEARCH
Title	**Mobile Phone Report**
Coverage	Quarterly review with statistics on phone use, penetration.
Frequency	Quarterly
Web Facilities	Detailed executive summaries with data on site.
Cost	£150
Comments	
Address	132-140 Goswell Road, London EC1V 7DP
Tel./e-mail	0207 490 9103 mail@continentalresearch.com
Fax / Web site	0207 490 1174 www.continentalresearch.com

296	CONTINENTAL RESEARCH
Title	**Internet Report**
Coverage	Quarterly review with statistics on Internet penetration, use.
Frequency	Quarterly
Web Facilities	Detailed executive summaries with data free on site.
Cost	£150
Comments	
Address	132-140 Goswell Road, London EC1V 7DP
Tel./e-mail	0207 490 9103 mail@continentalresearch.com
Fax / Web site	0207 490 1174 www.continentalresearch.com

297	CONTINENTAL RESEARCH
Title	**Medium and Large Businesses Omnibus**
Coverage	A monthly survey of director and managers in 200 businesses.
Frequency	Monthly
Web Facilities	Detailed executive summaries with data free on site.
Cost	On request
Comments	
Address	132-140 Goswell Road, London EC1V 7OP
Tel./e-mail	0207 490 9103 mail@continentalresearch.com
Fax / Web site	0207 490 9129 www.continentalresarch.com

298	
	CONTROL RISKS GROUP
Title	**Business Security Outlook**
Coverage	Based on a survey of senior executives in the UK and the USA, the report considers the main security issues for UK and US overseas investors.
Frequency	Annual
Web Facilities	
Cost	£158
Comments	
Address	83 Victoria Street, London SW1H 0HW
Tel./e-mail	0207 222 1552
Fax / Web site	0207 222 2296 www.crg.com

299	
	COOPERATIVE UNION LTD
Title	**Cooperative Statistics**
Coverage	Retail distribution by individual cooperative societies and other information on cooperative wholesaling, banking, and insurance. Based almost entirely on the organisation's own research.
Frequency	Annual
Web Facilities	
Cost	On request
Comments	
Address	Holyoake House, Hanover Street, Manchester M60 0AS
Tel./e-mail	0161 832 4300
Fax / Web site	0161 831 7684

300	
	CORRUGATED PACKAGING ASSOCIATION
Title	**Annual Production Statistics**
Coverage	Production by weight and area and the sales invoice value of solid and corrugated fibreboard produced in the UK. Based on a survey of members.
Frequency	Annual
Web Facilities	
Cost	Free but only available to members.
Comments	
Address	2 Saxon Court, Freeschool Street, Northampton NN1 1ST
Tel./e-mail	01604 621002 postbox@corrugated.org.uk
Fax / Web site	01604 620636 www.corrugated.org.uk

301	**CORRUGATED PACKAGING ASSOCIATION**
Title	**Accident Report and Statistics**
Coverage	Details of accidents and related incidents in the industry.
Frequency	Regular
Web Facilities	
Cost	Free but only available to members.
Comments	
Address	2 Saxon Court, Freeschool Street, Northampton NN1 1ST
Tel./e-mail	01604 621002 postbox@corrugated.org.uk
Fax / Web site	01604 620636 www.corrugated.org.uk

302	**COUNCIL OF MORTGAGE LENDERS**
Title	**Housing Finance**
Coverage	Includes articles and a diary of events plus a statistical section covering trends in housing, building, mortgage lending, prices, transactions, and savings. Also data on specific building societies.
Frequency	Quarterly
Web Facilities	Free press release data on site and details of publications.
Cost	£95, £40 for members
Comments	Based at the same address as the Building Societies Association and involved in some joint publications.
Address	3 Savile Row, London W1X 1AF
Tel./e-mail	0207 437 0075 pub@cml.org.uk
Fax / Web site	0207 734 3791 www.cml.org.uk

303	**COUNCIL OF MORTGAGE LENDERS**
Title	**Housing Finance National Market Review**
Coverage	Annual review of mortgage and housing trends in England, Wales, and Scotland.
Frequency	Annual
Web Facilities	Free press release data on site and details of publications.
Cost	£25, £15 for members. Free to Housing Finance subscribers.
Comments	Based at the same address as the Building Societies Association and involved in some joint publications.
Address	3 Savile Row, London W1X 1AF
Tel./e-mail	0207 437 0075 pub@cml.org.uk
Fax / Web site	0207 734 3791 www.cml.org.uk

304	COUNCIL OF MORTGAGE LENDERS
Title	**Mortgage Arrears and Re-possessions**
Coverage	A monthly summary of mortgage arrears produced as a press release.
Frequency	Monthly
Web Facilities	Free press release data on site and details of publications.
Cost	Free
Comments	Based at the same address as the Building Societies Association and involved in some joint publications.
Address	3 Savile Row, London W1X 1AF
Tel./e-mail	0207 437 0075 pub@cml.org.uk
Fax / Web site	0207 734 3791 www.cml.org.uk

305	COUNCIL OF MORTGAGE LENDERS
Title	**Market Briefing**
Coverage	A monthly review of economic and consumer trends and specific property and housing trends. Based on various sources.
Frequency	Monthly
Web Facilities	Free press release data on site and details of publications.
Cost	£170, £95 for members
Comments	Based at the same address as the Building Societies Association and involved in some joint publications.
Address	3 Savile Row, London W1X 1AF
Tel./e-mail	0207 437 0075 pub@cml.org.uk
Fax / Web site	0207 734 3791 www.cml.org.uk

306	COUNCIL OF MORTGAGE LENDERS
Title	**Mortgage Lending**
Coverage	A monthly summary of mortgage lending trends produced as a press release.
Frequency	Monthly
Web Facilities	Free press release data on site and details of publications.
Cost	Free
Comments	Based at the same address as the Building Societies Association and involved in some joint publications.
Address	3 Savile Row, London W1X 1AF
Tel./e-mail	0207 437 0075 pub@cml.org.uk
Fax / Web site	0207 734 3791 www.cml.org.uk

307		COUNCIL OF MORTGAGE LENDERS
	Title	**Housing Finance Review**
	Coverage	Various data and analysis on the housing sector and market in the UK.
	Frequency	Annual
	Web Facilities	Free press release data on site and details of publications.
	Cost	
	Comments	Based at the same address as the Building Societies Association and involved in some joint publications.
	Address	3 Savile Row, London W1X 1AF
	Tel./e-mail	0207 437 0075 pub@cml.org.uk
	Fax / Web site	0207 734 3791 www.cml.org.uk

308		CREMATION SOCIETY OF GREAT BRITAIN
	Title	**Directory of Crematoria**
	Coverage	Progress of cremation over the last 100 years. Facts and figures section includes number of crematoria, cremations carried out, fees etc. Based on the Society's own survey.
	Frequency	Annual
	Web Facilities	Free statistics on the Web site.
	Cost	£19 with binder, £15 loose-leaf
	Comments	
	Address	Brecon House (2nd Floor), 16/16a Albion Place, Maidstone ME14 5DZ
	Tel./e-mail	01622 688292 cremsoc@aol.com
	Fax / Web site	01622 686698 www.cremation.org.uk

309		CREMATION SOCIETY OF GREAT BRITAIN
	Title	**Cremation Statistics**
	Coverage	Historical data covering number of cremations and latest year data by region.
	Frequency	Annual
	Web Facilities	Free on the Web site.
	Cost	Free
	Comments	
	Address	Brecon House (2nd Floor), 16/16a Albion Place, Maidstone ME14 5DZ
	Tel./e-mail	01622 688292 cremsoc@aol.com
	Fax / Web site	01622 686698 www.cremation.org.uk

310	CROOKES HEALTHCARE LTD
Title	**Farley's Market Report**
Coverage	A review of the baby food market with statistics and commentary on various product sectors. Based on commissioned research.
Frequency	Regular
Web Facilities	
Cost	On request
Comments	
Address	Central Park, Lenton Lane, Nottingham NG7 2LJ
Tel./e-mail	0115 968 8529
Fax / Web site	0115 968 8838

311	CROP PROTECTION ASSOCIATION
Title	**CPA Handbook 20--**
Coverage	Contains a section on industry sales and pesticide usage in the UK plus data on the world agrochemicals market. Sales data is based on a survey of members with a time series covering the last seven years. Sales data broken down into herbicides, insecticides, fungicides, and others.
Frequency	Annual
Web Facilities	Free access to statistics on the Web site, plus online ordering facilities for publications.
Cost	Free
Comments	Changed name from British Agrochemicals Association.
Address	4 Lincoln Court, Lincoln Road, Peterborough PE1 2RP
Tel./e-mail	01733 349225 info@cropprotection.org.uk
Fax / Web site	01733 62523 www.cropprotection.org.uk

312	DATASTREAM INTERNATIONAL LTD
Title	**Economic Series Database**
Coverage	Datastream is primarily a provider of company information but it also has a database of economic statistics covering the UK and various other countries.
Frequency	Continuous
Web Facilities	Paid for access to data on site.
Cost	On request
Comments	
Address	Monmouth House, 58-64 City Road, London EC1Y 2AL
Tel./e-mail	0207 250 3000
Fax / Web site	0207 253 0207 www.datastream.com

313

	DEL MONTE FOODS (UK) LTD
Title	**Canned Fruit and Juices Report**
Coverage	Commentary and statistics on the canned fruit and juices market with data on market size, brands, consumer trends in specific product sectors. Based on commissioned research.
Frequency	Annual
Web Facilities	
Cost	On request
Comments	
Address	Del Monte House, London Road, Staines TW18 4JD
Tel./e-mail	01784 447400
Fax / Web site	01784 465301 www.delmonte-international.com

314

	DHL INTERNATIONAL (UK) LTD
Title	**Quarterly Export Indicator**
Coverage	This publication surveys the level of business confidence amongst the UK's manufacturing export industries and it is based on telephone interviews with approximately 500 directors and managers responsible for exports in British manufacturing. The survey results include export expectations over the next 3 and 12 months, trends in the main factors affecting exports, opinions on the role of the EU and the single European currency, trends in raw material costs.
Frequency	Quarterly
Web Facilities	
Cost	Free
Comments	The opinion survey is carried out by Gallup on behalf of DHL.
Address	Orbital Park, 178-188 Great South West Road, Hounslow, Middlesex TW4 6JS
Tel./e-mail	0208 818 8049
Fax / Web site	0208 818 8581 www.dhl.co.uk

315	**DIALOG CORPORATION**
Title	**Tradstat**
Coverage	An online database of UK import and export statistics with data on specific products. Based on data supplied by HM Customs and Excise and part of an international database of foreign trade statistics.
Frequency	Regular
Web Facilities	General details of services and paid for access to service on site.
Cost	On request
Comments	
Address	3rd Floor, Palace House, 3 Cathedral Street, London SE1 6EE
Tel./e-mail	0207 940 6900 contact@dialog.com
Fax / Web site	0207 940 6006 www.dialog.com

316	**DIRECT MAIL INFORMATION SERVICE**
Title	**Business to Business Direct Mail Trends 20--**
Coverage	A survey of business peoples' attitudes to direct mail. Includes the numbers of managers whose mail is "filtered", the quality of mail "filtered", the quality of addressing, and the amount of mail read and responded to.
Frequency	Annual
Web Facilities	Free access to statistics on the Web site, plus online ordering facilities for other data.
Cost	Free
Comments	
Address	5 Carlisle Street, London W1V 6JX
Tel./e-mail	0207 494 0483 jo@dmis.co.uk
Fax / Web site	0207 494 0455 www.dmis.co.uk

317	**DIRECT MAIL INFORMATION SERVICE**
Title	**The Letterbox Factfile 20--**
Coverage	Top line summary of information on the direct mail industry. Data on the consumer letterbox, levels of receipt, business to business direct mail, direct mail in Europe.
Frequency	Annual
Web Facilities	Free access on the Web site, plus online ordering facilities for other data.
Cost	Free
Comments	
Address	5 Carlisle Street, London W1D 3JX
Tel./e-mail	0207 494 0483 jo@dmis.co.uk
Fax / Web site	0207 494 0455 www.dmis.co.uk

318	
	DIRECT MAIL INFORMATION SERVICE
Title	**DMIS Factbook**
Coverage	Over 250 pages of data and information on the direct mail industry including historical data from the last 11 years.
Frequency	Regular
Web Facilities	General details on the Web site and online ordering facilities.
Cost	£250
Comments	
Address	5 Carlisle Street, London W1V 6JX
Tel./e-mail	0207 494 0483 jo@dmis.co.uk
Fax / Web site	0207 494 0455 www.dmis.co.uk

319	
	DIRECT MAIL INFORMATION SERVICE
Title	**Consumer Direct Mail Trends**
Coverage	Commentary and graphs on the volume of direct mail, mail opened, responses, purchases, awareness. Based on interviews with over 600 interviewees.
Frequency	Every two years
Web Facilities	Free access to statistics on the Web site,plus online ordering facilities for other data.
Cost	Free
Comments	Published every two years since 1985.
Address	5 Carlisle Street, London W1V 6JX
Tel./e-mail	0207 494 0483 jo@dmis.co.uk
Fax / Web site	0207 494 0455 www.dmis.co.uk

320	
	DIRECT MARKETING ASSOCIATION
Title	**DMA Census of the UK Direct Marketing Industry**
Coverage	A detailed survey of the industry covering structure, sales, postings etc based largely on original research.
Frequency	Annual
Web Facilities	List of publications on site.
Cost	Free - members, £285 - non-members
Comments	
Address	1 Oxenden Street, London SW1Y 4EE
Tel./e-mail	01780 762550 dma@dma.org.uk
Fax / Web site	01780 762040 www.dma.org.uk

321	DIRECT MARKETING ASSOCIATION
Title	**Direct Marketing Statistics**
Coverage	A compilation of statistics on direct marketing from a variety of non-official sources.
Frequency	Annual
Web Facilities	List of publications on site.
Cost	Free
Comments	
Address	1 Oxenden Street, London SW1Y 4EE
Tel./e-mail	01780 762550 dma@dma.org.uk
Fax / Web site	01780 762040 www.dma.org.uk

322	DIY SUPERSTORE
Title	**Review of the Year and Statistical Analysis**
Coverage	Commentary and statistics on developments in the DIY superstore sector with data on the number of superstores, openings during the year, and market shares.
Frequency	Annual in a monthly journal
Web Facilities	
Cost	£53
Comments	Usually appears in the November/December issue of the journal.
Address	Faversham House Group Ltd, Faversham House, 232a Addington Road, South Croydon CR2 8LE
Tel./e-mail	0208 651 7100 info@fav-house.com
Fax / Web site	0208 651 7117

323	DIY WEEK
Title	**DIY Trak Market Monitor**
Coverage	Statistics on DIY retail sales by product sector and by retail channels based on continuous research carried out by GfK Marketing Services (see other entry).
Frequency	Quarterly in a weekly journal
Web Facilities	
Cost	£82
Comments	The journal also has regular features and market reports on specific DIY product sectors and DIY retailers, wholesalers.
Address	Faversham House Group Ltd, Faversham House, 232a Addington Road, South Croydon CR2 8LE
Tel./e-mail	0208 651 7100 info@fav-house.com
Fax / Web site	0208 651 7117

324		**DODONA**
	Title	**Cinemagoing**
	Coverage	An annual review of cinema going trends in the UK and Ireland based on research by the company.
	Frequency	Annual
	Web Facilities	Free access to detailed summaries from the research, and other research, on site.
	Cost	On request
	Comments	Publishes various other European and international reports.
	Address	PO Box 450, Leicester LE2 2TE
	Tel./e-mail	customer.service@dodona.co.uk
	Fax / Web site	www.dodona.co.uk
325		**DONOVAN DATA SYSTEMS**
	Title	**Donovan Database Services**
	Coverage	Donovan has access to a number of media and consumer surveys held on computer, including the British Business Survey (see other entry), and other advertising and audience/readership surveys.
	Frequency	Continuous
	Web Facilities	General details of services on site.
	Cost	On request, depending on the nature and range of information required
	Comments	
	Address	7 Farm Street, London W1X 7RB
	Tel./e-mail	0207 255 7100 ukinfo@dds.co.uk
	Fax / Web site	0207 255 7171 www.dds.co.uk
326		**DTZ DEBENHAM THORPE**
	Title	**Regional Annual Property Reviews**
	Coverage	Regional trends in floorspace, rents, and availability. Based on surveys carried out by the company.
	Frequency	Annual
	Web Facilities	General access to latest reports on site.
	Cost	Free
	Comments	Publishes various other reports on key European cities and one-off reports on property issues, eg business parks, retailing, overseas investment in commercial property.
	Address	7 Curzon Street, London W1A 5PZ
	Tel./e-mail	0207 408 2756
	Fax / Web site	0207 643 6000 www.dtz.co.uk

327

	DTZ DEBENHAM THORPE
Title	**Central London Offices Research**
Coverage	Office floorspace and rent trends in the centre of London based on surveys by the company.
Frequency	Quarterly
Web Facilities	General access to latest reports on site.
Cost	Free
Comments	Publishes various other reports on key European cities and one-off reports on property issues, eg business parks, retailing, overseas investment in commercial property.
Address	7 Curzon Street, London W1A 5PZ
Tel./e-mail	0207 408 2756
Fax / Web site	0207 643 6000 www.dtz.co.uk

328

	DTZ DEBENHAM THORPE
Title	**Overseas Investment in UK Commercial Property**
Coverage	Analysis and data relating to overseas investment trends in UK property. Based on company research.
Frequency	Annual
Web Facilities	General access to the latest reports on site.
Cost	Free
Comments	
Address	1 Curzon Street, London W1A 5PZ
Tel./e-mail	0207 408 2756
Fax / Web site	0207 643 6000 www.dtz.co.uk

329

	DTZ DEBENHAM THORPE
Title	**Commercial Property Investment Transactions**
Coverage	Monitoring of investment levels in commercial property based on company's own research.
Frequency	Quarterly
Web Facilities	General access to latest publications on site.
Cost	Free
Comments	
Address	1 Curzon Street, London W1A 5PZ
Tel./e-mail	0207 408 2756
Fax / Web site	0207 643 6000 www.dtz.co.uk

330	**DTZ DEBENHAM THORPE**
Title	**Retail Park Investment**
Coverage	A review of investment trends for retail parks based on company research.
Frequency	Twice yearly
Web Facilities	General access to the latest publications on site.
Cost	Free
Comments	
Address	1 Curzon Street, London W1A 5PZ
Tel./e-mail	0207 408 2756
Fax / Web site	0207 643 6000 www.dtz.co.uk

331	**DTZ DEBENHAM THORPE**
Title	**Money into Property**
Coverage	An annual review of investment and capital flows into the UK property sector based on the company's own research.
Frequency	Annual
Web Facilities	General access to the latest publications on the site.
Cost	Free
Comments	
Address	1 Curzon Street, London W1A 5PZ
Tel./e-mail	0207 408 2756
Fax / Web site	0207 643 6000 www.dtz.co.uk

332	**DTZ DEBENHAM THORPE**
Title	**UK Industrial Land Values**
Coverage	A review of industrial land values and changes with data by region. Based on company's own research.
Frequency	Annual
Web Facilities	General access to the latest publications on site.
Cost	Free
Comments	
Address	1 Curzon Street, London W1A 5PZ
Tel./e-mail	0207 408 2756
Fax / Web site	0207 643 6000 www.dtz.co.uk

333	DTZ DEBENHAM THORPE
Title	**UK Industrial Land Rents**
Coverage	A review of industrial rents and changes with data by region. Based on company's own research.
Frequency	Annual
Web Facilities	General access to the latest publications on site.
Cost	Free
Comments	
Address	1 Curzon Street, London W1A 5PZ
Tel./e-mail	0207 408 2756
Fax / Web site	0207 643 6000 www.dtz.co.uk

334	DTZ DEBENHAM THORPE
Title	**UK Office Rents**
Coverage	A review of office rents and changes with data by region. Based on company's own research.
Frequency	Annual
Web Facilities	General access to the latest publications on site.
Cost	Free
Comments	
Address	1 Curzon Street, London W1A 5PZ
Tel./e-mail	0207 408 2756
Fax / Web site	0207 643 6000 www.dtz.co.uk

335	DUN AND BRADSTREET LTD
Title	**Key Business Ratios**
Coverage	20 key ratios arranged by SIC industry group with data for the latest three years available. Based on the company's own analysis of company financial data.
Frequency	Annual
Web Facilities	General details and some free basic data on site.
Cost	
Comments	
Address	Holmers Farm Way, High Wycombe HP12 4UL
Tel./e-mail	01494 423689
Fax / Web site	01494 422332 www.dunandbrad.co.uk

336

DUN AND BRADSTREET LTD

Title	**Business Failure Statistics**
Coverage	Company liquidations and bankruptcies analysed by sector and region. A commentary supports the data which comes from records maintained by the company.
Frequency	Quarterly
Web Facilities	General details and some free basic data on site.
Cost	Free
Comments	
Address	Holmers Farm Way, High Wycombe HP12 4UL
Tel./e-mail	01494 423689
Fax / Web site	01494 422332 www.dunandbrad.co.uk

337

DURLACHER CORPORATION PLC

Title	**Durlacher Quarterly Internet Report**
Coverage	Internet user surveys and profiles, analysis of Internet usage, and web-site growth statistics with the focus on the UK. Based on surveys by the company.
Frequency	Quarterly
Web Facilities	General details of, plus free access to summary statistics, on the Web site. Also paid-for access to other data, and online ordering facilities.
Cost	£75 per issue
Comments	Produces various other surveys and analysis of Internet developments and Internet companies.
Address	4 Chiswell Street, London EC1Y 4UP
Tel./e-mail	0207 459 3666 agc@durlacher com
Fax / Web site	www.durlacher.com

338

ECONOMIST PUBLICATIONS LTD

Title	**United Kingdom Quarterly Economic Review**
Coverage	Commentary and statistics on general economic trends and business conditions in the UK. Based mainly on official sources.
Frequency	Quarterly
Web Facilities	Free summary data and news, plus paid for access to detailed data and reports on site.
Cost	On request
Comments	Various other one-off and regular reports published on UK and international markets.
Address	15 Regent Street, London SW1Y 4LR
Tel./e-mail	0207 830 1007 london@eiu.com
Fax / Web site	0207 499 1023 www.eiu.com

339	**ECONOMIST PUBLICATIONS LTD**
Title	**UK Country Profile**
Coverage	An annual review of economic, political and business trends in the UK.
Frequency	Annual
Web Facilities	Free summary data and news plus paid for access to detailed data and reports on site.
Cost	On request
Comments	
Address	15 Regent Street, London SW1Y 4LR
Tel./e-mail	0207 830 1007 london@eiu.com
Fax / Web site	0207 499 1023 www.eiu.com
340	**ELECTRIC VEHICLE ASSOCIATION OF GREAT BRITAIN**
Title	**Yardstick Costs for Battery Electrics**
Coverage	Basic costs for electric vehicles used in warehouses and airports. Based on data collected by the association.
Frequency	Regular
Web Facilities	
Cost	On request
Comments	Also produces the EVA Manual.
Address	Alexandra House, Harrowden Road, Wellingborough NN8 5BD
Tel./e-mail	01933 276618
Fax / Web site	01933 276618
341	**ELECTRICITY ASSOCIATION**
Title	**Electricity Industry Review**
Coverage	An annual review of electricity production, consumption, prices and capacity based on data collected by the Association.
Frequency	Annual
Web Facilities	Some basic data free on the site, details of publications, and pdf version of this report.
Cost	£100
Comments	
Address	30 Millbank, London SW1P 4RD
Tel./e-mail	0207 963 5829
Fax / Web site	0207 963 5978 www.electricity.org.uk

342

	ELECTRICITY ASSOCIATION
Title	**UK Electricity Prices**
Coverage	The report produces simulated figures for the levels of demand and consumption, and prices.
Frequency	Annual
Web Facilities	Some basic data free, plus details of publications, and pdf version of this report on site.
Cost	On request
Comments	
Address	30 Millbank, London SW1P 4RD
Tel./e-mail	0207 963 5829
Fax / Web site	0207 963 5978 www.electricity.org.uk

343

	ELECTROLUX OUTDOOR PRODUCTS LTD
Title	**Garden Statistics**
Coverage	Regular reports, commissioned from research agencies such as NOP, on gardening trends.
Frequency	Regular
Web Facilities	Free reports on the Flymo brand Web site.
Cost	Free
Comments	
Address	Aycliffe Industrial Estate, Preston Road, Newton Aycliffe DL5 6UP
Tel./e-mail	01325 300303
Fax / Web site	01325 302577 www.flymo.com

344

	EMAP MEDIA LTD
Title	**British Rate and Data (BRAD)**
Coverage	Details of all UK media advertising rates, subscription rates, cover prices, circulation trends etc. Also general data on advertising expenditure, number of cinemas.
Frequency	Monthly
Web Facilities	Details of services on site, including new BRADnet web-based service.
Cost	£130 per issue
Comments	
Address	33-39 Bowling Green Lane, London EC1R 0DA
Tel./e-mail	0207 505 8275 william.fox@brad.co.uk
Fax / Web site	0207 505 8293 www.intellagencia.com

345	ENGINEERING EMPLOYERS' FEDERATION
Title	**Engineering Trends**
Coverage	Graphs, tables, and commentary on engineering output and sales and imports and exports. Some forecasts are included usually up to one year ahead and a commentary accompanies the data. Based on a combination of official and non-official sources.
Frequency	Quarterly
Web Facilities	Executive summary free on site.
Cost	£120, £35 per issue
Comments	
Address	Broadway House, Tothill Street, London SW1H 9NQ
Tel./e-mail	0207 222 7777
Fax / Web site	0207 222 2782 www.eef.org.uk
346	ENGLISH TOURISM COUNCIL
Title	**The Heritage Monitor**
Coverage	Includes details of the numbers of historic buildings and conservation areas, admission charges, and visitor trends.
Frequency	Annual
Web Facilities	Basic tourism facts and details of publications on staruk Web site.
Cost	£20
Comments	
Address	Research Department, Thames Tower, Black's Road, Hammersmith, London W6 9EL
Tel./e-mail	0208 563 3000
Fax / Web site	0208 563 0302 www.staruk.org.uk

347	**ENGLISH TOURISM COUNCIL**
Title	**The UK Tourist Statistics**
Coverage	An annual report based on the United Kingdom Tourism Survey (UKTS). Data includes the volume of UK residents' tourism, characteristics of their trips, and the people taking them. Subjects covered include purpose of trip, destinations, types of transport, accommodation used, categories of tourist spending. Also includes historical data.
Frequency	Annual
Web Facilities	Basic tourism facts and details of publications available on staruk Web site.
Cost	£90
Comments	
Address	Research Department, Thames Tower, Black's Road, Hammersmith, London W6 9EL
Tel./e-mail	0208 563 3000
Fax / Web site	0208 563 0302 www.staruk.org.uk

348	**ENGLISH TOURISM COUNCIL**
Title	**Visits to Tourist Attractions**
Coverage	Gives details of attendances at tourist attractions in the UK, seasonal opening, ownership, and information on free admission. Attractions include historic houses, gardens, museums and art galleries, wildlife attractions, country parks, steam railways, and workplaces.
Frequency	Annual
Web Facilities	Basic tourism facts and details of publications available on staruk.org.uk Web site.
Cost	£20
Comments	
Address	Research Department, Thames Tower, Black's Road, Hammersmith, London W6 9EL
Tel./e-mail	0208 563 3000
Fax / Web site	0208 563 0302 www.staruk.org.uk

349	ENGLISH TOURISM COUNCIL
Title	**UK Occupancy Survey**
Coverage	Statistics relating to national occupancy levels in serviced accommodation, seasonal variations, regional differences, types of accommodation and length of stay.
Frequency	Regular
Web Facilities	Basic tourism facts and details of publications available on staruk Web site
Cost	£25
Comments	
Address	Research Department, Thames Tower, Black's Road, Hammersmith, London W6 9EL
Tel./e-mail	0208 563 3000
Fax / Web site	0208 563 0302 www.staruk.org.uk

350	ENVIRONMENTAL TRANSPORT ASSOCIATION
Title	**Factsheets**
Coverage	Various factsheets relating to transport and the environment and based on various sources.
Frequency	Regular
Web Facilities	
Cost	Free
Comments	The association is relatively new, having been established in 1990.
Address	10 Church Street, Weybridge KT13 8RS
Tel./e-mail	01932 828882 eta@eta.co.uk
Fax / Web site	01932 829015 www.eta.co.uk

351	EQUIFAX EUROPE
Title	**Define**
Coverage	Define is a Census-based geodemographic system including 1991 Census data, financial data from the Equifax database, unemployment statistics, and electoral roll variables.
Frequency	Continuous
Web Facilities	General details of services on site.
Cost	On request, depending on the range and nature of the information required
Comments	
Address	Sentinel House, 16 Harcourt Street, London W1H 2AE
Tel./e-mail	0207 724 6116
Fax / Web site	0181 686 7777 www.equifax.com

352	**ERDMAN LEWIS**
Title	**Midsummer Retail Report**
Coverage	Analysis and statistics covering trends in the retailing sector and the retail property market. Based on data collected by the company.
Frequency	Annual
Web Facilities	
Cost	On request
Comments	Various other property reports and town reports produced.
Address	9 Marylebone Lane, London W1M 5FA
Tel./e-mail	0207 629 8191
Fax / Web site	0207 487 1904

353	**ERNST & YOUNG**
Title	**Analysis of Profit Warnings**
Coverage	An analysis of profit warnings issued by UK quoted companies with details of the number and percentage changes over the previous quarter. Regional analysis and focus on specific sectors in issues.
Frequency	Quarterly
Web Facilities	Free access to data and other reports on site.
Cost	Free
Comments	
Address	Becket House, 1 Lambeth Palace Road, London SE1 7EU
Tel./e-mail	0207 951 2000
Fax / Web site	www.ey.com/uk

354	**ERNST AND YOUNG ITEM CLUB**
Title	**UK Economic Prospects**
Coverage	A detailed review of economic trends and prospects with data on all the main economic indicators.
Frequency	Quarterly
Web Facilities	
Cost	£200 per issue
Comments	
Address	4th Floor, Abbey House, 121 St Aldates, Oxford OX1 1HB
Tel./e-mail	01865 268913 itemclub@oef.co.uk
Fax / Web site	01865 202533

355	ESA MARKET RESEARCH LTD
Title	**ESA Monthly Shopping Basket Report**
Coverage	A regular report analysing price differences between retailers during the current month and price differences over time. Based on a survey of 132 product categories at 85 outlets covering different retailing formats.
Frequency	Monthly
Web Facilities	
Cost	£195 per month
Comments	
Address	4 Woodland Court, Soothouse Spring, St Albans AL3 6NR
Tel./e-mail	01727 847572
Fax / Web site	01727 837337

356	ESRC DATA ARCHIVE
Title	**ESRC Data Archive**
Coverage	The archive holds surveys from various official and non-official sources including all the major ONS continuous surveys such as the Family Expenditure Survey, General Household Survey, National Food Survey plus many non-official surveys from organisations such as NOP, Gallup, Research Services etc.
Frequency	Continuous
Web Facilities	Details and news of data sources on site.
Cost	On request
Comments	Data can be supplied in various formats including diskette, magnetic tape, and CD-ROM.
Address	Wivenhoe Park, University of Essex, Colchester CO4 3SO
Tel./e-mail	01206 872001 archive@essex.ac.uk
Fax / Web site	01206 872003 www.dawww.essex.ac.uk

357	ESTATES GAZETTE
Title	**The Valuation Office Property Market Report**
Coverage	Based on data collected by the Valuation Office's 95 UK District Valuers. The publication contains facts, figures, and commentary on UK property trends.
Frequency	Twice yearly
Web Facilities	News and other information on site.
Cost	£80, £45 per issue
Comments	
Address	Estates Gazette Ltd, 151 Wardour Street, London W1F 8BN
Tel./e-mail	0207 411 2585 info@egi.co.uk
Fax / Web site	0207 411 2883 www.egi.co.uk

358

Title
Coverage

Frequency

Web Facilities
Cost

Comments

Address
Tel./e-mail
Fax / Web site

ESTATES GAZETTE
Figures and Figures
General data relating to the property market including house prices, farm prices, rent index, housing starts and completions, land prices, property yields, interest rates. Based mainly on various non-official sources supported by some official statistics.

Monthly in a weekly journal

News and other information on site.
£118, £2.10 for single issue

Estates Gazette Ltd, 151 Wardour Street, London   W1V 4BN
0207 411 2585   info@egi.co.uk
0207 411 2883   www.egi.co.uk

359

Title
Coverage

Frequency

Web Facilities

Cost

Comments

Address
Tel./e-mail
Fax / Web site

ESTATES GAZETTE
Estates Gazette and PSD Salary & Benefits Survey
Comprehensive annual guide to salaries and benefits in the property industry broken down by job.

Annual

News and other information on site.

£195

Published in association with NSM Research.

Estates Gazette Ltd, 151 Wardour Street, London   W1F 8BN
0207 411 2585   info@egi.co.uk
0207 411 2883   www.egi.co.uk

360

Title
Coverage

Frequency

Web Facilities

Cost

Comments

Address
Tel./e-mail
Fax / Web site

ESTATES GAZETTE
Shopping Centre Progress
Annual review of shopping centre developments including data on new openings, floorspace etc.

Annual

News and other information on site.

£30

Published by Estates Gazette for the British Council of Shopping Centres.

Estates Gazette Ltd, 151 Wardour Street, London   W1F 8BN
0207 411 2585   info@egi.co.uk
0207 411 2883   www.egi.co.uk

361	**ESTATES GAZETTE**
Title	**Office Trends**
Coverage	Annual review of trends in the commercial property sector in the UK.
Frequency	Annual
Web Facilities	News and other information on site.
Cost	£25
Comments	Published each year in June.
Address	Estates Gazette Ltd, 151 Wardour Street, London W1F 8BN
Tel./e-mail	0207 411 2585 info@egi.co.uk
Fax / Web site	0207 411 2883 www.egi.co.uk

362	**EULER TRADE INDEMNITY**
Title	**Quarterly Financial Trends Survey**
Coverage	Financial review of major sectors with details of late payments. Based on data collected by the company.
Frequency	Quarterly
Web Facilities	Online ordering of publications on site.
Cost	Free
Comments	
Address	1 Canada Square, London E14 5DX
Tel./e-mail	0207 860 2146
Fax / Web site	0207 860 2455 www.eulergroup.com

363	**EUREST**
Title	**Eurest Lunchtime Report**
Coverage	An annual review of the eating habits of workers and other activities during lunch times. Based on commissioned research.
Frequency	Annual
Web Facilities	
Cost	£20
Comments	Available from PR company E=MC2 at address below.
Address	High Street, Tisbury SP3 6HA
Tel./e-mail	01747 871752
Fax / Web site	01747 871960

364

EURODIRECT DATABASE MARKETING

Title **Define/CAMEO UK**

Coverage Define and CAMEO UK are demographic classification systems based on Census data with additional information from the electoral roll.

Frequency Continuous

Web Facilities General details of services on site.

Cost On request, and depending on the range and nature of the information required

Comments Additional services include CAMEO Financial, CAMEO Income, CAMEO Investment etc.

Address Onward House, 2 Baptist Place, Bradford   BD1 2PS

Tel./e-mail 01274 737144   sales@eddm.demon-co.uk

Fax / Web site 01274 741126   www.eurodirect.co.uk

365

EUROMONITOR

Title **Euromonitor Market and Media Guide**

Coverage A compilation of statistics covering economic trends, regional data, consumer trends, advertising, labour market data, transport, key markets etc. Based on Euromonitor data and statistics from other sources.

Frequency Monthly

Web Facilities Details of all reports, online ordering, and paid-for access to research on site.

Cost £450 (annual subscription to 'Market Research Great Britain')

Comments Included as part of 'Market Research Great Britain'. Various consumer reports on international markets also produced.

Address 60-61 Britton Street, London   EC1M 5NA

Tel./e-mail 0207 251 8024   info@euromonitor.com

Fax / Web site 0207 608 3149   www.euromonitor.com

366	EUROPEAN COSMETIC MARKETS
Title	**Market Reviews**
Coverage	Market reports are scheduled throughout the year and each report has a review of UK trends, alongside reviews of the other major European markets. The 1995 schedule is bathroom products (January), skin care (February), men's lines (March), sun care (April), women's fragrances (May), body care (June), deodorants (August), hair care (September), hair styling (October), colour cosmetics (November), oral hygiene (December). Mainly based on original consumer research.
Frequency	Monthly in a monthly journal
Web Facilities	General details of reviews on site.
Cost	£734
Comments	Publishers are considering paid-for access to reports online.
Address	Wilmington Publishing Ltd, 6-14 Underwood Street, London N1 7JQ
Tel./e-mail	0207 549 8626 ecm@wilmington.co.uk
Fax / Web site	0207 549 8622 www.cosmeticsbusiness.com
367	EUROPEAN PLASTICS NEWS
Title	**UK Plastics Annual Review**
Coverage	A commentary on the market performance of plastics raw materials in the UK with tables on the consumption of major plastics. A general outlook for the coming year is given.
Frequency	Annual in a monthly journal
Web Facilities	
Cost	£150, £16 per issue
Comments	
Address	EMAP Maclaren Ltd, 19th Floor, Leon House233 High StreetCroydon CR0 9XT
Tel./e-mail	0208 277 5000
Fax / Web site	0208 277 5531 www.plasticssearch.com

368	EXHIBITION VENUES ASSOCIATION
Title	**UK Exhibition Facts**
Coverage	Survey of exhibition visitors, exhibitor spending, exhibition numbers, international tourism. Data usually covers the last three years.
Frequency	Annual
Web Facilities	
Cost	£95
Comments	Produced by Exhibition Audience Audits Ltd.
Address	Mallards, Five Ashes, Mayfield TN20 6NN
Tel./e-mail	01435 872244 eva@martex.co.uk
Fax / Web site	01435 872696

369	EXPERIAN LTD
Title	**Neighbourhood Statistics**
Coverage	A new information service launched in 2001 offering academics free access to a database of annually updated neighbourhood statistics.
Frequency	Regular
Web Facilities	
Cost	Free to academics
Comments	Developed through an agreement with the Economic and Social Research Council (ESRC).
Address	Talbot House, Talbot Street, Nottingham NG1 5HF
Tel./e-mail	0115 934 4547
Fax / Web site	0115 934 4535 www.experian.com

370	FACTORS AND DISCOUNTERS ASSOCIATION
Title	**Annual and Half-Yearly Review**
Coverage	Revenues for UK factors and discounters from both their domestic and international businesses.
Frequency	Twice yearly
Web Facilities	Free access to statistics on the site.
Cost	Free
Comments	
Address	Boston House, The Little Green, Richmond TW9 1QE
Tel./e-mail	0208 332 9955 davidr@factors.org.uk
Fax / Web site	0208 332 2585 www.factors.org.uk

371	**FACTS INTERNATIONAL LTD**
Title	**Telefacts**
Coverage	An omnibus survey of 1,000 adults each month. It is a telephone survey covering the whole of the UK.
Frequency	Monthly
Web Facilities	
Cost	Varies according to questions and analysis
Comments	Results available on disc.
Address	Facts Centre, Kennington Road, Ashford TN24 0TD
Tel./e-mail	01233 643551 100141.322@compuserve.com
Fax / Web site	01233 626950 www.Facts.International.Ltd.uk

372	**FARMERS' WEEKLY**
Title	**Farmers' Weekly**
Coverage	Land value prices analysed over the previous six months. Includes a county-by-county analysis and the report is based on various sources.
Frequency	Weekly
Web Facilities	General market data free on Web site.
Cost	£1.50 per issue
Comments	The publication is produced jointly by 'Farmers' Weekly' and the Royal Institution of Chartered Surveyors.
Address	Quadrant House, The Quadrant, Sutton SM2 5AS
Tel./e-mail	0208 652 4911 farmers.weekly@rbi.co.uk
Fax / Web site	0208 652 4005 www.fwi.co.uk

373	**FAST FACTS LTD**
Title	**Factfinder**
Coverage	CD-ROM data base allowing access to all surveys published in 'Fast Food Facts' since 1985.
Frequency	Monthly
Web Facilities	
Cost	£2,200 (overall service cost)
Comments	
Address	Lower Green, Walgrave NN6 9QF
Tel./e-mail	01604 781 392 fastfacts@btinternet.com
Fax / Web site	01604 781 392

	374	FAST FACTS LTD
Title		**Fast Food Facts**
Coverage		Regular reports on various food sectors including meat, bakery products, savoury products, chocolate and sugar confectionery. Food sectors can be added when specified by the client.
Frequency		Monthly
Web Facilities		
Cost		£2,200 (overall service cost)
Comments		
Address		Lower Green, Walgrave NN6 9QF
Tel./e-mail		01604 781 392 fastfacts@btinternet.com
Fax / Web site		01604 781 392

	375	FAST FACTS LTD
Title		**Food Trends**
Coverage		Household consumption trends over the last ten years for over 200 product categories. Also includes projections for the next two years.
Frequency		Quarterly
Web Facilities		
Cost		£2,200 (overall service cost)
Comments		
Address		Lower Green, Walgrave NN6 9QF
Tel./e-mail		01604 781 392 fastfacts@btinternet.com
Fax / Web site		01604 781 392

	376	FEDERATION OF BAKERS
Title		**Annual Report**
Coverage		Includes a section with statistics on production trends in the UK bakery industry.
Frequency		Annual
Web Facilities		Free industry facts on site.
Cost		Free
Comments		
Address		6 Catherine Street, London WC2B 5JW
Tel./e-mail		0207 420 7190 info@bakersfederation.org.uk
Fax / Web site		0207 397 0542 www.bakersfederation.org.uk

FEDERATION OF BRITISH CREMATION AUTHORITIES

377

Title	**Annual Report**
Coverage	Includes cremation statistics for individual crematoria over a five year period. Based on the federation's own survey. A large amount of supporting text accompanies the data.
Frequency	Annual
Web Facilities	
Cost	Free
Comments	
Address	41 Salisbury Road, Carshalton SM5 3HA
Tel./e-mail	0208 669 4521
Fax / Web site	

FEDERATION OF MASTER BUILDERS

378

Title	**FMB State of Trade Survey**
Coverage	Results of a survey of member firms in England and Wales with data on workload for the previous quarter and predictions for the coming quarter. Various topical questions are also included in each survey. Text supports the data.
Frequency	Quarterly
Web Facilities	
Cost	On request
Comments	Also produces irregular factsheets.
Address	14 Great James Street, London WC1N 3DP
Tel./e-mail	0207 242 7583 central@fmb.org.uk
Fax / Web site	0207 404 0296 www.fmb.org.uk

FEDERATION OF OPTHALMIC & DISPENSING OPTICIANS

379

Title	**Optics at a Glance**
Coverage	General statistics on optics including the number of opticians, average spectacle prices. Based on a combination of the federation's own survey and Central Government data. Some supporting commentary.
Frequency	Annual
Web Facilities	General details of data on the site.
Cost	Free
Comments	
Address	113 Eastbourne Mews, London W2 6LQ
Tel./e-mail	0207 258 0240 optics@fodo.com
Fax / Web site	0207 724 1175 www.fodo.com

380	**FEDERATION OF SMALL BUSINESSES**
Title	**Small Business Surveys**
Coverage	Various regular surveys of the small business sector including a crime and small business survey and payment survey. Based mainly on member surveys.
Frequency	Regular
Web Facilities	
Cost	On request
Comments	A range of small business statistics on the web site.
Address	2 Catherine Place, London SW1E 6HF
Tel./e-mail	0207 233 7900 london@fsb.org.uk
Fax / Web site	0207 233 7899 www.fsb.org.uk

381	**FEDERATION OF THE ELECTRONICS INDUSTRY (FEI)**
Title	**The FEI Review**
Coverage	Mainly text describing the activities of the federation but the 'Focus on the Industry' section includes graphs and tables on sector value, and data on the components and business equipment sectors. Based on data collected by the federation.
Frequency	Annual
Web Facilities	Free summary statistics, online ordering facilities, and member access to more detailed statistics on the site.
Cost	Free
Comments	
Address	Russell Square House, 10-12 Russell Square, London WC1B 5EE
Tel./e-mail	0207 331 2000 feedback@fei.org.uk
Fax / Web site	0207 331 2040 www.fei.org.uk.

382	**FEDERATION OF THE ELECTRONICS INDUSTRY (FEI)**
Title	**Semiconductor Manufacturers Association Market Forecasts**
Coverage	Forecasts for the year ahead for the industry with forecasts for specific market segments. Based on the association's research.
Frequency	Annual
Web Facilities	Free summary statistics, online ordering, and member access to more detailed statistics on site.
Cost	On request
Comments	In Summer 2001, the federation announced a merger with the British Radio and Electronic Equipment Manufacturers Association (BREEMA).
Address	Russell Square House, 10-12 Russell Square, London WC1B 5EE
Tel./e-mail	0207 331 2000 feedback@fei.org.uk
Fax / Web site	0207 331 2040 www.fei.org.uk

383	**FERTILISER MANUFACTURERS' ASSOCIATION**
Title	**Fertiliser Review**
Coverage	Covers area of crops, consumption of inorganic fertilisers, straight fertilisers, and compound fertilisers. Also concentration, application rates, and usage of compound fertilisers. Based mainly on the association's own research with additional data from Central Government. Most of the review is made up of text.
Frequency	Annual
Web Facilities	Free summary information and tables on site.
Cost	£5
Comments	
Address	Great North Road, Peterborough PE8 6HJ
Tel./e-mail	01780 781360 enquiries@fma.org.uk
Fax / Web site	01780 781369 www.fma.org.uk

384	**FINANCE AND LEASING ASSOCIATION**
Title	**Annual Report**
Coverage	Contains commentary and statistics on trends in the credit and leasing market with most tables giving figures for the last two years. Based on transactions by FLA members.
Frequency	Annual
Web Facilities	
Cost	Free
Comments	
Address	15-19 Kingsway, London WC2B 6UN
Tel./e-mail	0207 836 6511 info@fla.org.uk
Fax / Web site	0207 420 9600 www.fla.org.uk

385	**FIRA INTERNATIONAL LTD**
Title	**Statistical Digest for the UK Furniture Industry**
Coverage	Statistics include turnover, sales, deliveries, consumption, imports, exports, prices, and advertising. Mainly based on Central Government data, supplemented by association and non-official sources.
Frequency	Annual
Web Facilities	
Cost	£100
Comments	Also produces statistics on the international market.
Address	Maxwell Road, Stevenage SG1 2EW
Tel./e-mail	01438 777700 info@fira.co.uk
Fax / Web site	01438 777800 www.fira.co.uk

386	**FISH TRADER**
Title	**Imports and Exports**
Coverage	Imports and exports of fish by volume and value broken down by type of fish. A short commentary accompanies the data which is based on official statistics.
Frequency	Quarterly in a monthly journal
Web Facilities	
Cost	£49.95
Comments	
Address	Oban Times Ltd, Royston House, Caroline Park, Edinburgh EH5 1QJ
Tel./e-mail	01631 568000 editor@specialpublications.co.uk
Fax / Web site	01631 568001

387	**FLOUR ADVISORY BUREAU**
Title	**Flour**
Coverage	A guide to flour in the UK with some basic data.
Frequency	Regular
Web Facilities	Basic data plus a downloadable copy of the 2001 Bread Values Report free on site.
Cost	Free
Comments	The Bread Values Report was published in Summer 2001 as an assessment of the UK bread market.
Address	21 Arlington Street, London SW1A 1RN
Tel./e-mail	0207 493 2521 info@fabflour.co.uk
Fax / Web site	0207 493 6785 www.fabflour.co.uk

388	**FLOWER BUSINESS INTERNATIONAL**
Title	**Annual Statistics**
Coverage	Cultivation and production data on non-edible horticultural products. Based on trade association data.
Frequency	Annual in a monthly journal
Web Facilities	
Cost	£41, or £2.50 per issue
Comments	
Address	Harling House, 47-51 Great Suffolk Street, London SE1 0BS
Tel./e-mail	0207 261 0717
Fax / Web site	0207 261 9252

389	FOOD FROM BRITAIN
Title	**Export Trade Review**
Coverage	A review of export trends and opportunities.
Frequency	Annual
Web Facilities	General details of statistics, online ordering, and access to statistics for members only on the site.
Cost	£450
Comments	
Address	123 Buckingham Palace Road, London SW1W 9SA
Tel./e-mail	0207 233 5111
Fax / Web site	0207 233 9515 www.foodfrombritain.com

390	FOOD FROM BRITAIN
Title	**Annual Report**
Coverage	Includes statistics on food exports and the key export markets for UK food companies plus general details of trends in the industry. Based primarily on official statistics.
Frequency	Annual
Web Facilities	General details of statistics, online ordering, and access to statistics for members only.
Cost	Free
Comments	
Address	123 Buckingham Palace Road, London SW1W 9SA
Tel./e-mail	0207 233 5111
Fax / Web site	0207 233 9515 www.foodfrombritain.com

391	FOODSERVICE INTELLIGENCE
Title	**Foodservice Barometer**
Coverage	A survey of meals served by caterers in each of nine sectors: hotels, restaurants, public houses, cafes, take-aways, leisure, staff catering, health care, education. Also includes a 'balance of confidence' indicator and a special feature in each issue.
Frequency	Monthly
Web Facilities	General details of surveys on Web site.
Cost	£1,250 plus VAT
Comments	Also publishes various one-off and occasional reports on the foodservice market.
Address	84 Uxbridge Road, London W13 8RA
Tel./e-mail	0208 799 3205 zcampion@fsintelligence.com
Fax / Web site	0208 566 2100 www.fsintelligence.com

392

FOODSERVICE INTELLIGENCE

Title	**Foodservice Industry Population File**
Coverage	A study of the structure of the catering industry giving number of outlets, value of caterers' food purchases, outlet sizes, number of meals served, sector buying concentration, and a regional analysis. Eleven catering sectors are covered in detail with historical trends over a ten-year period. Based on Marketpower research, non-official sources, and some official statistics.
Frequency	Annual
Web Facilities	General details of the surveys on the Web site.
Cost	£1,250 plus VAT
Comments	Also publishes various one-off and occasional reports on the foodservice market.
Address	84 Uxbridge Road, London W13 8RA
Tel./e-mail	0208 799 3205 zcampion@fsintelligence.com
Fax / Web site	0208 566 2100 www.fsintelligence.com

393

FOODSERVICE INTELLIGENCE

Title	**Foodservice Forecasts**
Coverage	Short-term forecasts for the UK catering industry based on research carried out amongst 700 caterers with trends given sector by sector.
Frequency	Annual
Web Facilities	General details of surveys on the Web site.
Cost	£850
Comments	Also publishes various one-off and occasional reports on the foodservice market.
Address	84 Uxbridge Road, London W13 8RA
Tel./e-mail	0208 799 3205 zcampoin@fsintelligence.com
Fax / Web site	0208 566 2100 www.fsintelligence.com

394

FORUM FOR PRIVATE BUSINESS

Title	**Private Businesses and their Banks**
Coverage	A regular survey of UK banks' attitudes to borrowings with a review of general attitudes towards specific sectors. Data for the latest quarter and earlier quarters.
Frequency	Quarterly
Web Facilities	Some press release data on the site.
Cost	On request
Comments	
Address	Ruskin Chambers, Drury Lane, Knutsford WA16 6HA
Tel./e-mail	01565 634467 fpbltdcommercial@fpb.co.uk
Fax / Web site	01565 650059 www.fpbltd.co.uk

395	FORUM FOR PRIVATE BUSINESS
Title	**FPB Quarterly Survey**
Coverage	A survey of member companies to obtain opinions on trends in the sector, and opinions on specific issues.
Frequency	Quarterly
Web Facilities	Some free press release data on the site.
Cost	On request
Comments	
Address	Ruskin Chambers, Drury Lane, Knutsford WA16 6HA
Tel./e-mail	01565 634467 fpbltdcommercial@fpb.co.uk
Fax / Web site	01565 650059 www.fpbltd.co.uk

396	FOUNDRY TRADE JOURNAL
Title	**Metal Prices**
Coverage	Prices of ferro-alloy and other metals and non-ferrous metals by type in the UK. Based on various non-official sources.
Frequency	Twice a month in a twice-monthly journal
Web Facilities	
Cost	£144.53, £16.50 per issue
Comments	
Address	DMG World Media Ltd, 2 Queensway, Redhill RH1 1QS
Tel./e-mail	01372 768611 foundry@dmg.co.uk
Fax / Web site	01732 855469 www.dmgworldmedia.com

397	FRASER OF ALLENDER INSTITUTE
Title	**Scottish Chambers' Business Survey**
Coverage	Trends in the Scottish economy and business sectors based on returns from a sample of members of Scottish chambers of commerce.
Frequency	Quarterly
Web Facilities	
Cost	£150
Comments	
Address	Strathclyde University, 100 Cathedral Street, Glasgow G4 0LN
Tel./e-mail	0141 548 3958 fraser@strath.ac.uk
Fax / Web site	0141 552 8347 www.fraser.strath.ac.uk

398	FRASER OF ALLENDER INSTITUTE
Title	**Quarterly Economic Commentary**
Coverage	Trends and outlook for the Scottish economy with individual reviews of industrial performance, service sector, labour market, and the regions. Also some feature articles. Based mainly on Central Government data and a supporting commentary.
Frequency	Quarterly
Web Facilities	
Cost	£60, £17.50 per issue
Comments	
Address	Strathclyde University, 100 Cathedral Street, Glasgow G4 0LN
Tel./e-mail	0141 548 3958 fraser@strath.ac.uk
Fax / Web site	0141 552 8347 www.fraser.strath.ac.uk
399	FRASER OF ALLENDER INSTITUTE
Title	**Business Forecasting Service**
Coverage	Forecasts of the Scottish economy and industry.
Frequency	Twice yearly
Web Facilities	
Cost	On request
Comments	
Address	Strathclyde University, 100 Cathedral Street, Glasgow G4 0LN
Tel./e-mail	0141 548 3958 fraser@strath.ac.uk
Fax / Web site	0141 552 8347 www.fraser.strath.ac.uk
400	FREIGHT TRANSPORT ASSOCIATION
Title	**Manager's Guide to Distribution Costs**
Coverage	Statistics on road transport costs including wages, vehicle operating costs, haulage rates. Actual costs and indices are included. Based on the association's own survey with supporting commentary.
Frequency	Quarterly
Web Facilities	
Cost	On request
Comments	Primarily for member companies.
Address	Hermes House, St John's Road, Tunbridge Wells TN4 9UZ
Tel./e-mail	01892 526171 inquiries@fta.org.uk
Fax / Web site	01892 534989 www.fta.co.uk

401

	FREIGHT TRANSPORT ASSOCIATION
Title	**Quarterly Transport Activity Survey**
Coverage	A review of freight transport by air, road, sea, and rail with data on demand, markets, prices, costs, safety, accidents, and forecasts. Based on Census returns from members, data from the Department of Transport, and other sources.
Frequency	Quarterly
Web Facilities	
Cost	On request
Comments	Primarily for member companies.
Address	Hermes House, St John's Road, Tunbridge Wells TN4 9UZ
Tel./e-mail	01892 526171 inquiries@fta.org.uk
Fax / Web site	01892 534989 www.fta.co.uk

402

	FREIGHT TRANSPORT ASSOCIATION
Title	**Manager's Fuel Price Information Service**
Coverage	Monthly monitor of prices for derv, gas, oil, and petrol. Based on the association's own survey.
Frequency	Monthly
Web Facilities	
Cost	On request
Comments	Primarily for member companies.
Address	Hermes House, St John's Road, Tunbridge Wells TN4 9UZ
Tel./e-mail	01892 526171 inquiries@fta.org.uk
Fax / Web site	01892 534989 www.fta.co.uk

403

	FRESH FRUIT AND VEGETABLE INFORMATION BUREAU
Title	**UK Fresh Fruit and Vegetable Market Review**
Coverage	Commentary and statistics on the fresh produce market with sections on specific fruits and vegetables.
Frequency	Annual
Web Facilities	
Cost	Free
Comments	
Address	126-128 Cromwell Road, London SW7 4ET
Tel./e-mail	0207 373 7734
Fax / Web site	0207 373 3926 www.ffvib.co.uk

404	FTSE INTERNATIONAL
Title	**UK Monthly Review**
Coverage	Data regularly updated on indices, securities, sector weightings etc.
Frequency	Monthly
Web Facilities	Various indices, news, and database records available on site.
Cost	On request
Comments	
Address	St Alphage House, Podium Floor, 2 Fore Street, London EC2Y 5DA
Tel./e-mail	0207 448 1810 info@ftse.com
Fax / Web site	0207 448 1804 www.ftse.com

405	GALLUP ORGANISATION
Title	**Gallup Omnibus**
Coverage	Sample surveys of around 1,000 adults form the basis of this omnibus survey. Based on face-to-face interviews with adults.
Frequency	Two or three times a week
Web Facilities	Summary data and analysis from polls on site.
Cost	On request
Comments	Results available in various machine-readable formats.
Address	Drapers Court, Kingston Hall Road, Kingston-upon-Thames KT1 2BG
Tel./e-mail	0208 939 7000 marianne-yates@gallup.co.uk
Fax / Web site	0208 939 7039 www.gallup.co.uk

406	GALLUP ORGANISATION
Title	**Gallup Political and Economic Index**
Coverage	Summary data on the various opinion polls carried out by Gallup on political, economic, and social issues.
Frequency	Monthly
Web Facilities	Summary data and analysis from polls free on site.
Cost	On request
Comments	Gallup data also available in machine readable formats.
Address	Drapers Court, Kingston Hall Road, Kingston-upon-Thames KT1 2BG
Tel./e-mail	0208 939 7000 marianne-yates@gallup.co.uk
Fax / Web site	0208 939 7039 www.gallup.co.uk

407

	GEOPLAN (UK) LTD
Title	**Geoplan**
Coverage	A service supplying statistical and geographical data, and the provision of Geographical Information Systems. Based on Census data and the postcode address file.
Frequency	Continuous
Web Facilities	General details of services on site.
Cost	On request, and depending on the range and nature of the information required
Comments	
Address	Bilton Court, Wetherby Road, Harrogate HG3 1GP
Tel./e-mail	01423 569538 sales@mi.co.uk
Fax / Web site	01423 819494 www.geoplan.com

408

	GIN AND VODKA ASSOCIATION OF GREAT BRITAIN
Title	**Annual Report**
Coverage	Gives production of gin, home trade sales and export sales to EU countries and non-EU countries for the last four six-month periods. Based on returns from members.
Frequency	Annual
Web Facilities	General details of statistics on site.
Cost	Free
Comments	Available primarily to members but other requests considered.
Address	Winchester House, Winchester Street, Andover SP10 2ET
Tel./e-mail	01264 337011 ginvodka@lineone.net
Fax / Web site	01264 350219 www.ginvodka.org

409

	GMAP LTD
Title	**GMAP**
Coverage	A geodemographic service based primarily on the Census population data and other specialist surveys.
Frequency	Continuous
Web Facilities	General details of services on site.
Cost	On request, and depending on the range and nature of the information required
Comments	
Address	15 Blenheim Terrace, Leeds LS2 9HN
Tel./e-mail	0113 229 4444
Fax / Web site	0113 2294455 www.gmap.co.uk

410	GOLDFISH
Title	**ePI - e-Tail Price Index**
Coverage	A monitor of prices for goods and services purchased on the Internet. Around 1,500 products are covered. Based on research by Datamonitor.
Frequency	Monthly
Web Facilities	Free access to the latest index on site and details of methodology.
Cost	Free
Comments	
Address	
Tel./e-mail	01256 492025 luc.warner@goldfish.com
Fax / Web site	www.goldfish.co.uk

411	HALIFAX
Title	**Halifax House Price Index**
Coverage	Commentary plus indices and average values for different types of houses. Also includes a regional analysis and additional data for first time buyers, mortgage demand etc. Based on Halifax records.
Frequency	Quarterly
Web Facilities	
Cost	Free
Comments	The separate regional price index publication is now included in this publication.
Address	Trinity Road, Halifax HX1 2RG
Tel./e-mail	01422 333333
Fax / Web site	01422 332039 www.halifax.co.uk

412	HARDWARE TODAY
Title	**Today's Trading Trends**
Coverage	Performance trends in various hardware sectors based on a summary of the results of a survey of members of the British Hardware Federation.
Frequency	Quarterly in a monthly journal
Web Facilities	
Cost	On request
Comments	
Address	Indices Publications Ltd, 14-16 Church Street, Rickmansworth WD3 1RQ
Tel./e-mail	01923 711434 htoday@moose.co.uk
Fax / Web site	01923 896063 www.bhfgroup.demon.co.uk

413	HARRIS RESEARCH
Title	**Young Persons' Omnibus**
Coverage	A quarterly omnibus survey of 1,500 young people aged between 12 and 24. Face-to-face interviews collect information on the purchasing trends, attitudes, and preferences of this consumer group.
Frequency	Quarterly
Web Facilities	
Cost	On request
Comments	
Address	34-38 Hill Rise, Richmond TW10 6UA
Tel./e-mail	0208 332 9898 general@harris-research.co.uk
Fax / Web site	0208 948 6335 www.harrisuk@org.1.demon.co.uk

414	HARRIS RESEARCH
Title	**55+ Omnibus**
Coverage	A quarterly face-to-face survey based on a sample of 1,500 adults aged 55 and over. A specialist service for those whose products and services are targeted at the 'grey' market.
Frequency	Quarterly
Web Facilities	
Cost	On request
Comments	
Address	34-38 Hill Rise, Richmond TW10 6UA
Tel./e-mail	0208 332 9898 general@harris-research.co.uk
Fax / Web site	0208 948 6335 www.harrisuk@org.1.demon.co.uk

415	HARRIS RESEARCH
Title	**Harris Response**
Coverage	A weekly omnibus survey involving face-to-face interviews with 1,000 adults. Demographic breakdowns and detailed information on purchasing, consumer attitudes etc.
Frequency	Weekly
Web Facilities	
Cost	On request
Comments	
Address	34-38 Hill Rise, Richmond TW10 6UA
Tel./e-mail	0208 332 9898 general@harris-research.co.uk
Fax / Web site	0208 948 6335 www.harrisuk@org.1.demon.co.uk

416	HAY MANAGEMENT CONSULTANTS LTD
Title	**Consumer Sector Salesforce Survey**
Coverage	A survey of salaries and benefits in fast-moving consumer goods (FMCG) companies. Based on a range of jobs in over 60 organisations.
Frequency	Annual
Web Facilities	General details of services on site.
Cost	£700
Comments	
Address	52 Grosvenor Gardens, London SW1W 0AU
Tel./e-mail	0207 881 7000 uk_infobus@haygroup.com
Fax / Web site	0207 881 7100 www.haygroup.com

417	HAY MANAGEMENT CONSULTANTS LTD
Title	**Accountants and Taxation Specialists**
Coverage	A salary and benefits survey of accountants and related professionals based around 19 job levels and sampling over 500 organisations. Based on a survey by the company.
Frequency	Annual
Web Facilities	General details of services on site.
Cost	£925
Comments	
Address	52 Grosvenor Gardens, London SW1W 0AU
Tel./e-mail	0207 881 7000 uk_infobus@haygroup.com
Fax / Web site	0207 881 7100 www.haygroup.com

418	HAY MANAGEMENT CONSULTANTS LTD
Title	**Investment Fund Remuneration**
Coverage	Covers the pay and benefits of investment fund managers and related jobs down to the level of investment analysts. Analyses available by sector, and geographical location. Based on data collected by the company.
Frequency	Annual
Web Facilities	General details of services on site.
Cost	£675
Comments	
Address	52 Grosvenor Gardens, London SW1W 0AU
Tel./e-mail	0207 881 7000 uk_infobus@haygroup.com
Fax / Web site	0207 881 7100 www.haygroup.com

419	HAY MANAGEMENT CONSULTANTS LTD
Title	**HAY/PA Publishers' Survey**
Coverage	A survey of salaries and benefits in the book and magazine publishing sectors. Based on data collected by the company and the Publishers' Association.
Frequency	Annual
Web Facilities	General details of services on site.
Cost	£860
Comments	
Address	52 Grosvenor Gardens, London SW1W 0AU
Tel./e-mail	0207 881 7000 uk_infobus@haygroup.com
Fax / Web site	0207 881 7100 www.haygroup.com

420	HAY MANAGEMENT CONSULTANTS LTD
Title	**Human Resources and Personnel Remuneration**
Coverage	A survey of salaries and benefits for personnel and human resources managers and related jobs. Based on a survey of over 600 organisations.
Frequency	Annual
Web Facilities	General details of services on site.
Cost	£720
Comments	
Address	52 Grosvenor Gardens, London SW1W 0AU
Tel./e-mail	0207 881 7000 uk_infobus@haygroup.com
Fax / Web site	0207 881 7100 www.haygroup.com

421	HAY MANAGEMENT CONSULTANTS LTD
Title	**Information Technology Remuneration**
Coverage	A survey of salaries and benefits for IT staff in over 400 organisations. Based on a survey by the company.
Frequency	Annual
Web Facilities	General details of services on site.
Cost	£720
Comments	
Address	52 Grosvenor Gardens, London SW1W 0AU
Tel./e-mail	0207 881 7000 uk_infobus@haygroup.com
Fax / Web site	0207 881 7100 www.haygroup.com

422	HAY MANAGEMENT CONSULTANTS LTD
Title	**Health Service Survey**
Coverage	A survey of salaries and benefits for 17 job levels in the health service. Based on a survey of around 70 hospitals.
Frequency	Annual
Web Facilities	General details of services on site.
Cost	£365
Comments	
Address	52 Grosvenor Gardens, London SW1W 0AU
Tel./e-mail	0207 881 7000 uk_infobus@haygroup.com
Fax / Web site	0207 881 7100 www.haygroup.com

423	HAY MANAGEMENT CONSULTANTS LTD
Title	**Local Authority Survey**
Coverage	A survey of salaries and benefits for various levels of local authority staff based on a survey of around 70 local authorities.
Frequency	Annual
Web Facilities	General details of services on site.
Cost	£675
Comments	
Address	52 Grosvenor Gardens, London SW1W 0AU
Tel./e-mail	0207 881 7000 uk_infobus@haygroup.com
Fax / Web site	0207 881 7100 www.haygroup.com

424	HAY MANAGEMENT CONSULTANTS LTD
Title	**Retail Survey**
Coverage	A survey of salaries and benefits for various jobs in the retailing sector. Based on a survey of almost 100 organisations.
Frequency	Annual
Web Facilities	General details of services on site.
Cost	£720
Comments	
Address	52 Grosvenor Gardens, London SW1W 0AU
Tel./e-mail	0207 881 7000 uk_infobus@haygroup.com
Fax / Web site	0207 881 7100 www.haygroup.com

425	HAY MANAGEMENT CONSULTANTS LTD
Title	**Engineers' Remuneration**
Coverage	A survey of salaries and benefits for engineers based on 22 job levels. Based on a survey by the company of over 300 organisations.
Frequency	Annual
Web Facilities	General details of services on site.
Cost	£675
Comments	
Address	52 Grosvenor Gardens, London SW1W 0AU
Tel./e-mail	0207 881 7000 uk_infobus@haygroup.com
Fax / Web site	0207 881 7100 www.haygroup.com

426	HAY MANAGEMENT CONSULTANTS LTD
Title	**Boardroom Guide - A Survey of Directors' Remuneration**
Coverage	A survey focusing on the remuneration of top management and directors with data on over 4,000 top jobs from over 400 companies. Based on salary data collected by the company with additional data on share options, cars, pensions and other benefits.
Frequency	Annual
Web Facilities	General details of services on site.
Cost	£1,750
Comments	
Address	52 Grosvenor Gardens, London SW1W 0AU
Tel./e-mail	0207 881 7000 uk_infobus@haygroup.com
Fax / Web site	0207 881 7100 www.haygroup.com

427	HAY MANAGEMENT CONSULTANTS LTD
Title	**Solicitors and Legal Executives' Remuneration**
Coverage	A survey of salaries and benefits of solicitors and related professionals based on data collected by the company.
Frequency	Annual
Web Facilities	General details of services on site.
Cost	£720
Comments	
Address	52 Grosvenor Gardens, London SW1W 0AU
Tel./e-mail	0207 881 7000 uk_infobus@haygroup.com
Fax / Web site	0207 881 7100 www.haygroup.com

428	HAY MANAGEMENT CONSULTANTS LTD
Title	**Employee Benefits Reports**
Coverage	Two reports on Industrial & Service Organisations and Financial Organisations.
Frequency	Regular
Web Facilities	Online ordering
Cost	£1,400 or £925 each if purchased separately
Comments	
Address	52 Grosvenor Gardens, London SW1W 0AU
Tel./e-mail	0207 881 7200 uk_infobase@haygroup.com
Fax / Web site	0207 881 7104 www.haygroup.com

429	HAY MANAGEMENT CONSULTANTS LTD
Title	**Hay Compensation Report**
Coverage	Statistics and analysis on the salaries and main benefits of executive, managerial, and supervisory positions. Analysis by major industrial and service sector, location, and function. Based on a quarterly updated database of over 500 companies and thousands of jobs.
Frequency	Quarterly
Web Facilities	General details of services on site.
Cost	£1,000, or £375 per quarterly report
Comments	
Address	52 Grosvenor Gardens, London SW1W 0AU
Tel./e-mail	0207 881 7000 uk_infobus@haygroup.com
Fax / Web site	0207 881 7100 www.haygroup.com

430	HAYS ACCOUNTANCY PERSONNEL
Title	**Guide to Salaries in Accountancy 431**
Coverage	Covers accountancy salaries and merchant and international banking salaries. Information based on surveys carried out in various regional centres in England and Wales. A general commentary accompanies the data.
Frequency	Twice yearly
Web Facilities	
Cost	£35
Comments	
Address	4th Floor, 141 Moorgate, London EC2M 6TX
Tel./e-mail	0207 628 6655 marketing@hays-ap.co.uk
Fax / Web site	0207 628 4736 www.hays-ap.com

431	HCIS
Title	**Fitzhugh Directory of Independent Healthcare**
Coverage	A directory of the independent healthcare sector which includes statistical data on market size and trends, plus details of the number of mergers and acquisitions.
Frequency	Annual
Web Facilities	
Cost	£240
Comments	
Address	12 Riverview Grove, London W4 3QJ
Tel./e-mail	0208 995 1752
Fax / Web site	0208 742 2418

432	HEALEY AND BAKER
Title	**Quarterly Market Report**
Coverage	Data on investment trends in the retail, office, and industrial property sectors. Commentary supported by various tables.
Frequency	Quarterly
Web Facilities	Free access to reports on site.
Cost	Free
Comments	
Address	29 St George Street, Hanover Square, London W1A 3BG
Tel./e-mail	0207 514 2290
Fax / Web site	0207 514 2366 www.healey-baker.com

433	HEALEY AND BAKER
Title	**Prime**
Coverage	Commentary and statistics on the trends in property rents with data for industrial, office, and retail property. Figures for the standard regions and a table of summary data covering a ten-year period. Based on the company's own research with supporting text.
Frequency	Annual
Web Facilities	Free access to reports on site.
Cost	Free
Comments	
Address	29 St George Street, Hanover Square, London W1A 3BG
Tel./e-mail	0207 514 2290
Fax / Web site	0207 514 2366 www.healey-baker.com

434	HESA SERVICES LTD
Title	**Higher Education Management Statistics - Sector Level**
Coverage	Data on applications and admissions, the student population, qualifications, first destinations etc.
Frequency	Annual
Web Facilities	Details of publications and free access to various statistics on site.
Cost	£22
Comments	Also available on disc (£25).
Address	18 Royal Crescent, Cheltenham GL50 3DA
Tel./e-mail	01242 255577 customer.services@hesa.ac.uk
Fax / Web site	01242 211122 www.hesa.ac.uk

435	HESA SERVICES LTD
Title	**Higher Education Management Statistics - Institution Level**
Coverage	A loose-leaf volume with data on finances, applications, admissions, student profiles and student outcomes.
Frequency	Regular
Web Facilities	Details of publications and free access to various statistics on site.
Cost	£65
Comments	Published in CD-ROM format.
Address	18 Royal Crescent, Cheltenham GL50 3DA
Tel./e-mail	01242 255577 customer.services@hesa.ac.uk
Fax / Web site	01242 211122 www.hesa.ac.uk

436	HESA SERVICES LTD
Title	**Statistics Focus**
Coverage	Analysis and data on key topics in higher education.
Frequency	Three issues a year
Web Facilities	Details of publications and free access to various statistics on site.
Cost	£75
Comments	
Address	18 Royal Crescent, Cheltenham GL50 3DA
Tel./e-mail	01242 255577 customer.services@hesa.ac.uk
Fax / Web site	01242 211122 www.hesa.ac.uk

437	HESA SERVICES LTD
Title	**Higher Education Statistics for the UK**
Coverage	Published in association with the Government Statistical Service and presenting an overview of higher education trends.
Frequency	Annual
Web Facilities	Details of publications and free access to various statistics on site.
Cost	£32
Comments	Also available on disc (£35).
Address	18 Royal Crescent, Cheltenham GL50 3DA
Tel./e-mail	01242 255577 customer.services@hesa.ac.uk
Fax / Web site	01242 211122 www.hesa.ac.uk

438	HESA SERVICES LTD
Title	**Reference Volume - First Destinations of Students Leaving Higher Education Institutions**
Coverage	Statistics about the first destinations of graduates including employment rates, participation in further study and training.
Frequency	Annual
Web Facilities	Details of publications and free access to various statistics on site.
Cost	£32
Comments	Also available on disc (£35).
Address	18 Royal Crescent, Cheltenham GL50 3DA
Tel./e-mail	01242 255577 customer.services@hesa.ac.uk
Fax / Web site	01242 211122 www.hesa.ac.uk

439	HESA SERVICES LTD
Title	**Reference Volume - Resources of Higher Education Institutions**
Coverage	Statistics covering the financing and staffing of HEIs.
Frequency	Annual
Web Facilities	Details of publications and free access to various statistics on site.
Cost	£32
Comments	Also available on disc (£35).
Address	18 Royal Crescent, Cheltenham GL50 3DA
Tel./e-mail	01242 255577 customer.services@hesa.ac.uk
Fax / Web site	01242 211122 www.hesa.ac.uk

440	HESA SERVICES LTD
Title	**Reference Volume - Students in Higher Education Institutions**
Coverage	Statistics on all aspects of students in higher education including examination results, subjects of study.
Frequency	Annual
Web Facilities	Details of publications and free access to various statistics on site.
Cost	£32
Comments	Also available on disc. (£35).
Address	18 Royal Crescent, Cheltenham GL50 3DA
Tel./e-mail	01242 255577 customer.services@hesa.ac.uk
Fax / Web site	01242 211122 www.hesa.ac.uk

441	HEWITT ASSOCIATES
Title	**Salary Increase Survey Report - UK**
Coverage	A survey of salary increases for various categories of jobs based on a sample of around 250 companies.
Frequency	Annual
Web Facilities	General details of services on site.
Cost	On request
Comments	The company carries out various specialist salary surveys, eg consumer electronics, consumer finance, and also maintains a salaries database. These services are available to clients only.
Address	Prospect House, Abbeyview, St Albans AL1 2QU
Tel./e-mail	01727 888200
Fax / Web site	01727 888333 www.hewitt.com

442	HGCA
Title	**Cereal Statistics**
Coverage	Production and supplies of specific types of cereals plus data on prices and imports and exports. Some international comparisons are included and there is a section of historical statistics. Based mainly on Central Government data with additional material from the authority and other non-official sources.
Frequency	Annual
Web Facilities	Free summary statistics and paid-for access to detailed data on site.
Cost	Annual subscription available for all data.
Comments	Home Grown Cereals Authority in previous edition.
Address	Caledonia House, 223 Pentonville Road, London N1 9HY
Tel./e-mail	0207 520 3926 communications@hgca.com
Fax / Web site	0207 520 3958 www.hgca.com

443

	HGCA
Title	**Annual Report**
Coverage	Mainly a general commentary on the cereals sector but includes some general statistics on production, supplies etc.
Frequency	Annual
Web Facilities	Free copy on site plus free summary statistics and paid-for access to detailed data.
Cost	Free
Comments	Home Grown Cereals Authority in previous edition.
Address	Caledonia House, 223 Pentonville Road, London N1 9HY
Tel./e-mail	0207 520 3926 communications@hgca.com
Fax / Web site	0207 520 3958 www.hgca.com

444

	HGCA
Title	**MI Prospects**
Coverage	Statistics and comments on grain market trends and policies. Based on a combination of Central Government statistics, data from the Authority, and other non-official sources.
Frequency	Weekly
Web Facilities	Free summary statistics and paid-for access to detailed data on site.
Cost	Annual subscription available for all data.
Comments	Home Grown Cereals Authority in previous edition.
Address	Caledonia House, 223 Pentonville Road, London N1 9HY
Tel./e-mail	0207 520 3926 communications@hgca.com
Fax / Web site	0207 520 3958 www.hgca.com

445

	HGCA
Title	**MI Bulletin**
Coverage	Statistics on prices, imports, exports, and the futures market for cereals. International data is also included.
Frequency	Weekly
Web Facilities	Free summary statistics and paid-for access to detailed data on site.
Cost	Annual subscription available for all data.
Comments	Home Grown Cereals Authority in previous edition.
Address	Caledonia House, 223 Pentonville Road, London N1 9HY
Tel./e-mail	0207 520 3926 communications@hgca.com
Fax / Web site	0207 520 3958 www.hgca.com

446	HGCA
Title	**MI Saturday**
Coverage	A two-page summary outlining key market trends and statistics in the cereals and grain markets.
Frequency	Weekly
Web Facilities	Free summary statistics and paid-for access to detailed data on site.
Cost	Annual subscription available for all data.
Comments	Home Grown Cereals Authority in previous edition.
Address	Caledonia House, 223 Pentonville Road, London N1 9HY
Tel./e-mail	0207 520 3926 communications@hgca.com
Fax / Web site	0207 520 3958 www.hgca.com

447	HGCA
Title	**MI Oilseeds**
Coverage	Statistics on prices, imports, exports and prospects for oilseeds. International data is also included.
Frequency	Weekly
Web Facilities	Free summary statistics plus paid-for access to detailed data on site.
Cost	Annual subscription available for all data.
Comments	Home Grown Cereals Authority in previous edition.
Address	Caledonia House, 223 Pentonville Road, London N1 9HY
Tel./e-mail	0207 520 3926 communications@hgca.com
Fax / Web site	0207 520 3958 www.hgca.com

448	HIGHER EDUCATION CAREERS SERVICES UNIT
Title	**What do Graduates Do?**
Coverage	Supply of graduates and those entering employment by employer, type of work and field of study. Comparative figures for earlier years. Based on data supplied by various institutions and some supporting text.
Frequency	Annual
Web Facilities	Free access to statistics on the site plus online ordering facilities. Email alerts about new statistics.
Cost	£9.95
Comments	
Address	Booth Street East, Manchester M13 9EP
Tel./e-mail	0161 2775325 d.Johnson@csu.ac.uk
Fax / Web site	0161 2775240 www.prospects.csu.ac.uk

449

	HIGHER EDUCATION CAREERS SERVICES UNIT
Title	**Graduate Market Trends**
Coverage	An analysis of graduate vacancies and salaries arranged by work type, employer type, subject of study, and location. Based on data collected by CSU. A commentary is included with the data.
Frequency	Quarterly
Web Facilities	Free access to statistics on the site, plus online ordering facilities. Email alerts about new statistics.
Cost	Free
Comments	
Address	Booth Street East, Manchester M13 9EP
Tel./e-mail	0161 2775325 d.Johnson@csu.ac.uk
Fax / Web site	0161 2775240 www.prospects.csu.ac.uk

450

	HOTEL CATERING AND INSTITUTIONAL MANAGEMENT ASSOCIATION
Title	**Hospitality Yearbook**
Coverage	Includes an Annual Review section with commentary and statistics on developments over the previous 12 months.
Frequency	Annual
Web Facilities	
Cost	On request
Comments	
Address	William Reed Publishing Ltd, Broadfield Park, Crawley RH11 9RT
Tel./e-mail	01293 610301
Fax / Web site	01293 613304

451

	HOUSE BUILDERS FEDERATION AND HOUSEBUILDER PUBLICATIONS
Title	**Housing Market Report**
Coverage	Includes a survey of housebuilding and a survey of confidence and affordability in the market. Also data on housing market activity, building, labour market trends, mortgages. News items on the housing market are also included and historical data is included in many tables.
Frequency	Monthly
Web Facilities	
Cost	£259, £195 for members of House Builders Federation
Comments	
Address	PO Box 2, Ellesmere Port, South Wirral L65 3AS
Tel./e-mail	0151 357 7707 holly.rickers@database-direct.co.uk
Fax / Web site	0151 357 2813 www.hbf.co.uk/hbf/index.html

452	HP FOODS LTD
Title	**HP Retail Sauce Report**
Coverage	Commentary and statistics on market trends, brands, product developments etc based on commissioned research.
Frequency	Annual
Web Facilities	
Cost	On request
Comments	
Address	45 Northampton Road, Market Harborough LE16 9BQ
Tel./e-mail	01858 410144
Fax / Web site	01858 410053

453	HSBC INVESTMENT BANK
Title	**UK Economics**
Coverage	Data for the current year, quarters and forecasts.Topics covered include inflation, PSBR, trade, earnings, banking etc.
Frequency	Quarterly
Web Facilities	Research and forecasts freely available on Web site.
Cost	Free
Comments	
Address	Thames Exchange, 10 Queen Street Place, London EC4R 1BL
Tel./e-mail	0207 621 0011
Fax / Web site	0207 336 4231 www.hsbcmarkets.com

454	HSBC INVESTMENT BANK
Title	**UK Chart Pack**
Coverage	UK performance evaluation and trends.
Frequency	Monthly
Web Facilities	Research and forecasts freely available on Web site.
Cost	Free
Comments	
Address	Thames Exchange, 10 Queen Street Place, London EC4R 1BL
Tel./e-mail	0207 621 0011
Fax / Web site	0207 336 4231 www.hsbcmarkets.com

455	HSBC INVESTMENT BANK
Title	**UK Performance Pack**
Coverage	FT All Share Index performance review.
Frequency	Monthly
Web Facilities	Research and forecasts freely available on Web site.
Cost	Free
Comments	
Address	Thames Exchange, 10 Queen Street Place, London EC4R 1BL
Tel./e-mail	0207 621 0011
Fax / Web site	0207 336 4231 www.hsbcmarkets.com

456	HUNT MARKETING RESEARCH
Title	**The UK Paint Market**
Coverage	An analysis of trends in various sectors of the paint market including DIY paints, motor vehicle paints, industrial coatings, trade paints, high performance coatings, vehicle refinishes. Based on research by the company.
Frequency	Every two years
Web Facilities	
Cost	£275
Comments	Latest issue published April 2001.
Address	Old Mill, Mill Street, Wantage OX12 9AB
Tel./e-mail	01235 772001
Fax / Web site	01235 772001

457	ICD MARKETING SERVICES
Title	**The National Lifestyle Report**
Coverage	ICD is a geodemographic service and the National Lifestyle Report is a customer profile analysis allocating every record on ICD's database into one of 100 cells, based on 280 lifestyle variables.
Frequency	Continuous
Web Facilities	
Cost	On request, and depending on the range and nature of the information required
Comments	
Address	Bain House, 16 Connaught Place, London W2 2EP
Tel./e-mail	0207 298 6300
Fax / Web site	

458	ICM RESEARCH
Title	**ICM Omnibus**
Coverage	An omnibus survey of 1,500 adults aged 15 and over at 103 sampling points around the country.
Frequency	Fortnightly
Web Facilities	Free access to various poll results on site.
Cost	On request
Comments	
Address	Knighton House, 56 Mortimer Street, London W1N 7DG
Tel./e-mail	0207 436 3114
Fax / Web site	0207 436 3179 www.icmresearch.co.uk

459	IMPERIAL CHEMICAL INDUSTRIES PLC
Title	**Dulux Paints Review**
Coverage	A review of the UK paints market with data on sales, distribution, and key brands. Based largely on market research sources.
Frequency	Regular
Web Facilities	
Cost	On request
Comments	
Address	9 Millbank, London SW1P 3JF
Tel./e-mail	0207 834 4444
Fax / Web site	0207 834 2042

460	INBUCON LTD
Title	**UK Survey of Executive Salaries and Benefits**
Coverage	A survey of salaries and benefits covering 56 executive job titles based in over 20 industrial groupings. Based on a survey carried out by the company.
Frequency	Annual
Web Facilities	
Cost	£550, £175 to participants
Comments	
Address	34 Paradise Road, Richmond TW9 1FE
Tel./e-mail	0208 334 5727 tbt@inbucon.co.uk
Fax / Web site	0208 334 5739 www.inbucon.co.uk

461	INCOMES DATA SERVICES
Title	**IDS Management Pay Review Pay and Progression for Graduates**
Coverage	A survey of salary and related trends in the graduate labour market based on a sample survey of over 100 organisations.
Frequency	Annual
Web Facilities	Free Statistics Zone on site mainly covering official data.
Cost	£202
Comments	
Address	77 Bastwick Street, London EC1V 3TT
Tel./e-mail	0207 250 3434 sales@incomesdata.co.uk
Fax / Web site	0207 608 0949 www.incomesdata.co.uk

462	INCOMES DATA SERVICES
Title	**IDS Management Pay Review Executive Pay Report**
Coverage	A survey of salary movements for management staff in FTSE 250 companies. Additional information on bonuses, share options, benefits, and contracts. Based on a survey by the company.
Frequency	Annual
Web Facilities	Free Statistics Zone on site mainly covering official data.
Cost	On request
Comments	
Address	77 Bastwick Street, London EC1V 3TT
Tel./e-mail	0207 250 3434 sales@incomesdata.co.uk
Fax / Web site	0207 608 0949 www.incomesdata.co.uk

463	INCOMES DATA SERVICES
Title	**Public Sector Labour Market Survey**
Coverage	An IDS survey of the public sector labour market based on a survey of employers' perceptions of the market and their recent recruitment and training experiences.
Frequency	Annual
Web Facilities	Free Statistics Zone on site mainly covering official data.
Cost	On request
Comments	The survey is included as a special feature in the twice-monthly 'IDS Report'. IDS publishes a range of reports on the UK and European labour market and conditions.
Address	77 Bastwick Street, London EC1V 3TT
Tel./e-mail	0207 250 3434 sales@incomesdata.co.uk
Fax / Web site	0207 608 0949 www.incomesdata.co.uk

464	INCOMES DATA SERVICES
Title	**Datable**
Coverage	General statistics on retail prices and average earnings, in index form, with historical data for previous months. Based on Central Government data.
Frequency	Twice monthly in a twice monthly journal
Web Facilities	Free Statistics Zone on site mainly covering official data.
Cost	On request
Comments	Published in the IDS journal, 'IDS Report'. IDS publishes a range of reports on the UK and European labour market and conditions.
Address	77 Bastwick Street, London EC1V 3TT
Tel./e-mail	0207 250 3434 sales@incomesdata.co.uk
Fax / Web site	0207 608 0949 www.incomesdata.co.uk

465	INCOMES DATA SERVICES
Title	**Pay Settlement Analysis**
Coverage	Data on trends in pay settlements with figures for changes in the level of settlements over a 12 month period. Based on data collected by IDS.
Frequency	Quarterly in a twice-monthly journal
Web Facilities	Free Statistics Zone on site mainly covering official data.
Cost	On request
Comments	The survey is included as a quarterly feature in the journal, 'IDS Report'. IDS publishes a range of reports on the UK and European labour market and conditions.
Address	77 Bastwick Street, London EC1V 3TT
Tel./e-mail	0207 250 3434 sales@incomesdata.co.uk
Fax / Web site	0207 608 0949 www.incomesdata.co.uk

466	INCOMES DATA SERVICES
Title	**Pay and Bargaining Prospects**
Coverage	Commentary and statistics on the outlook for pay and bargaining in the next twelve months. Based on an analysis of current and likely economic and pay trends by IDS.
Frequency	Annual
Web Facilities	Free Statistics Zone on site mainly covering official data.
Cost	On request
Comments	The survey is included as a special feature in the twice-monthly 'IDS Report', usually in a September issue.
Address	77 Bastwick Street, London EC1V 3TT
Tel./e-mail	0207 250 3434 sales@incomesdata.co.uk
Fax / Web site	0207 608 0949 www.incomesdata.co.uk

467	INCORPORATED SOCIETY OF BRITISH ADVERTISERS LTD
Title	**Advertiser Relationships with Direct Marketing Agencies**
Coverage	A review of opinions on direct marketing and a survey of services used from direct market agencies.
Frequency	Annual
Web Facilities	General details on site.
Cost	£250, £150 for members
Comments	Sponsored by Royal Mail.
Address	44 Hertford Street, London W1Y 8AE
Tel./e-mail	0207 499 7502 info@isba.org.uk
Fax / Web site	0207 629 5355 www.isba.org.uk

468	INCORPORATED SOCIETY OF BRITISH ADVERTISERS LTD
Title	**Paying for Advertising**
Coverage	A survey of the payment systems used to pay agencies and levels of remuneration.
Frequency	Regular
Web Facilities	General details on site.
Cost	£300, £100 for members.
Comments	Second in a series of tracking studies.
Address	44 Hertford Street, London W1Y 8AE
Tel./e-mail	0207 499 7502 info@isba.org.uk
Fax / Web site	0207 629 5355 www.isba.org.uk

469	INDEPENDENT HEALTHCARE ASSOCIATION
Title	**Survey of Acute Hospitals in the Independent Sector**
Coverage	Details of the size of, and growth trends for, the private hospital market in the UK. Regional data is also included. Based on information collected by the association.
Frequency	Annual
Web Facilities	Some free basic data on the site.
Cost	£25
Comments	
Address	Westminster Tower, 3 Albert Embankment, London SE1 7SP
Tel./e-mail	0207 793 4820 angela.salway@iha.org.uk
Fax / Web site	0207 820 3738 www.iha.org.uk

470	INDEPENDENT SCHOOLS INFORMATION SERVICE (ISIS)
Title	**ISIS Annual Census**
Coverage	General statistical information about the number of pupils in ISIS schools, spending, current trends in independent education etc. Based on a regular ISIS survey.
Frequency	Annual
Web Facilities	
Cost	£15
Comments	
Address	Grosvenor Gardens House, 35-37 Grosvenor Gardens, London SW1W 0BS
Tel./e-mail	0207 798 1500 national@isis.org.uk
Fax / Web site	0207 798 1501 www.isis.org.uk
471	INDEPENDENT TELEVISION COMMISSION (ITC)
Title	**ITC Cable Statistics**
Coverage	A press release giving figures for the take-up, homes passed, penetration of cable TV.
Frequency	Quarterly
Web Facilities	Free access to statistics on site.
Cost	Free
Comments	Also produces an annual report with a general review of viewing trends.
Address	33 Foley Street, London W1W 7TL
Tel./e-mail	0207 255 3000 publicaffairs@itc.org.uk
Fax / Web site	0207 306 7800 www.itc.org.uk
472	INDEPENDENT TELEVISION COMMISSION (ITC)
Title	**Television Audience Share Figures**
Coverage	Quarterly viewing figures broken down by TV channel.
Frequency	Quarterly
Web Facilities	Free access to statistics on site.
Cost	Free
Comments	Also produces an annual report with a general review of viewing trends.
Address	33 Foley Street, London W1W 7TL
Tel./e-mail	0207 255 3000 publicaffairs@itc.org.uk
Fax / Web site	0207 306 7800 www.itc.org.uk

473	**INDEPENDENT TELEVISION COMMISSION (ITC)**
Title	**Television: the Public's View**
Coverage	Annual survey, from 1970 onwards, of consumer opinions of television plus ownership levels. Includes data on the number of TV sets, subscriptions to cable and satellite television, programme selection, motives for choosing specific programmes, opinions on standards and quality, comments on specific types of programmes.
Frequency	Annual
Web Facilities	Free access to statistics on site.
Cost	£7.50
Comments	Also produces an annual report with a general review of viewing trends.
Address	33 Foley Street, London W1W 7TL
Tel./e-mail	0207 255 3000 publicaffairs@itc.org.uk
Fax / Web site	0207 306 7800 www.itc.org.uk

474	**INDICES PUBLICATIONS LTD**
Title	**The New Grey List**
Coverage	Market prices for over 30,000 hardware and DIY products based on a survey by Indices Publications of prices throughout the country.
Frequency	Monthly
Web Facilities	
Cost	£119, £99 to British Hardware Federation members
Comments	
Address	14-16 Church Street, Rickmansworth WD3 1WD
Tel./e-mail	01923 711434
Fax / Web site	01923 896063

475	**INDUSTRIAL RELATIONS SERVICES (IRS)**
Title	**IRS Employment Review**
Coverage	The Employment Review comprises five journals which have been brought together under one cover. These include 'Pay' and 'Benefits Bulletin', with data on earnings, settlements, prices etc. and 'IRS Employment Trends'.
Frequency	Twice a month
Web Facilities	General details of publications and services on site.
Cost	On request
Comments	
Address	18-20 Highbury Place, London N5 1QP
Tel./e-mail	0207 354 5858
Fax / Web site	0207 359 4000 www.irseclipse.co.uk

476	ING CHARTERHOUSE SECURITIES
Title	**Scotch Whisky Review**
Coverage	A detailed analysis of the sector with data on home and export prices, costs and profit margins, sales, distillers, market shares, brand and company information, exports, and forecasts of future trends. Based on various sources.
Frequency	Annual
Web Facilities	
Cost	£395
Comments	
Address	Lismore House, 127 George Street, Edinburgh EH2 4JX
Tel./e-mail	0131 527 3000
Fax / Web site	0131 527 3001
477	INGLEBY TRICE KENNARD
Title	**City Floorspace Survey**
Coverage	Details of floorspace in the centre of London with a geographical breakdown into three areas: city, central city, city fringe. Based on data held by the company.
Frequency	Monthly
Web Facilities	Web site currently under development.
Cost	£500, £240 to some libraries and other organisations
Comments	Ingleby Trice was previously Richard Saunders & Partners.
Address	11 Old Jewry, London EC2R 8DU
Tel./e-mail	0207 606 7461 a.fell@inglebytk.co.uk
Fax / Web site	0207 726 2578
478	INSIGNIA RICHARD ELLIS
Title	**London Office Market Bulletin**
Coverage	Rents, values and property availability in various areas of London, eg Docklands, West End, City, Mid-Town etc. Based on data collected by the company.
Frequency	Quarterly
Web Facilities	Free access to all reports (except the Monthly Index) on site.
Cost	Free
Comments	Occasional reports on property trends and issues.
Address	Berkeley Square House, London W1X 6AN
Tel./e-mail	0207 629 6290
Fax / Web site	0207 493 3734 www.richardellis.co.uk

479	INSIGNIA RICHARD ELLIS
Title	**Monthly Index**
Coverage	General commentary and statistics on property values and yields with a monthly index covering the latest 12 months. Based on data collected by the company.
Frequency	Monthly
Web Facilities	Free access to all reports (except the Monthly Index) on site.
Cost	On request
Comments	Occasional reports on property trends and issues.
Address	Berkeley Square House, London W1X 6AN
Tel./e-mail	0207 629 6290
Fax / Web site	0207 493 3734 www.richardellis.co.uk
480	INSTITUTE FOR EMPLOYMENT STUDIES
Title	**IES Graduate Review**
Coverage	Statistics on graduates and the graduate recruitment market, plus characteristics of the student population. Also examines major issues relevant to graduate recruitment. Based on data collected and analysed by the institute.
Frequency	Annual
Web Facilities	General details of all publications on site.
Cost	£27.50
Comments	Various other reports on the labour market produced and a publications catalogue is available.
Address	Mantell Building, University of Sussex, Falmer, Brighton BN1 9RF
Tel./e-mail	01273 686751 enquiries@employment-studies.co.uk
Fax / Web site	01273 690430 www.employment-studies.co.uk
481	INSTITUTE FOR EMPLOYMENT STUDIES
Title	**Graduate Salaries and Vacancies**
Coverage	A twice-yearly review of trends in graduate salaries and vacancies. Based on data collected and analysed by the
Frequency	Twice yearly
Web Facilities	General details of all publications on site.
Cost	On request
Comments	
Address	Mantell Building, University of Sussex, Falmer, Brighton BN1 9RF
Tel./e-mail	01273 686751 enquiries@employment-studies.co.uk
Fax / Web site	01273 690430 www.employment-studies.co.uk

482	INSTITUTE OF GROCERY DISTRIBUTION
Title	**Grocery Wholesaling**
Coverage	A regularly updated report on grocery wholesaling with commentary and statistics covering sales, wholesaling sectors, companies, employment, and new developments. Based on various sources.
Frequency	Regular
Web Facilities	Free Fact Sheets on site with market data on grocery trade. Paid for online access to reports.
Cost	£650, £500 to members
Comments	Various other occasional and one-off reports are produced on the grocery sector.
Address	Grange Lane, Letchmore Heath, Watford WD2 8DQ
Tel./e-mail	01923 857141 igd@igd.org.uk
Fax / Web site	01923 852531 www.igd.com

483	INSTITUTE OF GROCERY DISTRIBUTION
Title	**Grocery Retailing**
Coverage	A regularly updated report on grocery retailing in the UK with details of sales and sectors, companies, consumer trends, and new developments. Based on various sources.
Frequency	Regular
Web Facilities	Free Fact Sheets on site with market data on grocery trade. Paid-for online access to reports.
Cost	£650, £500 to members
Comments	Various other occasional and one-off reports are produced on the grocery sector.
Address	Grange Lane, Letchmore Heath, Watford WD2 8DQ
Tel./e-mail	01923 857141 igd@igd.org.uk
Fax / Web site	01923 852531 www.igd.com

484	INSTITUTE OF INFORMATION SCIENTISTS (IIS)
Title	**IIS Remuneration Survey**
Coverage	Salary statistics for institute members in full time employment. Analysis by grade of membership, age, and sectors of employment. A commentary accompanies the data.
Frequency	Every two years
Web Facilities	News and general publications on site.
Cost	£15, free to members
Comments	
Address	39-41 North Road, London N7 9DP
Tel./e-mail	0207 619 0624 iis@dial.pipex.com
Fax / Web site	0207 619 0626 www.iis.org.uk

485	INSTITUTE OF PETROLEUM
Title	**IP Statistical Service**
Coverage	A folder with data sheets providing summary information on the main indicators relating to the UK petroleum sector. Based largely on the institute's own data.
Frequency	Quarterly
Web Facilities	Available from the Web site for £80 annual subscription (also in traditional hard copy).
Cost	£125
Comments	Also publishes the monthly 'Petroleum Review' which contains some statistics.
Address	61 New Cavendish Street, London W1G 7AR
Tel./e-mail	0207 467 7100 ip@petroleum.co.uk
Fax / Web site	0207 255 1472 www.petroleum.co.uk

486	INSTITUTE OF PETROLEUM
Title	**UK Consumption and Refining Production: Ten-Year Cumulation**
Coverage	Historical statistics for a ten-year period covering the key indicators in the UK petroleum sector.
Frequency	Annual
Web Facilities	General details of publications on the Web site.
Cost	£8 members, £12 non-members
Comments	Also publishes the monthly 'Petroleum Review' which contains some statistics.
Address	61 New Cavendish Street, London W1G 7AR
Tel./e-mail	0207 467 7100 ip@petroleum.co.uk
Fax / Web site	0207 255 1472 www.petroleum.co.uk

487	INSTITUTE OF PETROLEUM
Title	**Petroleum Review: Retail Marketing Survey**
Coverage	Statistics and commentary on the retail market for petrol with data on sites, sales, company performance, and new developments and sites. Also data on forecourt retailing.
Frequency	Annual
Web Facilities	General details of publications on the Web site.
Cost	£90, free to members
Comments	Published in March each year. Also publishes the monthly 'Petroleum Review' which contains some statistics.
Address	61 New Cavendish Street, London W1G 7AR
Tel./e-mail	0207 467 7100 ip@petroleum.co.uk
Fax / Web site	0207 255 1472 www.petroleum.co.uk

488	INSTITUTE OF PETROLEUM
Title	**Oil Data Sheet - Monthly Update Services**
Coverage	Some selected statistics showing oil price and address changes are updated monthly.
Frequency	Monthly
Web Facilities	General details of publications on the Web site.
Cost	£18 per sheet electronically delivered, £25 hard copy
Comments	Also publishes the monthly 'Petroleum Review' which contains some statistics.
Address	61 New Cavendish Street, London W1G 7AR
Tel./e-mail	0207 467 7100 ip@petroleum.co.uk
Fax / Web site	0207 255 1472 www.petroleum.co.uk

489	INSTITUTE OF PHYSICS
Title	**Remuneration Survey**
Coverage	Analysis of salaries of members by class of membership, age, sex, type of work etc. Based on a survey of members and supported by a brief commentary.
Frequency	Annual
Web Facilities	
Cost	£20
Comments	Available in the house journal Physics World.
Address	47 Belgrave Square, London SW1X 8QX
Tel./e-mail	0207 470 4800 john.brindley@iop.org
Fax / Web site	0207 470 4848 www.physicsweb.org

490	INSTITUTE OF PRACTITIONERS IN ADVERTISING
Title	**IPA Agency Census**
Coverage	Estimated number of people employed in IPA member advertising agencies categorised by location, staff category, size of agency. Based on the IPA's own survey with some supporting text. Usually published early in the year following a survey in autumn of the previous year.
Frequency	Annual
Web Facilities	Publication details and press releases on site.
Cost	£15
Comments	Also produces surveys of agency costs usually only available to members.
Address	44 Belgrave Square, London SW1X 8QS
Tel./e-mail	0207 235 7020 dawn@ipa.co.uk
Fax / Web site	0207 245 9904 www.ipa.co.uk

491	INSTITUTE OF PRACTITIONERS IN ADVERTISING
Title	**IPA Monitor of Attitudes to Advertising Effectiveness**
Coverage	A survey of perceptions of advertising awareness.
Frequency	Regular
Web Facilities	Publication details and press releases on site.
Cost	£15
Comments	
Address	44 Belgrave Square, London SW1X 8QS
Tel./e-mail	0207 235 7020 dawn@ipa.co.uk
Fax / Web site	0207 245 9904 www.ipa.co.uk

492	INSTITUTE OF PRACTITIONERS IN ADVERTISING
Title	**Bellwether Report**
Coverage	A quarterly review of advertising and marketing activities by companies to offer an indication of business confidence and economic growth.
Frequency	Quarterly
Web Facilities	Publications details and press releases on site.
Cost	On request
Comments	
Address	44 Belgrave Square, London SW1X 8QS
Tel./e-mail	0207 235 7020 dawn@ipa.co.uk
Fax / Web site	0207 245 9904 www.ipa.co.uk

493	INSTITUTION OF CHEMICAL ENGINEERS
Title	**Salary Survey**
Coverage	Remuneration and employment trends for members of the institution based on the organisation's own survey.
Frequency	Every two years
Web Facilities	
Cost	£105, free to members
Comments	
Address	Davis Building, 165-171 Railway Terrace, Rugby CV21 3HQ
Tel./e-mail	01788 578214
Fax / Web site	01788 560833 www.icheme.org

494	**INSTITUTION OF CIVIL ENGINEERS**
Title	**ICE Salary Survey**
Coverage	An analysis by employer, age, type of work, overtime payments, location, firm size, qualifications etc. Based on a survey of members.
Frequency	Annual
Web Facilities	
Cost	£130
Comments	Produced in association with 'New Civil Engineer'.
Address	1 Great George Street, London SW1P 3AA
Tel./e-mail	0207 232 7722
Fax / Web site	0207 282 7500 www.ice.org.uk

495	**INSTITUTION OF ELECTRICAL ENGINEERS (IEE)**
Title	**IEE Salary Survey**
Coverage	A random sample of members, analysed by age, position, class, type of work, levels of responsibility, size of work, qualifications, location of employment, fringe benefits etc. A small amount of supporting text.
Frequency	Annual
Web Facilities	
Cost	£50, £30 to members
Comments	
Address	Savoy House, London WC2R 0BL
Tel./e-mail	0207 240 1871 postmaster@iee.org.uk
Fax / Web site	0207 240 7735 www.iee.org.uk

496	**INSTITUTION OF MECHANICAL ENGINEERS**
Title	**Salary Survey**
Coverage	Salary survey of the members of the institution with data by type of work, sector, type of member, and geographical location. Also includes data on fringe benefits and overtime.
Frequency	Every two years
Web Facilities	
Cost	£60
Comments	
Address	1 Birdcage Walk, London SW1H 9JJ
Tel./e-mail	0207 222 7899 s_macdonald@imeche.org.uk
Fax / Web site	0207 222 4557 www.imeche.org.uk

497	INSTITUTIONAL FUND MANAGERS' ASSOCIATION
Title	**Fund Management Survey**
Coverage	A survey of IFMA members with data on fund ownership, funds under management, client analysis, overseas earnings, and staff.
Frequency	Regular
Web Facilities	
Cost	On request
Comments	First published in 1992.
Address	Roman House, Wood Street, London EC2Y 5BA
Tel./e-mail	0207 588 0588
Fax / Web site	0207 588 7100

498	INVESTMENT PROPERTY DATABANK
Title	**Residential Index**
Coverage	A regular index examining trends in the value of residential property with an analysis by region.
Frequency	Regular
Web Facilities	Latest copies of reports on site and details of services.
Cost	On request
Comments	Also offers a telephone inquiry service.
Address	7-8 Greenland Place, London NW1 0AP
Tel./e-mail	0207 482 5149
Fax / Web site	0207 267 0208 www.ipdindex.co.uk

499	INVESTMENT PROPERTY DATABANK
Title	**Quarterly Review**
Coverage	A quarterly review of the trends in the value of commercial property with an analysis by region and sector. Based on data collected by IPD.
Frequency	Quarterly
Web Facilities	Latest copies of reports on site and details of services.
Cost	£1000
Comments	Also offers a telephone inquiry service.
Address	7-8 Greenland Place, London NW1 0AP
Tel./e-mail	0207 482 5149
Fax / Web site	0207 267 0208 www.ipdindex.co.uk

500	INVESTMENT PROPERTY DATABANK
Title	**Monthly Index**
Coverage	A monthly index examining the trends in the value of commercial property analysed by region and sector. Based on data collected by IPD.
Frequency	Monthly
Web Facilities	Latest copies of reports on site and details of services.
Cost	£350
Comments	Also offers a telephone inquiry service.
Address	7-8 Greenland Place, London NW1 0AP
Tel./e-mail	0207 482 5149
Fax / Web site	0207 267 0208 www.ipdindex.co.uk

501	INVESTMENT PROPERTY DATABANK
Title	**IPD Annual Index**
Coverage	Presents and interprets statistics about current trends in the commercial property market. Utilises records of over 9,000 properties on the IPD and includes ten-years worth of data on total returns, capital growth, income return, value growth, fund strategies etc. A large amount of text accompanies the
Frequency	Annual
Web Facilities	Latest copies of reports on site and details of services.
Cost	Free
Comments	Also offers a telephone inquiry service.
Address	7-8 Greenland Place, London NW1 0AP
Tel./e-mail	0207 482 5149
Fax / Web site	0207 267 0208 www.ipdindex.co.uk

502	IPSOS-RSL LTD
Title	**Signpost**
Coverage	A monthly monitor of the effectiveness of outdoor advertising posters based on a consumer survey by the company.
Frequency	Monthly
Web Facilities	Details of surveys on site.
Cost	On request
Comments	RSL also publish the British Business Survey for the Business Media Research Committee (see other entry).
Address	Kings House, Kymberley Road, Harrow HA1 1PT
Tel./e-mail	0208 861 8099 information@ipsos-rsl.com
Fax / Web site	0208 863 6647 www.ipsos.rslmedia.com

503	IPSOS-RSL LTD
Title	**Capibus**
Coverage	A weekly omnibus survey of 2,000 adults based on face-to-face interviews in the home.
Frequency	Weekly
Web Facilities	Details of surveys on site.
Cost	On request
Comments	Capibus was the UK's first computer assisted face-to-face omnibus, launched in 1992. RSL also publish the British Business Survey for the Business Media Research Committee (see other entry).
Address	Kings House, Kymberley Road, Harrow HA1 1PT
Tel./e-mail	0208 861 8099 information@ipsos-rsl.com
Fax / Web site	0208 863 6647 www.ipsos.rslmedia.com

504	IPSOS-RSL LTD
Title	**Flexifarm Livestock Omnibus**
Coverage	An omnibus survey of 800 cattle farmers, 500 sheep farmers, and 400 pig farmers based on telephone and face-to-face interviews.
Frequency	Annual and twice yearly
Web Facilities	Details of surveys on site.
Cost	On request
Comments	RSL also publish the British Business Survey for the Business Media Research Committee (see other entry).
Address	Kings House, Kymberley Road, Harrow HA1 1PT
Tel./e-mail	0208 861 8099 information@ipsos-rsl.com
Fax / Web site	0208 863 6647 www.ipsos.rslmedia.com

505	IRN SERVICES LTD
Title	**Travelstat**
Coverage	Detailed statistics covering inbound and outbound tourist profiles, tourist flows by origin and destination, tourist flows by purpose of visit, expenditure breakdowns, traffic by mode of transport, market shares etc. Based primarily on Central Government's International Passenger Survey plus IRN's own database of travel and tourism data.
Frequency	Continuous
Web Facilities	Links to various non-governmental statistics on site.
Cost	Varies according to the nature and range of data required
Comments	Available in hard copy or disc formats.
Address	Field House, 72 Oldfield Road, Hampton TW12 2HQ
Tel./e-mail	0208 481 8750 info@irn-research.com
Fax / Web site	0208 783 0049 www.irn-research.com

506	IRN SERVICES LTD
Title	**Ferrystat: PSA Monthly Digest of Ferry Statistics**
Coverage	Statistics on passenger, car, and coach carrying by ferries. Based on regular survey of PSA members.
Frequency	Monthly
Web Facilities	Links to various non-governmental statistics on site.
Cost	£475
Comments	Produced on behalf of the Passenger Shipping Association. Various other cruise, and general travel reports available.
Address	Field House, 72 Oldfield Road, Hampton TW12 2HQ
Tel./e-mail	0208 481 87507107 info@irn-research.com
Fax / Web site	0208 783 0049 www.irn-research.com

507	IRN SERVICES LTD
Title	**Market Research on the Web**
Coverage	Web site offering links to over 600 non-governmental sites providing statistics or market data. Mainly UK but also European, US, and international sites.
Frequency	Continuous
Web Facilities	Links to various non-governmental statistics on site.
Cost	Free
Comments	
Address	Field House, 72 Oldfield Road, Hampton TW12 2HQ
Tel./e-mail	0208 481 8750 info@irn-research.com
Fax / Web site	0208 783 0049 www.irn-research.com

508	IRN SERVICES LTD
Title	**Annual Cruise Review**
Coverage	A detailed statistical analysis of the UK cruise market.
Frequency	Annual
Web Facilities	Links to various non-governmental statistics on site.
Cost	On request
Comments	Produced in association with the Passenger Shipping Association. Various other cruise, and general travel reports available.
Address	Field House, 72 Oldfield Road, Hampton. TW12 2HQ
Tel./e-mail	0208 481 8750 info@irn-research.com
Fax / Web site	0208 783 0049 www.irn-research.com

509	ISSB LTD
Title	**UK Steel Exports**
Coverage	A monthly volume showing cumulative exports for the year to date. Covering 190 products in 100 countries.
Frequency	Monthly
Web Facilities	Selected key statistics free on the site plus details of publications and online ordering facilities.
Cost	£350
Comments	Also publishes regular statistics on steel in specific countries. Name changed from UK Iron and Steel Statistics Bureau.
Address	Millbank Tower, 21-24 Millbank, London SW1P 4QP
Tel./e-mail	0207 343 3900 enquiries@issb.co.uk
Fax / Web site	0207 343 3901 www.issb.co.uk

510	ISSB LTD
Title	**UK Steel Imports**
Coverage	Published in two separate versions either showing individual months or cumulative figures. Series covers 190 products from 38 countries.
Frequency	Monthly
Web Facilities	Selected key statistics free on the site plus publication details and online ordering facilities.
Cost	£350 per series
Comments	Also publishes regular statistics on steel in specific countries. Name changed from UK Iron and Steel Statistics Bureau.
Address	Millbank Tower, 21-24 Millbank, London SW1P 4QP
Tel./e-mail	0207 343 3900 enquiries@issb.co.uk
Fax / Web site	0207 343 3901 www.issb.co.uk

511	ISSB LTD
Title	**UK Iron and Steel Industry: Annual Statistics**
Coverage	Figures on production, consumption, trade of iron and steel products. Also details of raw materials consumed, cokemaking, iron foundries, and manpower. Historical figures given in most tables and based almost entirely on the bureau's own data.
Frequency	Annual
Web Facilities	Selected key statistics free on the site plus publication details and online ordering facilities.
Cost	£150
Comments	Also publishes regular statistics on steel in specific countries. Name changed from UK Iron and Steel Statistics Bureau.
Address	Millbank Tower, 21-24 Millbank, London SW1P 4QP
Tel./e-mail	0207 343 3900 enquiries@issb.co.uk
Fax / Web site	0207 343 3901 www.issb.co.uk

512	JOINT INDUSTRY COMMITTEE FOR REGIONAL PRESS RESEARCH (JICREG)
Title	**Readership Surveys**
Coverage	Regular readership surveys relating to regional and local newspapers.
Frequency	Regular
Web Facilities	Free access to readership reports by location and title on site.
Cost	Free
Comments	
Address	Bloomsbury House, 74-77 Great Russell Street, London WC1B 3DA
Tel./e-mail	0207 636 7014
Fax / Web site	0107 436 3873 www.jicreg.co.uk

513	JONES LANG LASALLE
Title	**50 Centres: Office, Industrial and Retail Rents**
Coverage	Statistics on 50 main urban centres based on JLW's Centres database which records transactions at the top end of the prime property market. Some supporting text.
Frequency	Twice yearly
Web Facilities	Free access to copies of latest reports on site.
Cost	Free
Comments	Publications also cover London City offices and West End offices.
Address	22 Hanover Square, London W1A 2BN
Tel./e-mail	0207 493 6040 info@jlw.co.uk
Fax / Web site	0207 408 0220 www.joneslanglassale.co.uk

514	JONES LANG LASALLE
Title	**Auction Results Analysis**
Coverage	Analysis of the results of commercial property auctions of six London-based auctioneers.
Frequency	Quarterly
Web Facilities	Free access to copies of latest reports on site.
Cost	Free
Comments	Publications also cover London City offices and West End offices.
Address	22 Hanover Square, London W1A 2BN
Tel./e-mail	0207 493 6040 info@jlw.co.uk
Fax / Web site	0207 408 0220 www.joneslanglassale.co.uk

515	**JONES LANG LASALLE**
Title	**Monthly Property Monitor**
Coverage	Review of financial, economic, and property trends with data and commentary.
Frequency	Monthly
Web Facilities	Free access to latest copies of reports on site.
Cost	Free
Comments	Publications also cover London City offices and West End offices.
Address	22 Hanover Square, London W1A 2BN
Tel./e-mail	0207 493 6040 info@jlw.co.uk
Fax / Web site	0207 408 0220 www.joneslanglasalle.co.uk

516	**JONES, ALAN & ASSOCIATES**
Title	**Charities Salary Survey**
Coverage	A survey by the company of salaries for various jobs in 30 charities.
Frequency	Annual
Web Facilities	
Cost	On request
Comments	
Address	Apex House, Wonastow Road, Monmouth NP5 4YE
Tel./e-mail	01600 716916
Fax / Web site	

517	**JOSEPH ROWNTREE FOUNDATION**
Title	**Monitoring Poverty and Social Exclusion**
Coverage	A review of poverty trends which monitors 50 indicators of povery and social exclusion. These are grouped into six categories: income, children, young adults, adults, older people, and communities.
Frequency	Annual
Web Facilities	
Cost	£16.95
Comments	First published in 1998, these are the findings of a four-year project with results published each year. The final report in the series is at the end of 2001.
Address	The Homestead, 40 Water End, York YO3 6WP
Tel./e-mail	01904 629241 publications@jrf.org.uk
Fax / Web site	01904 615922 www.jrf.org.uk

518	JOSEPH ROWNTREE FOUNDATION
Title	**The State of UK Housing**
Coverage	A factfile of housing conditions and housing renewal policies in the UK drawing together data from the National House Condition Surveys and other evidence.
Frequency	Regular
Web Facilities	
Cost	£16.95
Comments	The second edition was published in 2000 following an earlier edition in the 1990s.
Address	The Homestead, 40 Water End, York YO30 6WP
Tel./e-mail	01904 629241 publications@jrf.org.uk
Fax / Web site	01904 615922 www.jrf.org.uk

519	JOSEPH ROWNTREE FOUNDATION
Title	**Housing Finance Review**
Coverage	A compendium of data on the housing sector with 150 tables covering key housing issues. Based on data collected from various sources.
Frequency	Annual
Web Facilities	
Cost	£26
Comments	Published in association with Chartered Institute of Housing and Council of Mortgage Lenders.
Address	The Homestead, 40 Water End, York YO3 6WP
Tel./e-mail	01904 629241 publications@jrf.org.uk
Fax / Web site	01904 615922 www.jrf.org.uk

520	KADENCE (UK) LTD
Title	**Retail and Hospitality Omnibus**
Coverage	Omnibus surveys of specific retailing and hospitality sectors.
Frequency	Quarterly
Web Facilities	Details of services on site.
Cost	On request
Comments	
Address	Kadence House, 748 Fulham Road, London SW6 5SN
Tel./e-mail	0207 610 6464
Fax / Web site	0207 610 6565 www.kadence.com

521	KADENCE (UK) LTD
Title	**Corporate and Financial Omnibus**
Coverage	Omnibus survey of the professional business and corporate financial markets based on telephone interviews.
Frequency	Quarterly
Web Facilities	Details of services on site.
Cost	On request
Comments	
Address	Kadence House, 748 Fulham Road, London SW6 5SN
Tel./e-mail	0207 610 6464
Fax / Web site	0207 610 6565 www.kadence.com
522	KEY NOTE PUBLICATIONS
Title	**Key Note Market Reviews**
Coverage	These are reviews of general market sectors in the UK, such as food, drinks, catering, clothing, leisure and recreation, and travel and tourism. Within each report, the market sector is broken down into its main segments. There is also a section profiling the major companies in the sector and, normally, some original consumer data. Most market reviews are updated regularly and there are approximately 40 titles in the series.
Frequency	Regular
Web Facilities	Free executive summaries, details of all reports, and email newsletter covering new reports on site.
Cost	£540
Comments	
Address	Field House, 72 Oldfield Road, Hampton TW12 2HQ
Tel./e-mail	0208 481 8750
Fax / Web site	0208 783 0049 www.keynote.co.uk

523

	KEY NOTE PUBLICATIONS
Title	**Key Note Reports**
Coverage	A range of over 200 reports on UK markets and sectors, with many of the reports updated every 12 to 18 months. Each report follows a standard format with sections on market definition, market size, industry background, competitor analysis, SWOT analysis, buying behaviour, outside suppliers, current issues, forecasts, and company profiles. Based on various sources including official statistics, trade association data, company reports, TGI data, and, occasionally, commissioned research.
Frequency	Regular
Web Facilities	Free executive summaries, details of all reports, and email newsletter covering new reports on site.
Cost	£325, £435 for Key Note Plus reports
Comments	
Address	Field House, 72 Oldfield Road, Hampton TW12 2HQ
Tel./e-mail	0208 481 8750
Fax / Web site	0208 783 0049 www.keynote.co.uk

524

	KING STURGE & CO
Title	**UK Industrial Floorspace Today**
Coverage	Commentary on the industrial floorspace market with data sheets giving statistics by region.
Frequency	Three issues a year
Web Facilities	Reports can be freely viewed on Web site.
Cost	Free
Comments	Pan-European and global reports also available.
Address	7 Stratford Place, London W1N 9AE
Tel./e-mail	0207 493 4933
Fax / Web site	0207 409 0469 www.kingsturge.co.uk

525

	KING STURGE & CO
Title	**Office Markets**
Coverage	An annual review of the commercial property sector.
Frequency	Annual
Web Facilities	Reports can be freely viewed on Web site.
Cost	Free
Comments	Pan-European and global reports also available.
Address	7 Stratford Place, London W1N 9AE
Tel./e-mail	0207 493 4933
Fax / Web site	0207 409 0469 www.kingsturge.co.uk

526	KNIGHT FRANK
Title	**Central London**
Coverage	Property development trends, including rents and floorspace, in Central London.
Frequency	Quarterly
Web Facilities	Free access to, and downloading of, reports on the site.
Cost	Free
Comments	
Address	20 Hanover Square, London W15 1HZ
Tel./e-mail	0207 629 8171
Fax / Web site	0207 629 1610 www.knightfrank.com

527	KNIGHT FRANK
Title	**UK Industrial Focus**
Coverage	A review of industrial property trends with a regional assessment.
Frequency	Twice yearly
Web Facilities	Free access to, and downloading of, reports on the site.
Cost	Free
Comments	
Address	20 Hanover Square, London W15 1HZ
Tel./e-mail	0207 629 8171
Fax / Web site	0207 629 1610 www.knightfrank.com

528	KNIGHT FRANK
Title	**Quarterly UK Investment Commentary**
Coverage	An economic overview is followed by data on property investment trends and a property overview.
Frequency	Quarterly
Web Facilitie	Free access to, and downloading of, reports on the site.
Cost	Free
Comments	
Address	20 Hanover Square, London W15 1HZ
Tel./e-mail	0207 629 8171
Fax / Web site	0207 629 1610 www.knightfrank.com

529	KPMG
Title	**Building Society Database**
Coverage	Mainly information on specific societies but there is also a statistical section with eight-year industry trends.
Frequency	Annual
Web Facilities	
Cost	On request
Comments	
Address	1 The Embankment, Leeds LS1 4DW
Tel./e-mail	0113 231 3000
Fax / Web site	0113 231 3139

530	KPMG CORPORATE FINANCE
Title	**New Issue Statistics**
Coverage	Commentary and statistics on UK flotations, new issues by quarter. Also contains details of specific new issues. Based on an analysis of Stock Exchange data.
Frequency	Quarterly
Web Facilities	Details and copies of various reports on site.
Cost	On request
Comments	
Address	8 Salisbury Square, London EC4Y 8BB
Tel./e-mail	0207 236 8805
Fax / Web site	0207 248 6552 www.kpmg.co.uk

531	KPMG CORPORATE FINANCE
Title	**Management Buyout Bulletin**
Coverage	Commentary and statistics on the total value of buy-outs plus data by category, size of buy-out.
Frequency	Quarterly
Web Facilities	Details and copies of various reports on site.
Cost	On request
Comments	
Address	8 Salisbury Square, London EC4Y 8BB
Tel./e-mail	0207 236 8805
Fax / Web site	0207 248 6552 www.kpmg.co.uk

532	KPMG CORPORATE FINANCE
Title	**Alternative Investment Market (AIM)**
Coverage	Commentary and statistics on trends in the alternative investment market including total size, companies etc.
Frequency	Quarterly
Web Facilities	Details and copies of various reports on site.
Cost	On request
Comments	
Address	8 Salisbury Square, London EC4Y 8BB
Tel./e-mail	0207 236 8805
Fax / Web site	0207 248 6552 www.kpmg.co.uk

533	KPMG CORPORATE FINANCE
Title	**Management Buy-Out Commentary**
Coverage	A detailed review of buy-outs with historical data by region and for Europe.
Frequency	Regular
Web Facilities	Details and copies of various reports on site.
Cost	On request
Comments	
Address	8 Salisbury Square, London EC4Y 8BB
Tel./e-mail	0207 236 8805
Fax / Web site	0207 248 6552 www.kpmg.co.uk

534	LABOUR RESEARCH DEPARTMENT
Title	**Labour Research Fact Service**
Coverage	A weekly pamphlet containing news and statistics relating to the labour market. Based on various sources.
Frequency	Weekly
Web Facilities	Paid-for access to data on site.
Cost	£54.75
Comments	Also publishes reports on directors' pay and bargaining plus a monthly journal, 'Labour Research'.
Address	78 Blackfriars Road, London SE1 8HF
Tel./e-mail	0207 928 3649 info@lrd.org.uk
Fax / Web site	0207 928 0621 www.lrd.org.uk

535	LABOUR RESEARCH DEPARTMENT
Title	**Bargaining Report**
Coverage	News and articles on bargaining issues plus 'Bargaining - Key Statistics' with economic, labour market, and earnings data.
Frequency	Eleven issues a year
Web Facilities	Paid-for access to data on site.
Cost	£46.75
Comments	Also publishes reports on directors' pay and bargaining plus a monthly journal, 'Labour Research'.
Address	78 Blackfriars Road, London SE1 8HF
Tel./e-mail	0207 928 3649 info@lrd.org.uk
Fax / Web site	0207 928 0621 www.lrd.org.uk

536	LAING & BUISSON PUBLICATIONS LTD
Title	**Private Medical Insurance - UK Market Sector Report**
Coverage	A review of the healthcare insurance market with details of market trends, market segments, suppliers etc. Based on research by the company.
Frequency	Annual
Web Facilities	Free statistical pages covering hospitals, clinics, insurance, and care homes on site.
Cost	£320
Comments	
Address	29 Angel Gate, City Road, London EC1V 2PT
Tel./e-mail	0207 833 9123 info@laingbuisson.co.uk
Fax / Web site	0207 833 9129 www.laingbuisson.co.uk

537	LAING & BUISSON PUBLICATIONS LTD
Title	**Laing's Healthcare Market Review**
Coverage	Analysis and statistics covering the private healthcare market with information on three sectors: acute healthcare services, medical insurance, and long-term care of the elderly. Based on research by the company.
Frequency	Annual
Web Facilities	Free statistical pages covering hospitals, clinics, insurance, and care homes on site.
Cost	£170
Comments	
Address	29 Angel Gate, City Road, London EC1V 2PT
Tel./e-mail	0207 833 9123 info@laingbuisson.co.uk
Fax / Web site	0207 833 9129 www.laingbuisson.co.uk

538	**LAING & BUISSON PUBLICATIONS LTD**
Title	**Care of Elderly People - UK Market Survey**
Coverage	A review of trends in the elderly healthcare market with data for market segments, suppliers etc. Based on research by the company.
Frequency	Annual
Web Facilities	Free statistical pages covering hospitals, clinics, insurance and care homes on site.
Cost	£410
Comments	
Address	29 Angel Gate, City Road, London EC1V 2PT
Tel./e-mail	0207 833 9123 info@laingbuisson.co.uk
Fax / Web site	0207 833 9129 www.laingbuisson.co.uk

539	**LEATHER MAGAZINE**
Title	**Leather Magazine**
Coverage	Leather and hide prices in the UK based on data collected from leather markets.
Frequency	Monthly in a monthly journal
Web Facilities	
Cost	£84
Comments	The journal also has regular surveys of the UK leather industry and similar surveys of European and international markets.
Address	Polygon Media Ltd, Tubs Hill House, London Road, Sevenoaks TN13 1BY
Tel./e-mail	01732 470024
Fax / Web site	01732 470045

540	**LEATHERHEAD FOOD RA**
Title	**UK Food and Drinks Report**
Coverage	The report reviews the UK food market, industry, and new product trends by sector. There are 17 food sectors covered in the report. Based on a combination of original research and various published sources.
Frequency	Annual
Web Facilities	General details of research reports on site plus paid-for access to market intelligence and other information on www.foodlineweb.com.
Cost	£350, £295 for members
Comments	UK Foods and Drinks Report is usually published in April. Also publishes various one-off reports on the UK and European food industry.
Address	Randalls Road, Leatherhead KT22 7RY
Tel./e-mail	01372 376761 publications@lfra.co.uk
Fax / Web site	01372 386228 www.lfra.co.uk

541	LEISURE INDUSTRIES RESEARCH CENTRE
Title	**Sport Market Forecasts**
Coverage	Detailed forecasts for specific sports sectors.
Frequency	Annual
Web Facilities	General details of statistics on site plus online ordering. Email alerts about new statistics.
Cost	£250
Comments	
Address	Unit 1, Sheffield Science Park, Howard Street, Sheffield S1 2LX
Tel./e-mail	0114 225 2023 lirc@shu.ac.uk
Fax / Web site	0114 225 4488 www.shu.ac.uk/schools/slm/lirc

542	LEISURE INDUSTRIES RESEARCH CENTRE
Title	**Leisure Forecasts**
Coverage	Published in two volumes with the first volume covering leisure away from the home and the second volume relating to leisure in the home. Forecasts are given for five years ahead for consumer spending, prices, and key market indicators. Based largely on the company's own research with some supporting commentary.
Frequency	Annual
Web Facilities	General details of statistics on site plus online ordering. Email alerts about new statistics.
Cost	£250
Comments	
Address	Unit 1, Sheffield Science Park, Howard Street, Sheffield S1 2LX
Tel./e-mail	0114 225 2023 lirc@shu.ac.uk
Fax / Web site	0114 225 4488 www.shu.ac.uk/schools/slm/lirc

543	LEX SERVICE PLC
Title	**RAC Report on Motoring**
Coverage	A sample survey of approximately 1,500 drivers providing information on purchasing, ownership, attitudes etc. It also includes forecasts relating to the motoring sector.
Frequency	Annual
Web Facilities	Online ordering of statistics/publications on the site.
Cost	£395
Comments	Published in January.
Address	Lex House, Boston Drive, Bourne End SL8 5YS
Tel./e-mail	01628 843888 lex@lex.co.uk
Fax / Web site	01628 810294 www.lex.co.uk

544	LEX SERVICE PLC
Title	**Lex Vehicle Leasing Report on Company Motoring**
Coverage	A report of detailed research on company car drivers, fleets, and fleet managers.
Frequency	Annual
Web Facilities	Online ordering of statistics/publications on site.
Cost	£345
Comments	Published in October.
Address	Lex House, Boston Drive, Bourne End SL8 5YS
Tel./e-mail	01628 843888 lex@lex.co.uk
Fax / Web site	01628 810294 www.lex.co.uk

545	LEX SERVICE PLC
Title	**Lex Transfleet Report on Freight**
Coverage	A report of research on British freight activity and the freight market.
Frequency	Annual
Web Facilities	Online ordering of statistics/publications on site.
Cost	£395
Comments	Published in February.
Address	Lex House, Boston Drive, Bourne End SL8 5YS
Tel./e-mail	01628 843888 lex@lex.co.uk
Fax / Web site	01628 810294 www.lex.co.uk

546	LIBRARY AND INFORMATION STATISTICS UNIT (LISU)
Title	**LISU Annual Library Statistics**
Coverage	A compendium of statistics on UK libraries including public libraries, university libraries, the national libraries, and the book trade. Historical statistics are included for the last ten years and the data is based on returns to CIPFA, UFC, and SCONUL supplemented by some special surveys.
Frequency	Annual
Web Facilities	Publication details and some statistics freely available on the site.
Cost	£32
Comments	LISU also publishes a range of occasional and one-off surveys of the library and publishing sectors.
Address	Loughborough University of Technology, Loughborough LE11 3TU
Tel./e-mail	01509 223071 lisu@lboro.ac.uk
Fax / Web site	01509 223072 www.lboro.ac.uk/departments/dils/lisu/lisuhp html

547	LIBRARY AND INFORMATION STATISTICS UNIT (LISU)
Title	**Survey of Library Services to Schools and Children in the UK**
Coverage	An analysis of services based on a questionnaire survey carried out with guidance from AMDECL, SOCCEL, and other groups of specialist librarians. It includes tables of detailed information by authority with explanatory comments, summaries, and per capita indicators. The delegation effect of local management of schools on the Schools Library Service is monitored.
Frequency	Annual
Web Facilities	Publication details and some statistics freely available on the site.
Cost	£27.50, £22.50 to contributing institutions
Comments	LISU also publishes a range of occasional and one-off surveys of the library and publishing sectors.
Address	Loughborough University of Technology, Loughborough LE11 3TU
Tel./e-mail	01509 223071 lisu@lboro.ac.uk
Fax / Web site	01509 223072

548	LIBRARY AND INFORMATION STATISTICS UNIT (LISU)
Title	**Public Library Materials Fund and Budget Survey**
Coverage	Originally concentrating on public library book funds, this survey now also covers audio and video material, service points, opening hours, and staffing levels. Comparisons are presented between individual authorities responding to the survey, and the latest year's budgets are compared to the previous year.
Frequency	Annual
Web Facilities	Publication details and some statistics freely available on the site.
Cost	£27.50, £22.50 to contributing institutions
Comments	Published in July each year. LISU also publishes a range of occasional and one-off surveys of the library and publishing sectors.
Address	Loughborough University of Technology, Loughborough LE11 3TU
Tel./e-mail	01509 223071 lisu@lboro.ac.uk
Fax / Web site	01509 223072 www.lboro.ac.uk/departments/dils/lisu/lisuhp html

549	LIBRARY AND INFORMATION STATISTICS UNIT (LISU)
Title	**A Survey of NHS Libraries**
Coverage	A survey of the operations and performance of NHS libraries with data on expenditure, funding sources, user populations, stocks, loans, electronic searches.
Frequency	Regular
Web Facilities	Publication details and some statistics freely available on the site.
Cost	£17.50
Comments	LISU also publishes a range of occasional and one-off surveys of the library and publishing sectors.
Address	Loughborough University of Technology, Loughborough LE11 3TU
Tel./e-mail	01509 223071 lisu@lboro.ac.uk
Fax / Web site	01509 223072 www.lboro.ac.uk/departments/dils/lisu/lisuhp html

550	LIBRARY AND INFORMATION STATISTICS UNIT (LISU)
Title	**Average Prices of British & US Academic Books**
Coverage	A survey of thousands of published titles with prices analysed by various subject categories, and academic and calender year indexing.
Frequency	Twice yearly
Web Facilities	Publication details and some statistics freely available on the site.
Cost	£24.50, £13.75 per issue
Comments	The survey is published in February and August each year. LISU also publishes a range of occasional and one-off surveys of the library and publishing sectors.
Address	Loughborough University of Technology, Loughborough LE11 3TU
Tel./e-mail	01509 223071 lisu@lboro.ac.uk
Fax / Web site	01509 223072 www.lboro.ac.uk/departments/dils/lisu/lisuhp html

551

	LIBRARY ASSOCIATION RECORD
Title	**Annual Periodical Prices**
Coverage	Brief commentary and statistics of periodical prices arranged by subject, with figures for the latest year and the previous year. Based on data collected by Blackwells from a broad selection of journals.
Frequency	Annual
Web Facilities	
Cost	£79.50
Comments	Usually published in July.
Address	7 Ridgmount Street, London WC1E 7AE
Tel./e-mail	0207 636 7543 record@la-hq.org.uk
Fax / Web site	0207 323 6675 www.la-hq.org.uk/record

552

	LIVERPOOL MACROECONOMIC RESEARCH LTD
Title	**Quarterly Economic Bulletin**
Coverage	Quarterly commentary on economic trends supported by statistics and forecasts of future trends.
Frequency	Quarterly
Web Facilities	Web site under construction.
Cost	£325
Comments	Published in March, June, October, and December.
Address	Liverpool Macroeconomic Research Ltd, 5 Cable Road, Whiston, Liverpool L35 5AN
Tel./e-mail	0151 290 0194
Fax / Web site	0151 290 0194

553

	LLP LTD
Title	**Lloyds' Nautical Yearbook**
Coverage	Includes a section on the 'Year in Shipping', plus casualty statistics, port statistics, and country information. Based on various sources.
Frequency	Annual
Web Facilities	Details of publications on site.
Cost	On request
Comments	Publishes various regular statistical reports on international shipping trends.
Address	LLP Limited, Sheepen Place, Colchester CO3 3LP
Tel./e-mail	01206 772061
Fax / Web site	01206 46273 www.llplimited.com

554	LONDON CHAMBER OF COMMERCE
Title	**Annual Review of the London Economy**
Coverage	A review of economic trends in the capital based on data from the chamber and other sources.
Frequency	Annual
Web Facilities	Basic free data on the London economy on site.
Cost	On request
Comments	
Address	33 Queen Street, London EC4R 1AP
Tel./e-mail	0207 248 4444 lc@londonchamber.co.uk
Fax / Web site	0207 489 0391 www.londonchamber.co.uk

555	LONDON CHAMBER OF COMMERCE
Title	**Quarterly Review of the London Economy**
Coverage	A review of economic and business trends in London including statistics on domestic business, investment, profits, exports, labour. Based on a survey of around 250 companies in the capital with additional data from official sources.
Frequency	Quarterly
Web Facilities	Basic free data on the London economy on site.
Cost	On request
Comments	
Address	33 Queen Street, London EC4R 1AP
Tel./e-mail	0207 248 4444 lc@londonchamber.co.uk
Fax / Web site	0207 489 0391 www.londonchamber.co.uk

556	LONDON CLEARING HOUSE
Title	**London Clearing House Statistics**
Coverage	Statistics relating to cleared volumes with monthly figures for the latest year. Based on data collected by the clearing house.
Frequency	Monthly
Web Facilities	Some clearing data and details of services on site.
Cost	On request
Comments	
Address	Aldgate House, 33 Aldgate High Street, London EC3N 1EA
Tel./e-mail	0207 426 7000
Fax / Web site	0207 426 7001 www.lch.co.uk

557	**LONDON CORN CIRCULAR**
Title	**Market Prices**
Coverage	Prices of cereals and various other crops with some forecasts of future prices.
Frequency	Weekly in a weekly journal
Web Facilities	
Cost	£80
Comments	
Address	Palace Hall, Darthill Road, March PE35 8HP
Tel./e-mail	01354 661976
Fax / Web site	01354 660055

558	**LONDON METAL EXCHANGE**
Title	**Statistics at a Glance**
Coverage	A regular market report including data on price movements, liquidity, and volume. Based on the exchange's own data.
Frequency	Monthly
Web Facilities	Free price data on site with historical series.
Cost	£100
Comments	
Address	56 Leadenhall Street, London EC3A 2BJ
Tel./e-mail	0207 264 5555 james.oliver@lme.co.uk
Fax / Web site	0207 680 0505 www.lme.co.uk

559	**LONDON STOCK EXCHANGE**
Title	**Primary Fact Sheet**
Coverage	News, statistics on new issues, shares, equity values, market trends.
Frequency	Monthly
Web Facilities	All statistics can be viewed and downloaded from the site.
Cost	
Comments	Historical statistics also on web site.
Address	Stock Exchange, London EC2N 1HP
Tel./e-mail	0207 797 1000
Fax / Web site	0891 437052 www.londonstockexchange.com

560	LONDON STOCK EXCHANGE
Title	**Secondary Fact Sheet**
Coverage	News, statistics on turnover, market movements etc.
Frequency	Monthly
Web Facilities	All statistics can be viewed and downloaded from the site.
Cost	
Comments	Historical statistics also on web site.
Address	Stock Exchange, London EC2N 1HP
Tel./e-mail	0207 797 1000
Fax / Web site	0891 437052 www.londonstockexchange.com

561	LONDON STOCK EXCHANGE
Title	**Trading Summary Fact Sheet**
Coverage	Trading data by security for all UK listed, FTSE UK index, and AIM admitted companies.
Frequency	Monthly
Web Facilities	All statistics can be viewed and downloaded from the site.
Cost	
Comments	Historical statistics also on web site.
Address	Stock Exchange, London EC2N 1HP
Tel./e-mail	0207 797 1000
Fax / Web site	0891 437052 www.londonstockexchange.com

562	LONDON STOCK EXCHANGE
Title	**AIM Market Statistics**
Coverage	Statistics covering trends in the recently established AIM market based on information maintained by the Stock Exchange.
Frequency	Monthly
Web Facilities	All statistics can be viewed and downloaded from the site.
Cost	
Comments	Historical statistics also on web site.
Address	Stock Exchange, London EC2N 1HP
Tel./e-mail	0207 797 1000
Fax / Web site	0891 437052 www.londonstockexchange.com

563	LONDON STOCK EXCHANGE
Title	**Quarterly Fact File**
Coverage	A review of the exchange's market on a year-to-year basis.
Frequency	Quarterly
Web Facilities	All statistics can be viewed and downloaded free from the site.
Cost	
Comments	Historical statistics are also available on the web site.
Address	Stock Exchange, London EC2N 1HP
Tel./e-mail	0207 797 1000
Fax / Web site	0891 437052 www.londonstockexchange.com

564	LONDON STOCK EXCHANGE
Title	**Quarterly Review**
Coverage	The publication contains a selection of key graphs and statistics which summarise the market's performance.
Frequency	Quarterly
Web Facilities	All statistics can be viewed and downloaded free from the site.
Cost	
Comments	Historical statistics are also available on the web site.
Address	Stock Exchange, London EC2N 1HP
Tel./e-mail	0207 797 1000
Fax / Web site	0891 437052 www.londonstockexchange.com

565	MACHINE TOOL TECHNOLOGIES ASSOCIATION
Title	**Statistical Report on Trade Figures**
Coverage	Detailed import and export statistics accompanying the regular press release on overseas trade.
Frequency	Quarterly
Web Facilities	
Cost	Free
Comments	
Address	62 Bayswater Road, London W2 3PS
Tel./e-mail	0207 298 6400 mtta@:mtta.co.uk
Fax / Web site	0207 298 6430 www.mtta.co.uk

566	MACHINE TOOL TECHNOLOGIES ASSOCIATION
Title	**Basic Facts**
Coverage	Basic figures on production, sales, investment, imports, exports, and consumption over a ten-year period. Also information on the leading export markets and leading import sources plus the UK's share of total world production and exports. Based on a mixture of Central Government and non-official sources.
Frequency	Annual
Web Facilities	Free access to Basic Facts on site.
Cost	Free
Comments	Produced in pocketbook format.
Address	62 Bayswater Road, London W2 3PS
Tel./e-mail	0207 298 6400 mtta@:mtta.co.uk
Fax / Web site	0207 298 6430 www.mtta.co.uk

567	MACHINE TOOL TECHNOLOGIES ASSOCIATION
Title	**MTTA Press Release**
Coverage	Review of machine tool import/export trends.
Frequency	Quarterly
Web Facilities	
Cost	Free
Comments	
Address	62 Bayswater Road, London W2 3PS
Tel./e-mail	0207 298 6400 mtta@:mtta.co.uk
Fax / Web site	0207 298 6430 www.mtta.co.uk

568	MACMILLAN DAVIES HODES
Title	**The Value of Safety and Health**
Coverage	An annual survey of salaries and attitudes of health and safety practitioners.
Frequency	Annual
Web Facilities	
Cost	£75, £20 for members of the Institute of Occupational Safety and Health
Comments	Produced in association with the Institute of Occupational Safety and Health.
Address	Television House, Mount Street, Manchester M2 5WS
Tel./e-mail	01992 552552
Fax / Web site	www.mdh.co.uk

569

Title	**MALTSTERS' ASSOCIATION OF GREAT BRITAIN** **Malting Statistics**
Coverage	Some statistics available to members.
Frequency	Regular
Web Facilities	Basic statistics on site.
Cost	On request
Comments	
Address	31B Castle Gate, Newark NG24 1AZ
Tel./e-mail	01636 700781
Fax / Web site	01636 701836 www.breworld.com/maltsters/magb/ht

570

Title	**MANAGEMENT CONSULTANCIES ASSOCIATION** **Annual Report**
Coverage	Includes some pages of statistical data with details of total turnover, numbers of clients, number of consultants employed, and a breakdown of turnover by service category. Based on a survey of members.
Frequency	Annual
Web Facilities	Free summary data on site
Cost	Free
Comments	
Address	11 West Halkin Street, London SW1X 8JL
Tel./e-mail	0207 235 3897 mca@mca.org.uk
Fax / Web site	0207 235 0825 www.mca.org.uk

571

Title	**MANAGEMENT CONSULTANCIES ASSOCIATION** **Quarterly Survey**
Coverage	Surveys of member company's turnover, workload trends.
Frequency	Quarterly
Web Facilities	Free summary statistics on site.
Cost	Free
Comments	
Address	11 West Halkin Street, London SW1X 8JL
Tel./e-mail	0207 235 3897 mca@mca.org.uk
Fax / Web site	0207 235 0825 www.mca.org.uk

572	MANAGEMENT CONSULTANCY
Title	**Surveys**
Coverage	Regular surveys of the management consultancy sector with surveys of particular types of consultants and specific work areas. Based on various sources and some research by the journal.
Frequency	Regular in a monthly journal
Web Facilities	
Cost	£95
Comments	Controlled circulation journal.
Address	VNU Business Publications, VNU House, 32-34 Broadwick Street, London W1A 2HG
Tel./e-mail	0207 316 9032 mc@vnu.co.uk
Fax / Web site	0207 316 9250 www.managementconsultancy.co.uk
573	MANAGEMENT CONSULTANCY INFORMATION SERVICE
Title	**Management Consultancy Salary Survey**
Coverage	A survey of consultancy salaries across different functions, different consultancy sizes etc.
Frequency	Every 18 months
Web Facilities	
Cost	£30
Comments	
Address	38 Blenheim Avenue, Gants Hill, Ilford IG2 6JQ
Tel./e-mail	0208 554 4695 annemallach@cwcom.net
Fax / Web site	0208 554 4695 www.mcis.mcmail.com

574

MANAGEMENT CONSULTANCY INFORMATION SERVICE

Title	**Management Consultancy Fee Rate Survey**
Coverage	The survey analyses fees charged by management consultants ranging in size from sole practitioners to major international practices. The results are analysed by seven different practice areas and by four sector groups, as well as geographical variations, analysis by size of consultancy, fees charged for different levels of consultant, recruitment charges, and terms of working. Based on original research.
Frequency	Every 18 months
Web Facilities	
Cost	£30
Comments	A relatively new survey, first published in 1992.
Address	38 Blenheim Avenue, Gants Hill, Ilford IG2 6JQ
Tel./e-mail	0208 554 4695 annemallach@cwcom.net
Fax / Web site	0208 554 4695 www.mcis.mcmail.com

575

MANPOWER PLC

Title	**Survey of Employment Prospects**
Coverage	Short-term forecasts of employment for specific sectors in manufacturing, services, and the public sector based on the stated intentions of over 2,000 companies and organisations. Data by region is included and a commentary accompanies the statistics.
Frequency	Quarterly
Web Facilities	The latest survey is available free on the site.
Cost	Free
Comments	
Address	International House, 66 Chiltern Street, London W1M 1PR
Tel./e-mail	0207 224 6688 info@manpower.co.uk
Fax / Web site	0207 224 5267 www.manpower.co.uk

576	MANUFACTURING CHEMIST
Title	**Aerosol Review**
Coverage	Listing of all aerosols filled in the UK and imported. Also lists all types of aerosols filled by company, brand name, type etc. Based on non-official sources.
Frequency	Annual and as a separate item from the journal
Web Facilities	
Cost	£24
Comments	
Address	Polygon Media Ltd, Tubs Hill House, Sevenoaks TN13 1BY
Tel./e-mail	01732 470028 shennessy@wilmington.co.uk
Fax / Web site	01732 470047 www.dotfinechem.com

577	MARKET & BUSINESS DEVELOPMENT (MBD)
Title	**MBD UK Market Research Reports**
Coverage	MBD publishes over 120 reports covering business to business, building, engineering, and professional/office services markets and these are updated quarterly.
Frequency	Quarterly
Web Facilities	General details and sample pages on site.
Cost	£495, £395 for single copy.
Comments	
Address	Barnett House, 53 Fountain Street, Manchester M2 2AN
Tel./e-mail	0161 247 8000 nataliegrogan@mbdltd.co.uk
Fax / Web site	0161 247 8606 www.mbdltd.co.uk

578	MARKET ASSESSMENT INTERNATIONAL
Title	**Market Reports**
Coverage	Over 100 regular reports are published on UK consumer markets with data and analysis on market value, brands, market segments, consumers, advertising, companies, distribution, and forecasts. Based on various sources.
Frequency	Regular
Web Facilities	
Cost	£695
Comments	
Address	Field House, 72 Oldfield Road, Hampton TW12 2HQ
Tel./e-mail	0208 481 8710
Fax / Web site	0208 783 0049

579	MARKET ASSESSMENT INTERNATIONAL
Title	**Market Forecasts**
Coverage	Forecasts over a five-year period of trends in 150 markets covered in the MAPS market research report series.
Frequency	Annual
Web Facilities	
Cost	£695
Comments	
Address	Field House, 72 Oldfield Road, Hampton TW12 2HQ
Tel./e-mail	0208 481 8710
Fax / Web site	0208 783 0049

580	MARKET ASSESSMENT INTERNATIONAL
Title	**Top Markets**
Coverage	A digest of statistics and commentary on the top 150 markets covered in the MAPS market research report series. Each market summary has data on value, trade, brands, advertising, and general trends.
Frequency	Annual
Web Facilities	
Cost	£695
Comments	
Address	Field House, 72 Oldfield Road, Hampton TW12 2HQ
Tel./e-mail	0208 481 8710
Fax / Web site	0208 783 0049

581	MARKET LOCATION LTD
Title	**Industry Analysis**
Coverage	Tables giving the distribution of industry by region and SIC classification. Based on Market Location's Primefile plus database of establishments.
Frequency	Regular
Web Facilities	General details of services on site.
Cost	On request
Comments	
Address	1 Warwick Street, Leamington Spa CV32 5LW
Tel./e-mail	01926 887744 enquiries@marketlocation.com
Fax / Web site	01926 430590 www.marketlocation.com

582	MARKET RESEARCH SCOTLAND
Title	**Scottish Consumer Omnibus**
Coverage	An omnibus survey based around a sample of 1,000 consumers in Scotland.
Frequency	Monthly
Web Facilities	
Cost	On request
Comments	
Address	9 Park Quadrant, Glasgow G3 6BS
Tel./e-mail	0141 332 5751
Fax / Web site	0141 332 3035

583	MARKETING WEEK
Title	**Ball and Hoolahan Salary Survey**
Coverage	Volume 1 supplies key information on average salary levels by industry sector. Volume 2 supplies more detailed information on 11 different job titles from marketing director through to marketing executive.
Frequency	Annual
Web Facilities	
Cost	£129, £2.20 for single copy
Comments	
Address	Centaur Communications, 50 Poland Street, London W1E 6JZ
Tel./e-mail	0207 970 4000
Fax / Web site	0207 970 4392 www.marketing-week.co.uk

584	MDS TRANSMODAL
Title	**Overseas Trade Data**
Coverage	Detailed product information for imports and exports plus details of trading partners and port of entry and exit.
Frequency	Monthly
Web Facilities	General details of services on site.
Cost	Depends on amount of information required
Comments	Available in various machine readable formats. The company also offers overseas trade forecasting services and is an agent for the International Passenger Survey.
Address	6 Hunter's Walk, Canal Street, Chester CH1 4EB
Tel./e-mail	01244 348301 queries@mdst.co.uk
Fax / Web site	01244 348471 www.mdst.co.uk

585	**MEAT TRADES JOURNAL**
Title	**Market Prices**
Coverage	Wholesale and retail prices for different types of meat and livestock and the data usually refers to prices at the end of the previous week.
Frequency	Weekly in a weekly journal
Web Facilities	
Cost	£60, £1.20 per week
Comments	
Address	Quantum Publishing, Quantum House, 19 Scarbrook Road, Croydon CR9 1LX
Tel./e-mail	0208 565 4255 mtj@qpp.co.uk
Fax / Web site	0208 565 4250 www.mtj.co.uk

586	**METAL BULLETIN PLC**
Title	**Metal Bulletin**
Coverage	Every issue contains 800 prices for metals, ferro-alloys, ores, steel, scrap.
Frequency	Twice a week
Web Facilities	Paid for access to data on site.
Cost	£460
Comments	Various other market reports on metals and geographical markets.
Address	Park House, Park Terrace, Worcester Park KT4 7HY
Tel./e-mail	0207 827 9977 subscriptions@metalbulletin.plc.uk
Fax / Web site	0207 337 8943 www.metalbulletin.com

587	**METAL PACKAGING MANUFACTURERS' ASSOCIATION**
Title	**Annual Report**
Coverage	Includes a review of the year with statistics on sales of packaging materials, sales by end-user sector, sales by type of packaging, exports, and employees. Based mainly on data collected by the association.
Frequency	Annual
Web Facilities	Free access to various statistics on site.
Cost	Free
Comments	
Address	Siena Court, The Broadway, Maidenhead SL6 1NJ
Tel./e-mail	01628 509029 mpma.enquiries@btinternet.com
Fax / Web site	01628 509100 www.mpma.org.uk

588	METALWORKING PRODUCTION
Title	**Survey of Machine Tools and Production Equipment**
Coverage	Trends in sales and use of the various types of machine tools with a detailed breakdown by industrial sector and a regional analysis. Based on returns from over 4,000 companies. A detailed commentary introduces the statistics.
Frequency	Every five years, published separately from the journal
Web Facilities	
Cost	On request
Comments	
Address	Centaur Publications, 50 Poland Street, London W1V 4AX
Tel./e-mail	0207 970 4000
Fax / Web site	0207 970 4189 www.e4engineering.com

589	MIL MOTORING RESEARCH
Title	**MIL Motoring Telephone Omnibus**
Coverage	An omnibus survey of a national representative sample of motorists in Great Britain. Based on a sample of 500 and the results include a wide range of motoring demographics plus consumer results.
Frequency	Weekly
Web Facilities	
Cost	On request
Comments	
Address	1-2 Berners Street, London W1P 3AG
Tel./e-mail	0207 612 0265
Fax / Web site	0207 612 0263

590	MILPRO
Title	**Pharmaceutical Development Service**
Coverage	A monthly omnibus survey of 200 NHS general practitioners with data on prescribing trends for various products and therapeutic groups. Analysis available by regional health authority, practice size, date of qualification, practice type etc.
Frequency	Monthly
Web Facilities	
Cost	On request
Comments	
Address	NOP Research Group, Evelyn House, 62 Oxford Street, London W1N 9LD
Tel./e-mail	0207 612 0153
Fax / Web site	0207 612 0159

591	MINTEL
Title	**Market Intelligence**
Coverage	A series of regular reports on the UK food, drink, white/brown goods sectors with detailed market data and forecasts in addition to key consumer trends.
Frequency	Monthly
Web Facilities	Details of all publications and press releases on site. Access to report contents for clients.
Cost	From £495 per report
Comments	Special reports, services covering specific markets, ad-hoc reports and analyses are also available.
Address	18-19 Long Lane, London EC1A 9HE
Tel./e-mail	0207 606 6000 info@mintel.co.uk
Fax / Web site	0207 606 5932 www.mintel.co.uk

592	MINTEL
Title	**Leisure Intelligence**
Coverage	A series of regular reports on the UK leisure sector with basic data updated regularly and analytical articles updated every few years.
Frequency	Regular
Web Facilities	Details of all publications and press releases on site. Access to report contents for clients
Cost	From £545 per report
Comments	Special reports, services covering specific markets, ad-hoc reports and analyses are also available.
Address	18-19 Long Lane, London EC1A 9HE
Tel./e-mail	0207 606 6000 info@mintel.co.uk
Fax / Web site	0207 606 5932 www.mintel.co.uk

593	MINTEL
Title	**Retailing Intelligence**
Coverage	A series of regular reports on the UK retailing sector with basic retailing data updated regularly and specific reports updated every few years.
Frequency	Regular
Web Facilities	Details of all publications and press releases on site. Access to report contents for clients.
Cost	From £645 per report
Comments	Special reports, services covering specific markets, ad-hoc reports and analyses are also available.
Address	18-19 Long Lane, London EC1A 9HE
Tel./e-mail	0207 606 6000 info@mintel.co.uk
Fax / Web site	0207 606 5932 www.mintel.co.uk

594

	MINTEL
Title	**Finance Intelligence**
Coverage	A series of regular reports on the UK financial services sector with basic data updated regularly and analytical articles updated every few years.
Frequency	Regular
Web Facilities	Details of all publications and press releases on site. Access to report contents for clients.
Cost	From £495 per report
Comments	Special reports, services covering specific markets, ad-hoc reports and analyses are also available.
Address	18-19 Long Lane, London EC1A 9HE
Tel./e-mail	0207 606 6000 info@mintel.co.uk
Fax / Web site	0207 606 5932 www.mintel.co.uk

595

	MONEYFACTS GROUP
Title	**Business Money Facts**
Coverage	A range of economic and monetary statistics including retail prices, annual inflation rates, average earnings, base rates, tax and price index, finance house base rates, commercial rents, employment statistics, and house price data from the Halifax. Based on various official and non-official sources.
Frequency	Regular
Web Facilities	
Cost	£59.80, £14.95 per issue
Comments	
Address	Moneyfacts House, 66-70 Thorpe Road, Norwich NR1 1BJ
Tel./e-mail	01603 476476 mfacts:dircon.co.uk
Fax / Web site	01603 476477

596

	MONKS PARTNERSHIP
Title	**Survey of Non-Executive Director Practices and Fees**
Coverage	A survey of non-executive director salaries and benefits, and other issues, based on a survey by the company.
Frequency	Annual
Web Facilities	General details of publications on site.
Cost	On request
Comments	Other reports available on remuneration in specific sectors.
Address	The Mill House, Wendens Ambo, Saffron Walden CB11 4JX
Tel./e-mail	01799 54222 info@monkspartnership.com
Fax / Web site	01799 541805 www.monkspartnership.com

597

MONKS PARTNERSHIP

Title **Board Earnings in FTSE 100 Companies**

Coverage A survey of salary trends based on an analysis of company annual reports and other published data.

Frequency Annual

Web Facilities General details of publications on site.

Cost On request

Comments Other reports available on remuneration in specific sectors.

Address The Mill House, Wendens Ambo, Saffron Walden   CB11 4JX

Tel./e-mail 01799 54222   info@monkspartnership.com

Fax / Web site 01799 541805   www.monkspartnership.com

598

MONKS PARTNERSHIP

Title **Financial Sector Pay Guide**

Coverage A review of pay in the financial sector.

Frequency Annual

Web Facilities General details of publications on site.

Cost On request

Comments Other reports available on remuneration in specific sectors.

Address The Mill House, Wendens Ambo, Saffron Walden   CB11 4JX

Tel./e-mail 01799 54222   info@monkspartnership.com

Fax / Web site 01799 541805   www.monkspartnership.com

599

MONKS PARTNERSHIP

Title **Company Car UK**

Coverage Details of policies, benefits, changes based on a survey by the company.

Frequency Annual

Web Facilities General details of publications on site.

Cost On request

Comments Other reports available on remuneration in specific sectors.

Address The Mill House, Wendens Ambo, Saffron Walden   CB11 4JX

Tel./e-mail 01799 54222   info@monkspartnership.com

Fax / Web site 01799 541805   www.monkspartnership.com

600	MONKS PARTNERSHIP
Title	**Management Pay UK**
Coverage	Pay and benefits of directors and managers in various industries and sectors. Also details of incentives, company cars. Based on the company's own research.
Frequency	Regular
Web Facilities	General details of publications on site.
Cost	On request
Comments	Published in five volumes. Other reports available on remuneration in specific sectors.
Address	The Mill House, Wendens Ambo, Saffron Walden CB11 4JX
Tel./e-mail	01799 54222 info@monkspartnership.com
Fax / Web site	01799 541805 www.monkspartnership.com

601	MONSTER CO UK
Title	**HR Salary Survey**
Coverage	A regular salary survey based on data for 1,000 HR jobs and results from over 1,000 companies.
Frequency	Regular
Web Facilities	Free access to data on site.
Cost	Free
Comments	Produced in association with the Personnel Today.
Address	
Tel./e-mail	0800 169 5015
Fax / Web site	www.hr.monster.co.uk

602	MORI
Title	**British Public Opinion**
Coverage	A digest of some of the major polls carried out by MORI in previous weeks.
Frequency	Ten issues a year
Web Facilities	Summary data from various surveys on site.
Cost	£100
Comments	Various other research services available.
Address	95 Southwark Street, London SE1 0HX
Tel./e-mail	0207 928 5955 mori@mori.com
Fax / Web site	0207 955 0670 www.mori.com

603

	MORI
Title	**MORI Omnibus**
Coverage	Face-to-face omnibus survey of 2,000 adults in the UK. Detailed analysis of results covering purchasing trends, consumer attitudes, consumer awareness etc.
Frequency	Fortnightly
Web Facilities	Summary data from various surveys on site.
Cost	On request
Comments	Various other research services available.
Address	95 Southwark Street, London SE1 0HX
Tel./e-mail	0207 928 5955 mori@mori.com
Fax / Web site	0207 955 0670 www.mori.com

604

	MORTGAGE FINANCE GAZETTE
Title	**Loans Figures and Figures/Indicators**
Coverage	Details of the number of mortgage loans by type of loan and other indicators of the housing market. Based on various sources.
Frequency	Monthly in a monthly journal
Web Facilities	
Cost	£54
Comments	
Address	Charterhouse Communications Ltd, Arnold House, 36-41 Holywood Lane, London EC2A 3SF
Tel./e-mail	0207 827 5457
Fax / Web site	0207 827 0567

605

	MOTOR CYCLE INDUSTRY ASSOCIATION
Title	**Annual Report**
Coverage	The annual report contains some basic statistics on the motor cycle industry.
Frequency	Annual
Web Facilities	Some basic data on site.
Cost	On request
Comments	
Address	Starley House, Eaton Road, Coventry CV6 2GH
Tel./e-mail	0870 0706242 mcia@mcia.co.uk
Fax / Web site	0870 0703291 www.mcia.co.uk

606	MOTOR CYCLE INDUSTRY ASSOCIATION
Title	**New Powered Two Wheeler Registrations - UK**
Coverage	A monthly review of new registrations by model, type etc.
Frequency	Monthly
Web Facilities	Some basic data on site.
Cost	Free to members, £160 non-members
Comments	
Address	Starley House, Eaton Road, Coventry CV6 2GH
Tel./e-mail	0870 0706242 mcia@mcia.co.uk
Fax / Web site	0870 070 3291 www.mcia.co.uk

607	MOTOR CYCLE INDUSTRY ASSOCIATION
Title	**UK Industry Statistics**
Coverage	Statistics to order on production, registrations etc.
Frequency	Monthly
Web Facilities	Some basic data on site.
Cost	On request
Comments	
Address	Starley House, Eaton Road, Coventry CV6 2GH
Tel./e-mail	0870 0706242 mcia@mcia.co.uk
Fax / Web site	0870 0703291 www.mcia.co.uk

608	MOTOR TRANSPORT
Title	**Market Intelligence**
Coverage	Summary statistics and news covering vehicles and road transport with data collected from various sources.
Frequency	Weekly in a weekly journal
Web Facilities	
Cost	£72, £2.20 for single copy
Comments	
Address	Reed Business Information, Windsor Court, East Grinstead House, East Grinstead RH19 1XA
Tel./e-mail	01342 326972
Fax / Web site	01342 335612 www.roadtransport.net

609	MOTOR TRANSPORT
Title	**20-- Road Transport Market Survey**
Coverage	A survey of companies, vehicles, haulage trends in the road transport sector carried out for Motor Transport by NOP. The survey also includes comparative data for previous years.
Frequency	Annual in a weekly journal
Web Facilities	
Cost	£72, £2.50 for single copy
Comments	
Address	Reed Business Information, Windsor Court, East Grinstead House, East Grinstead RH19 1XA
Tel./e-mail	01342 326972
Fax / Web site	01342 335612 www.roadtransport.net

610	MSI MARKETING RESEARCH FOR INDUSTRY
Title	**MSI Data Reports**
Coverage	MSI publishes over a 100 reports per year on UK consumer and industrial sectors and many of these are updated on a regular basis. Based primarily on research by the company supported by data from official non-official sources.
Frequency	Regular
Web Facilities	
Cost	£375 - £795 depending on number of data units in each report.
Comments	
Address	Viscount House, River Dee Business Park, River Lane, Saltney, Chester CH4 8RH
Tel./e-mail	01244 681186 enquiries@msi-marketingresearch.co.uk
Fax / Web site	01244 681457

611	MUSHROOM GROWERS' ASSOCIATION
Title	**Industry Survey**
Coverage	Production and manpower figures for the sector plus a cost analysis, methods of growing, and industry yield figures. Based on a survey of members, and accompanied by a commentary.
Frequency	Annual
Web Facilities	
Cost	
Comments	Primarily for members.
Address	2 St Pauls Street, Stamford PE9 2BE
Tel./e-mail	01780 766888
Fax / Web site	01780 766558

612	
Title	NATIONAL ASSOCIATION OF ESTATE AGENTS **Market Trends**
Coverage	A review of trends in the housing market based on a survey of a sample of members, plus data from other sources.
Frequency	Monthly
Web Facilities	A general summary is available free on the site.
Cost	Free
Comments	The survey is normally only available to members but some summary data on web site.
Address	Arbon House, 21 Jury Street, Warwick CV34 4EH
Tel./e-mail	01926 496800 info@naea.co.uk
Fax / Web site	01926 400953 www.naea.co.uk

613	
Title	NATIONAL ASSOCIATION OF PAPER MERCHANTS **Merchanting Statistics**
Coverage	Detailed statistics on sales based on returns from member companies.
Frequency	Regular
Web Facilities	Some basic free statistics and member access to detailed data on the site.
Cost	On request
Comments	
Address	Hamilton Court, Cogmore Lane, Chertsey KT16 9AP
Tel./e-mail	01932 569797 info@napm.org.uk
Fax / Web site	01932 569749 www.napm.org.uk

614	
Title	NATIONAL ASSOCIATION OF PENSION FUNDS **Annual Survey of Occupational Pension Schemes**
Coverage	A survey of various schemes with data on income, expenditure, size of fund, the nature of the schemes, benefits provided. The data is collected via a postal survey to all members of the association. A supporting commentary is included with the statistics.
Frequency	Annual
Web Facilities	Free summary statistics and paid-for access to detailed statistics on site. Online ordering facilities and email alerts about new statistics.
Cost	£120 members, £160 non-members
Comments	
Address	NIOC House, 4 Victoria Street, London SW1H 0NX
Tel./e-mail	0207 808 1300 publications@napf.co.uk
Fax / Web site	0207 222 7585 www.napf.co.uk

615	NATIONAL ASSOCIATION OF PENSION FUNDS
Title	**NAPF Year Book**
Coverage	Basically a directory of NAPF members but there are also some summary statistics on the industry.
Frequency	Annual
Web Facilities	Free summary statistics and paid-for access to detailed statistics on the site. Online ordering facilities and email alerts about new statistics.
Cost	£65, free to members
Comments	
Address	NIOC House, 4 Victoria Street, London SW1H 0NX
Tel./e-mail	0207 808 1300 publications@napf.co.uk
Fax / Web site	0207 222 7585 www.napf.co.uk
616	NATIONAL ASSOCIATION OF STEEL STOCKHOLDERS
Title	**NASS Business trends**
Coverage	Monthly survey of members with analysis of prospects for the next three months.
Frequency	Monthly
Web Facilities	Some basic market information free on the site and details of statistics.
Cost	On request
Comments	Usually only available to members.
Address	6th Floor, McLaren Building, Dale End, Birmingham B4 7LN
Tel./e-mail	0121 200 2288 info@nass.org.uk
Fax / Web site	0121 236 7444 www.nass.org.uk
617	NATIONAL ASSOCIATION OF STEEL STOCKHOLDERS
Title	**NASS Trading Summary**
Coverage	Regular review of opening and closing stocks in the industry based on member's returns.
Frequency	Regular
Web Facilities	
Cost	On request
Comments	Usually only available to members.
Address	6th Floor, McLaren Building, Dale End, Birmingham B4 7LN
Tel./e-mail	0121 200 2288 info@nass.org.uk
Fax / Web site	0121 236 7444 www.nass.org.uk

618

	NATIONAL CENTRE FOR SOCIAL RESEARCH
Title	**British Social Attitudes**
Coverage	A survey of social values and attitudes in the UK in the 1980s and 1990s, based on interviews with approximately 3,000 people. Supported by detailed analysis.
Frequency	Annual
Web Facilities	Details of all surveys on site.
Cost	£25
Comments	The 2000 survey was the 17th annual survey. Published by Sage Publications, 6 Bonhill Street, London EC2A 4PS. Tel. 0207 374 0645.
Address	35 Northampton Square, London ECV 0AX
Tel./e-mail	0207 250 1866
Fax / Web site	0207 250 1524 www.natcen.ac.uk

619

	NATIONAL COMPUTING CENTRE
Title	**Business Information Security Survey**
Coverage	A review of security issues related to the use of IT.
Frequency	Annual
Web Facilities	Paid-for access to statistics and online ordering facilities on site.
Cost	Free
Comments	This report can be downloaded from the site.
Address	Oxford House, Oxford Road, Manchester M1 7ED
Tel./e-mail	0161 228 6333 surveys@ncc.co.uk
Fax / Web site	0161 242 2499 www.ncc.co.uk

620

	NATIONAL COMPUTING CENTRE
Title	**Survey of IT Users**
Coverage	A regular survey of IT users based on research by the organisation.
Frequency	Twice yearly
Web Facilities	Paid-for access to statistics on site. Online ordering facilities.
Cost	£200, free to members
Comments	
Address	Oxford House, Oxford Road, Manchester M1 7ED
Tel./e-mail	0161 228 6333 surveys@ncc.co.uk
Fax / Web site	0161 242 2499 www.ncc.co.uk

621	NATIONAL COMPUTING CENTRE
Title	**Salaries and Staff Issues in IT**
Coverage	A survey of salaries and benefits for 34 IT job titles based on questionnaires sent to 12,000 individuals in 600 organisations.
Frequency	Annual
Web Facilities	Paid-for access to statistics on site. Online ordering facilities.
Cost	£260
Comments	
Address	Oxford House, Oxford Road, Manchester M1 7ED
Tel./e-mail	0161 228 6333 surveys@ncc.co.uk
Fax / Web site	0161 242 2499 www.ncc.co.uk

622	NATIONAL DAIRY COUNCIL
Title	**Dairy Facts and Figures**
Coverage	Statistics covering the prices, consumption, and general market for milk and other dairy products. Data from various sources with a significant amount of supporting text.
Frequency	Annual
Web Facilities	Some basic facts free on the site.
Cost	£50
Comments	
Address	5-7 John Princes Street, London W1M 0AP
Tel./e-mail	0207 499 7822 info@dairycouncil.org.uk
Fax / Web site	0207 408 1353 www.milk.co.uk

623	NATIONAL ENVIRONMENT RESEARCH COUNCIL
Title	**UK Minerals Yearbook**
Coverage	A review of UK mineral production and consumption with sections for specific raw materials and products. Some historical data.
Frequency	Annual
Web Facilities	General details of publications on site.
Cost	£35
Comments	
Address	Polaris House, North Star Avenue, Swindon SN2 1EU
Tel./e-mail	01793 411500
Fax / Web site	01793 411501 www.nerc.ac.uk

624	NATIONAL FARMERS' UNION
Title	**National Weekly Egg Market Intelligence Report**
Coverage	Weekly report on egg production and output trends.
Frequency	Weekly
Web Facilities	General details of reports, and basic data from press releases on site.
Cost	On request
Comments	Also publishes an annual review of farm incomes.
Address	164 Shaftesbury Avenue, London WC2H 8HL
Tel./e-mail	0207 331 7200
Fax / Web site	0207 331 7313 www.nfu.org.uk

625	NATIONAL HOUSE BUILDING COUNCIL
Title	**New House-Building Statistics**
Coverage	Covers dwelling starts and completions, prices, market share of timber frame, first time buyers' ability to buy, and some regional trends. Largely based on the council's own survey plus some Central Government data. Usually published two to three weeks after the quarter to which it relates, and some historical data is included.
Frequency	Quarterly
Web Facilities	Free summary data from survey on site.
Cost	£50, £12.50 per issue
Comments	
Address	Buildmark House, Chiltern Avenue, Amersham HP6 5AP
Tel./e-mail	01494 434477
Fax / Web site	01494 735201 www.nhbc.co.uk

626	NATIONAL INSTITUTE OF ECONOMIC AND SOCIAL RESEARCH (NIESR)
Title	**National Institute Economic Review**
Coverage	General analysis of the UK and world economy with forecasts usually up to 18 months ahead. Special articles on relevant topics. A separate statistical section is included in each issue along with some tables in the text.
Frequency	Quarterly
Web Facilities	Free summary data and analysis on site plus paid-for access to monthly GDP estimates service.
Cost	£156, £40 per issue
Comments	Publication available from Sage Publications, 6 Bonhill Street, London EC2A 4PU. Tel. 0207 374 0645. Also offers paid-for subscription access on the web site to monthly GDP estimates.
Address	2 Dean Trench Street, Smith Square, London SW1P 3HE
Tel./e-mail	0207 222 7665 hbarnes@niesr.ac.uk
Fax / Web site	0207 654 1900 www.niesr.ac.uk

627	NATIONAL ON-LINE MANPOWER INFORMATION SYSTEM (NOMIS)
Title	**NOMIS**
Coverage	A database of approximately 19 billion monthly, quarterly, annual, and triennial population and labour statistics and, with the appropriate software, users can access the data, manipulate it, and produce graphs, charts etc. Based on data supplied by Central Government departments.
Frequency	Regular
Web Facilities	From summer 2001, NOMIS is no longer charging for data and access is free on the site to users who register.
Cost	On Request
Comments	
Address	Suite 1L, Mountjoy Research Centre, Durham University DH1 3SW
Tel./e-mail	0191 374 2468 support@nomisweb.co.uk
Fax / Web site	0191 374 3741 www.nomisweb.co.uk

628	NATIONAL READERSHIP SURVEY
Title	**National Readership Survey**
Coverage	Statistics on the readership of national newspapers and various consumer magazines based on a stratified random sample of over 28,000 individuals. Results are published a few months after the survey. Some commentary supports the text.
Frequency	Annual
Web Facilities	Top line survey data for newspapers, general magazines, women's magazines is free on the site. Also details of services, demographics, methodology etc.
Cost	On request
Comments	
Address	42 Drury Lane, London WC2B 5RT
Tel./e-mail	0207 632 2915
Fax / Web site	0207 632 2916 www.nrs.co.uk
629	NATIONAL TYRE DISTRIBUTORS' ASSOCIATION
Title	**Quarterly Tyre Statistics**
Coverage	Statistics on sales of new tyres, retreads, exhausts, and batteries. Based on research by the association.
Frequency	Quarterly
Web Facilities	Some data from survey on site.
Cost	On request
Comments	
Address	Elsinore House, Buckingham Street, Aylesbury HP20 2NQ
Tel./e-mail	0870 9000600 ntda@ndirect.co.uk
Fax / Web site	0870 90000610 www.ntda.co.uk

630	NATIONWIDE
Title	**Monthly Review**
Coverage	A review of the UK housing market with commentary and statistics on house prices, types of houses purchased, mortgage lending, regional house prices, and house prices by type of house. Based on data collected and analysed by the building society.
Frequency	Monthly
Web Facilities	Free access to latest data on site plus historical data.
Cost	Free
Comments	Nationwide also has summary sheets of house price data available back to 1952 for national data and back to 1973 for regional data. A guide to the house price methodology used by Nationwide is available free from the address below.
Address	Nationwide House, Pipers Way, Swindon SN38 1NW
Tel./e-mail	01793 455196
Fax / Web site	01793 455903 www.nationwide.co.uk

631	NATIONWIDE
Title	**Quarterly Review**
Coverage	Data on the housing market, including housing market forecasts, and economic and consumer trends. Based on various sources.
Frequency	Quarterly
Web Facilities	Free access to latest data on site plus free access to historical data.
Cost	Free
Comments	Nationwide also has summary sheets of house price data available back to 1952 for national data and back to 1973 for regional data. A guide to the house price methodology used by Nationwide is available free from the address below.
Address	Nationwide House, Pipers Way, Swindon SN38 1NW
Tel./e-mail	01793 455196
Fax / Web site	01793 455903 www.nationwide.co.uk

632

	NESTLE (UK) LTD
Title	**National Drinks Survey**
Coverage	A review of the drinks market covering tea, coffee, chocolate, food drinks, carbonates, fruit juices, alcoholic drinks. Includes details of market value, brands, retailing, and new developments.
Frequency	Annual
Web Facilities	
Cost	Free
Comments	A multi-volume report with specific volumes on individual markets.
Address	St George's House, Park Lane, Croydon CR9 1NR
Tel./e-mail	0208 667 5616
Fax / Web site	0208 668 9471

633

	NET PROFIT PUBLICATIONS
Title	**Net Figures**
Coverage	Figures on web site use, Internet use, mobile access, b-to-b and b-to-c web sales, forecasts etc.
Frequency	Continuous
Web Facilities	General details and some summary data on site.
Cost	On request
Comments	International data also available. Other ad-hoc surveys on Internet use produced.
Address	PO Box 11155, London SE22 0LY
Tel./e-mail	0208 516 4630 figures@net-profit.co.uk
Fax / Web site	www.net-profit.co.uk

634

	NOP CONSUMER MARKET RESEARCH
Title	**NOP Quota Omnibus**
Coverage	An omnibus survey covering a sample of 1,500 adults carried out face-to-face in households.
Frequency	Twice monthly
Web Facilities	Details and some survey results free on site.
Cost	On request
Comments	
Address	Ludgate House, 245 Blackfriars Road, London SE1 9UL
Tel./e-mail	0207 890 9000 nopinfo@nopres.co.uk
Fax / Web site	0207 890 9362 www.nopres.co.uk

635	NOP CONSUMER MARKET RESEARCH
Title	**NOP Random Omnibus Survey**
Coverage	A weekly omnibus survey covering 2,000 adults and based around face-to-face in-home interviews. Demographic and lifestyle analysis plus details of purchasing trends, consumer habits etc.
Frequency	Weekly
Web Facilities	Details and some survey results free on site.
Cost	On request
Comments	
Address	Ludgate House, 245 Blackfriars Road, London SE1 9UL
Tel./e-mail	0207 890 9000 nopinfo@nopres.co.uk
Fax / Web site	0207 890 9362 www.nopres.co.uk

636	NOP CONSUMER MARKET RESEARCH
Title	**NOP Telebus**
Coverage	A weekly omnibus survey of 1,000 adults based on telephone interviews. The data analysis follows the same breakdown as the Random Omnibus Survey (see previous entry).
Frequency	Weekly
Web Facilities	Details and some survey results free on site.
Cost	On request
Comments	
Address	Ludgate House, 245 Blackfriars Road, London SE1 9UL
Tel./e-mail	0207 890 9000 nopinfo@nopres.co.uk
Fax / Web site	0207 890 9362 www.nopres.co.uk

637	NOP CORPORATE AND FINANCIAL
Title	**Office Equipment Dealer Omnibus**
Coverage	A survey of 300 office equipment dealers covering products such as copiers, computers, telecommunications equipment, office furniture, and other office supplies.
Frequency	Regular
Web Facilities	Details and some survey results free on site.
Cost	On request
Comments	
Address	Ludgate House, 245 Blackfriars Road, London SE1 9UL
Tel./e-mail	0207 890 9000 nopinfo@nopres.co.uk
Fax / Web site	0207 890 9362 www.nopres.co.uk

638	NOP CORPORATE AND FINANCIAL
Title	**NOP Financial Research Survey (FRS)**
Coverage	An omnibus survey monitoring trends in the personal finance sector based on a regular sample of 2,000 people. Analysis of customer bases, products, and cross holdings.
Frequency	32 surveys per year
Web Facilities	Details and some survey results on site.
Cost	On request
Comments	
Address	Ludgate House, 245 Blackfriars Road, London SE1 9UL
Tel./e-mail	0207 890 9000 nopinfo@nopres.co.uk
Fax / Web site	0207 890 9362 www.nopres.co.uk

639	NOP CORPORATE AND FINANCIAL
Title	**National Architects' Survey**
Coverage	A survey of a sample of architects with results covering journal readership, information sources used, etc.
Frequency	Six issues per year
Web Facilities	Details and some survey results free on site.
Cost	On request
Comments	
Address	Ludgate House, 245 Blackfriars Road, London SE1 9UL
Tel./e-mail	0207 890 9000 nopinfo@nopres.co.uk
Fax / Web site	0207 890 9362 www.nopres.co.uk

640	NOP HEALTHCARE
Title	**Healthcare Surveys**
Coverage	Various continuous surveys of the healthcare sector usually based on interviews with medical staff.
Frequency	Continuous
Web Facilities	Details and some survey results free on site.
Cost	On request
Comments	
Address	Ludgate House, 245 Blackfriars Road, London SE1 9UL
Tel./e-mail	0207 890 9000 nopinfo@nopres.co.uk
Fax / Web site	0207 890 9362 www.nopres.co.uk

641	NORMAN CHESTER CENTRE FOR FOOTBALL RESEARCH
Title	**Factsheets**
Coverage	Details of attendances, match receipts, other financial data, miscellaneous data. Based mainly on non-official sources.
Frequency	Regular
Web Facilities	Free Factsheet data on site.
Cost	Free
Comments	
Address	University of Leicester, University Road, Leicester LE1 7RH
Tel./e-mail	01533 522741
Fax / Web site	www.le.ac.uk/snccfr/research/fsheets

642	NTC PUBLICATIONS LTD
Title	**Public Relations Pocket Book**
Coverage	A general review of the public relations sector with accompanying data.
Frequency	Annual
Web Facilities	Details, and online ordering of most publications on site.
Cost	£28
Comments	
Address	Farm Road, Henley-on-Thames RG9 1EJ
Tel./e-mail	01491 411000 info@ntc.co.uk
Fax / Web site	01491 571188 www.warc.com

643	NTC PUBLICATIONS LTD
Title	**London Pocket Book**
Coverage	A pocket book of data on market,economic, social and demographic trends in London. Based on various sources but a strong reliance on Nielsen data.
Frequency	Annual
Web Facilities	Details, and online ordering of most publications on site.
Cost	£28
Comments	Published in association with the Advertising Association.
Address	Farm Road, Henley-on-Thames RG9 1EJ
Tel./e-mail	01491 411000 info@ntc.co.uk
Fax / Web site	01491 571188 www.warc.com

644	NTC PUBLICATIONS LTD
Title	**Lifestyle Pocket Book**
Coverage	Lifestyle data for the UK with sections on shopping habits, consumption patterns, leisure, holidays, media usage, personal finance, housing and households, transport, communications, employment, education, health, crime, economics, and demographics. A final section provides some summary data on the rest of Europe. Based on various official and non-official sources.
Frequency	Annual
Web Facilities	Details, and online ordering of most publications on site.
Cost	£24
Comments	Published in association with the Advertising Association.
Address	Farm Road, Henley-on-Thames RG9 1EJ
Tel./e-mail	01491 411000 info@ntc.co.uk
Fax / Web site	01491 571188 www.warc.com

645	NTC PUBLICATIONS LTD
Title	**Regional Marketing Pocket Book**
Coverage	Statistics on consumer spending, health, media use, leisure activities, personal finance, demographics, tourism, transport, communications, economic trends, crime, education by region. Based on various sources with some additional information on Europe's regions.
Frequency	Annual
Web Facilities	Details, and online ordering of most publications on site.
Cost	£24
Comments	Published in association with the Advertising Association.
Address	Farm Road, Henley-on-Thames RG9 1EJ
Tel./e-mail	01491 411000 info@ntc.co.uk
Fax / Web site	01491 571188 www.warc.com

646	**NTC PUBLICATIONS LTD**
Title	**Marketing Pocket Book**
Coverage	A statistical profile of the marketing, distribution, and consumption of goods and services in the UK, with some additional data on Europe and other areas. Based on various sources, including official and market research publications.
Frequency	Annual
Web Facilities	Details, and online ordering of most publications on site.
Cost	£24
Comments	Published in association with the Advertising Association. A companion volume, European Marketing Pocket Book, is also available.
Address	Farm Road, Henley-on-Thames RG9 1EJ
Tel./e-mail	01491 411000 info@ntc.co.uk
Fax / Web site	01491 571188 www.warc.com

647	**NTC PUBLICATIONS LTD**
Title	**Geodemographic Pocket Book**
Coverage	A profile of Britain's towns, counties, products, and consumer spending patterns based primarily on data collected by CACI (see other entry).
Frequency	Annual
Web Facilities	Details, and online ordering of most publications on site.
Cost	£32
Comments	Published in association with CACI.
Address	Farm Road, Henley-on-Thames RG9 1EJ
Tel./e-mail	01491 411000 info@ntc.co.uk
Fax / Web site	01491 571188 www.warc.com

648	**NTC PUBLICATIONS LTD**
Title	**The Drink Forecast**
Coverage	Data, analysis, and forecasts for the beer, wine, cider, spirits, and soft drinks markets of the UK. Based on a range of sources.
Frequency	Quarterly
Web Facilities	Details, and online ordering of most publications on site.
Cost	£695
Comments	
Address	Farm Road, Henley-on-Thames RG9 1EJ
Tel./e-mail	01491 411000 info@ntc.co.uk
Fax / Web site	01491 571188 www.warc.com

649	NTC PUBLICATIONS LTD
Title	**Drink Pocket Book**
Coverage	Basic data on the drinks sector including general statistics on the market followed by sections on specific drinks and drink outlets. Some international data is included. Based on various sources but a strong reliance on data from Stats MR.
Frequency	Annual
Web Facilities	Details, and online ordering of most publications on site.
Cost	£35
Comments	Published in association with Stats MR.
Address	Farm Road, Henley-on-Thames RG9 1EJ
Tel./e-mail	01491 411000 info@ntc.co.uk
Fax / Web site	01491 571188 www.warc.com

650	NTC PUBLICATIONS LTD
Title	**The Food Forecast**
Coverage	Information, analysis, and forecasts for the food markets of the UK. Analysis and commentary accompanies the data.
Frequency	Quarterly
Web Facilities	Details, and online ordering of most publications on site.
Cost	£595
Comments	
Address	Farm Road, Henley-on-Thames RG9 1EJ
Tel./e-mail	01491 411000 info@ntc.co.uk
Fax / Web site	01491 571188 www.warc.com

651	NTC PUBLICATIONS LTD
Title	**Manager's Pocket Book**
Coverage	Data on management and business trends from various sources.
Frequency	Monthly
Web Facilities	Details, and online ordering of most publications on site.
Cost	£28
Comments	
Address	Farm Road, Henley-on-Thames RG9 1EJ
Tel./e-mail	01491 411000 info@ntc.co.uk
Fax / Web site	01491 571188 www.warc.com

652 NTC PUBLICATIONS LTD

Title	**Pensions Pocket Book**
Coverage	Statistics on pension schemes, the legal background, and current pension issues.
Frequency	Regular
Web Facilities	Details, and online ordering of most publications on site.
Cost	£24
Comments	Published in association with Bacon & Woodrow.
Address	Farm Road, Henley-on-Thames RG9 1EJ
Tel./e-mail	01491 411000 info@ntc.co.uk
Fax / Web site	01491 571188 www.warc.com

653 NTC PUBLICATIONS LTD

Title	**Recruitment Pocket Book**
Coverage	A compilation of labour market and recruitment data based on various sources.
Frequency	Regular
Web Facilities	Details, and online ordering of most publications on site.
Cost	£24
Comments	
Address	Farm Road, Henley-on-Thames RG9 1EJ
Tel./e-mail	01491 411000 info@ntc.co.uk
Fax / Web site	01491 571188 www.warc.com

654 NTC PUBLICATIONS LTD

Title	**Parliament and Government Pocket Book**
Coverage	Information on the UK and EU parliaments with data on their spending of public money and the public's attitude to them.
Frequency	Regular
Web Facilities	Details, and online ordering of most publications on site.
Cost	£32
Comments	
Address	Farm Road, Henley-on-Thames RG9 1EJ
Tel./e-mail	01491 411000 info@ntc.co.uk
Fax / Web site	01491 571188 www.warc.com

655

	NTC PUBLICATIONS LTD
Title	**Media Pocket Book**
Coverage	A statistical profile of British commercial media. Coverage includes advertising spending by media and product category, circulation and readership data, publisher information, titles, stations, audiences, viewing, reach, indices of media rates and cover prices.
Frequency	Regular
Web Facilities	Details, and online ordering of most publications on site.
Cost	£26
Comments	
Address	Farm Road, Henley-on-Thames RG9 1EJ
Tel./e-mail	01491 411000 info@ntc.co.uk
Fax / Web site	01491 571188 www.warc.com

656

	NTC PUBLICATIONS LTD
Title	**Insurance Pocket Book**
Coverage	Basic data on the insurance sector including an overview and detailed sections on life insurance, general insurance, the London insurance market, corporate risk management, specialised insurance carriers and the international insurance market.
Frequency	Regular
Web Facilities	Details, and online ordering of most publications on site.
Cost	£35
Comments	
Address	Farm Road, Henley-on-Thames RG9 1EJ
Tel./e-mail	01491 411000 info@ntc.co.uk
Fax / Web site	01491 571188 www.warc.com

657

	NTC PUBLICATIONS LTD
Title	**Financial Marketing Pocket Book**
Coverage	Published in association with NOP Financial, a guide to the UK personal finance sector. Includes data from NOP research and covers personal incomes, wealth and savings, consumers' expenditure, personal investments, life assurance, general insurance, consumer credit, mortgages, banking, credit cards, and advertising.
Frequency	Regular
Web Facilities	Details, and online ordering of most publications on site.
Cost	£32
Comments	
Address	Farm Road, Henley-on-Thames RG9 1EJ
Tel./e-mail	01491 411000 info@ntc.co.uk
Fax / Web site	01491 571188 www.warc.com

658

	NTC PUBLICATIONS LTD
Title	**Retail Pocket Book**
Coverage	Statistics on specific retail markets and the major retailers plus advertising trends and developments in retailing. A final section covers international retailing. Based on data collected from various sources.
Frequency	Annual
Web Facilities	Details, and online ordering of most publications on site.
Cost	£32
Comments	Published in association with Nielsen.
Address	Farm Road, Henley-on-Thames RG9 1EJ
Tel./e-mail	01491 411000 info@ntc.co.uk
Fax / Web site	01491 571188 www.warc.com

659

	OPINION LEADER RESEARCH
Title	**Opinion Leader Panel**
Coverage	A panel survey of over 100 key opinion leaders such as directors in industry, politicians, media, trade unionists, city analysts etc.
Frequency	Regular
Web Facilities	
Cost	On request
Comments	
Address	Alliance House, 30-32 Grays Inn Road, London WC1X 8HR
Tel./e-mail	0207 242 2222
Fax / Web site	0207 404 7250

660	OUTDOOR ADVERTISING ASSOCIATION
Title	**Free Facts**
Coverage	Summary data on the outdoor advertising sector including expenditure, sector advertising, types of posters etc.
Frequency	Regular
Web Facilities	Free access to data on site.
Cost	Free
Comments	
Address	Summit House, 27 Sale Place, London W2 1YR
Tel./e-mail	0207 973 0315 enquiries@oaa.org.uk
Fax / Web site	0207 973 0318 www.oaa.org.uk

661	OVUM HOLWAY
Title	**System House**
Coverage	A monthly review of the financial performance of the UK computing service industry.
Frequency	Monthly
Web Facilities	General details of research surveys on site plus paid-for access to detailed data. News on site.
Cost	£340
Comments	Ovum acquired Richard Holway in 2000.
Address	2 St Georges Yard, Farnham GU9 7LW
Tel./e-mail	01252 740900 mail@ovumholway.com.
Fax / Web site	01252 740919 www.ovumholway.com

662	OVUM HOLWAY
Title	**UK IT Staff Agency Market Report**
Coverage	First published in 2000, the report is now an annual volume with research results covering the IT staffing and contractor market.
Frequency	Annual
Web Facilities	
Cost	£1,750
Comments	Ovum acquired Richard Holway in 2000.
Address	2 St Georges Yard, Farnham GU9 7LW
Tel./e-mail	01252 740900 mail@ovumholway.com
Fax / Web site	01252 740919 www.ovumholway.com

663	OVUM HOLWAY
Title	**Holway Report**
Coverage	A two volume report on the software and computing services industry. Volume 1 contains general market data and analysis, including projections for the next four years. Volume 2 has profiles of 800 leading companies. Based largely on research by the company.
Frequency	Annual
Web Facilities	General details of research surveys on site plus paid-for access to detailed data. News on site.
Cost	£6,000
Comments	Published in June. Ovum acquired Richard Holway in 2000.
Address	2 St Georges Yard, Farnham GU9 7LW
Tel./e-mail	01252 740900 mail@ovumholway.com
Fax / Web site	01252 740919 www.ovumholway.com

664	OXFORD ECONOMIC FORECASTING LTD
Title	**UK Economic Outlook**
Coverage	Detailed forecasts of the UK economy, along with other major world economies. Summary articles and features on trends.
Frequency	Quarterly
Web Facilities	Summary data, details of all publications, and paid for online access on site.
Cost	£346, £104 per issue
Comments	
Address	Abbey House, 121 St Aldates, Oxford OX1 1HB
Tel./e-mail	01865 202828 mailbox@oef.com
Fax / Web site	01865 202533 www.oef.com

665	OXFORD ECONOMIC FORECASTING LTD
Title	**UK Industrial Prospects**
Coverage	An analysis, with forecasts, of 70 UK sectors based on a model developed by the company.
Frequency	Twice yearly
Web Facilities	Summary data, details of all publications, and paid for online access to data on site.
Cost	On request
Comments	
Address	Abbey House, 121 St Aldates, Oxford OX1 1HB
Tel./e-mail	01865 202828 mailbox@oef.co.uk
Fax / Web site	01865 202533 www.oef.com

666	OXFORD ECONOMIC FORECASTING LTD
Title	**UK Regional Prospects**
Coverage	An analysis, with forecasts, of the economies of 13 Government Standard Office regions.
Frequency	Twice yearly
Web Facilities	Summary data, details of all publications, and paid for online access to data on site.
Cost	On request
Comments	
Address	Abbey House, 121 St Aldates, Oxford OX1 1HB
Tel./e-mail	01865 202828 mailbox@oef.co.uk
Fax / Web site	01865 202533 www.oef.com

667	OXFORD ECONOMIC FORECASTING LTD
Title	**UK Weekly Brief**
Coverage	A review of key economic trends based on various sources.
Frequency	Weekly
Web Facilities	Summary data, details of all publications, and paid for online access to data on site.
Cost	On request
Comments	
Address	Abbey House, 121 St Aldates, Oxford OX1 1HB
Tel./e-mail	01865 202828 mailbox@oef.co.uk
Fax / Web site	01865 202533 www.oef.com

668	OXFORD ECONOMIC FORECASTING LTD
Title	**UK Consumer Outlook**
Coverage	An analysis, with forecasts, of trends in 50 consumer sectors.
Frequency	Twice yearly
Web Facilities	Summary data, details of all publications, and paid for online access to data on site.
Cost	On request
Comments	
Address	Abbey House, 121 St Aldates, Oxford OX1 1HB
Tel./e-mail	01865 202828 mailbox@oef.co.uk
Fax / Web site	01865 202533 www.oef.com

669

	PA CONSULTING
Title	**Telesales and Customer Services Sales Survey**
Coverage	A survey of salaries in telesales and customer services based around 18 job categories. Based on a survey carried out by the company.
Frequency	Annual
Web Facilities	General details of services on site.
Cost	£375
Comments	
Address	123 Buckingham Palace Road, London SW1W 9SR
Tel./e-mail	0207 730 9000 info@paconsulting.com
Fax / Web site	0207 333 5050 www.paconsulting.com

670

	PA CONSULTING
Title	**Survey of Graduate Salaries and Recruitment Trends**
Coverage	Statistics and analysis of trends in the graduate labour market based on research by the company.
Frequency	Annual
Web Facilities	General details of services on site.
Cost	£445, £295 for participants
Comments	
Address	123 Buckingham Palace Road, London SW1W 9SR
Tel./e-mail	0207 730 9000 info@paconsulting.com
Fax / Web site	0207 333 5050 www.paconsulting.com

671

	PAPER FEDERATION OF GREAT BRITAIN
Title	**Market Statistics**
Coverage	Detailed tables and charts on consumption, production, sales, stocks, imports, exports of paper and board plus consumption, production, stocks and imports of raw materials. Based on a combination of sources.
Frequency	Monthly
Web Facilities	Some free statistics pages on site plus details of all publications.
Cost	£900, £100 for individual copies, individual tables and sections can also be supplied on request
Comments	Enquiry service can deal with ad hoc enquiries.
Address	Papermakers House, Rivenhall Road, Swindon SN5 7BD
Tel./e-mail	01793 889600 fedn@paper.org.uk
Fax / Web site	01793 886182 www.paper.org.uk

672		PAPER FEDERATION OF GREAT BRITAIN
	Title	**Reference Statistics**
	Coverage	Ten-year series of tables and charts with data on production, consumption, sales, stocks, imports and exports of paper and board plus consumption, production, stocks, and imports of raw materials. Also data on employment, energy, and finance. Based on various sources.
	Frequency	Annual
	Web Facilities	Some free statistics pages on site plus details of all publications.
	Cost	£150
	Comments	Enquiry service can deal with ad hoc enquiries.
	Address	Papermakers House, Rivenhall Road, Swindon SN5 7BD
	Tel./e-mail	01793 889600 fedn@paper.org.uk
	Fax / Web site	01793 886182 www.paper.org.uk

673		PAPER FEDERATION OF GREAT BRITAIN
	Title	**Capacity Report**
	Coverage	Historical data for the last few years and forecasts for three or four years ahead of capacity in the industry.
	Frequency	Annual
	Web Facilities	Some free statistics pages on site plus details of all publications.
	Cost	£250
	Comments	Enquiry service can deal with ad hoc enquiries.
	Address	Papermakers House, Rivenhall Road, Swindon SN5 7BD
	Tel./e-mail	01793 889600 fedn@paper.org.uk
	Fax / Web site	01793 886182 www.paper.org.uk

674		PAPER FEDERATION OF GREAT BRITAIN
	Title	**Energy Report**
	Coverage	Analysis and statistics on energy use and costs in the paper and board sector.
	Frequency	Annual
	Web Facilities	Some free statistics pages on site plus details of all publications.
	Cost	£150
	Comments	Enquiry service can deal with ad hoc enquiries.
	Address	Papermakers House, Rivenhall Road, Swindon SN5 7BD
	Tel./e-mail	01793 889600 fedn@paper.org.uk
	Fax / Web site	01793 886182 www.paper.org.uk

675	PAPER FEDERATION OF GREAT BRITAIN
Title	**Apparent Consumption of Paper and Board**
Coverage	Monthly figures on apparent consumption plus a commentary on trends.
Frequency	Monthly
Web Facilities	Some free statistics pages on site plus details of all publications.
Cost	£150
Comments	Enquiry service can deal with ad hoc enquiries.
Address	Papermakers House, Rivenhall Road, Swindon SN5 7BD
Tel./e-mail	01793 889600 fedn@paper.org.uk
Fax / Web site	01793 886182 www.paper.org.uk

676	PAPER FEDERATION OF GREAT BRITAIN
Title	**Production of Paper and Board**
Coverage	Monthly data and analysis on production, sales, and stocks of paper and board.
Frequency	Monthly
Web Facilities	Some free statistics pages on site plus details of all publications.
Cost	£250
Comments	Enquiry service can deal with ad hoc enquiries.
Address	Papermakers House, Rivenhall Road, Swindon SN5 7BD
Tel./e-mail	01793 889600 fedn@paper.org.uk
Fax / Web site	01793 886182 www.paper.org.uk

677	PAPER FEDERATION OF GREAT BRITAIN
Title	**Consumption of Paper and Board**
Coverage	Monthly statistics and commentary on paper and board consumption in the UK.
Frequency	Monthly
Web Facilities	Some free statistics pages on site plus details of all publications.
Cost	£125
Comments	Enquiry service can deal with ad hoc enquiries.
Address	Papermakers House, Rivenhall Road, Swindon SN5 7BD
Tel./e-mail	01793 889600 fedn@paper.org.uk
Fax / Web site	01793 886182 www.paper.org.uk

678	PAPER FEDERATION OF GREAT BRITAIN
Title	**Imports of Paper and Board**
Coverage	Detailed monthly import statistics for paper and board based on Central Government data.
Frequency	Monthly
Web Facilities	Some free statistics pages on site plus details of all publications.
Cost	£250
Comments	Enquiry service can deal with ad hoc enquiries.
Address	Papermakers House, Rivenhall Road, Swindon SN5 7BD
Tel./e-mail	01793 889600 fedn@paper.org.uk
Fax / Web site	01793 886182 www.paper.org.uk

679	PAPER FEDERATION OF GREAT BRITAIN
Title	**Recovered Fibre Consumption, Stocks and Trade**
Coverage	Monthly statistics on waste paper demand, stocks, and overseas trade based on various sources.
Frequency	Monthly
Web Facilities	Some free statistics on site plus details of all publications.
Cost	£250
Comments	Enquiry service can deal with ad hoc enquiries.
Address	Papermakers House, Rivenhall Road, Swindon SN5 7BD
Tel./e-mail	01793 889600 fedn@paper.org.uk
Fax / Web site	01793 886182 www.paper.org.uk

680	PAPER FEDERATION OF GREAT BRITAIN
Title	**Fact Card**
Coverage	Summary data on the paper and board industry based on the various statistics produced by the federation.
Frequency	Annual
Web Facilities	Some free statistics on site plus details of all publications.
Cost	£4 for paper edition, prices on request for transparencies, 35mm slides, electronic graphics file
Comments	Enquiry service can deal with ad hoc enquiries.
Address	Papermakers House, Rivenhall Road, Swindon SN5 7BD
Tel./e-mail	01793 889600 fedn@paper.org.uk
Fax / Web site	01793 886182 www.paper.org.uk

681

	PAPER FEDERATION OF GREAT BRITAIN
Title	**Industry Facts**
Coverage	Key figures on industry, production and consumption plus a commentary on trends.
Frequency	Annual
Web Facilities	Some free statistics pages on site plus details of all publications.
Cost	£25
Comments	Enquiry service can deal with ad-hoc enquiries.
Address	Papermakers House, Rivenhall Road, Swindon SN5 7BD
Tel./e-mail	01793 889600 fedn@paper.org.uk
Fax / Web site	01793 886182 www.paper.org.uk

682

	PAPER FEDERATION OF GREAT BRITAIN
Title	**Pulp Consumption Stocks and Trade**
Coverage	Monthly statistics covering pulp demand, stocks, and trade based on various sources.
Frequency	Monthly
Web Facilities	Some free statistics on site plus details of all publications.
Cost	£250
Comments	Enquiry service can deal with ad hoc enquiries.
Address	Papermakers House, Rivenhall Road, Swindon SN5 7BD
Tel./e-mail	01793 889600 fedn@paper.org.uk
Fax / Web site	01793 886182 www.paper.org.uk

683

	PAY AND WORKFORCE RESEARCH (PWR)
Title	**Care Sector Managers Pay, Terms and Conditions**
Coverage	A survey of salaries, benefits, and conditions based on a survey of almost 100 organisations and over 800 posts.
Frequency	Regular
Web Facilities	General details of various publications on site.
Cost	£38
Comments	Publishes various reports on pay and conditions.
Address	30 Victoria Avenue, Harrogate HG1 5PR
Tel./e-mail	01423 720200 info@payandwork.co.uk
Fax / Web site	01423 720222 www.payandwork.co.uk

684	PEARSON PROFESSIONAL LTD
Title	**Unit Trust Yearbook**
Coverage	Includes a market commentary plus a statistical section on sales, total funds, performance, income from unit trusts etc. The official yearbook of the Association of Unit Trusts and Investment Funds and many figures are taken from this source.
Frequency	Annual
Web Facilities	
Cost	On request
Comments	An 'FT Financial Publishing' imprint.
Address	Maple House, 149 Tottenham Court Road, London W1P 9LL
Tel./e-mail	0207 896 2222
Fax / Web site	0207 896 2274

685	PEDDER ASSOCIATES
Title	**Operating Systems Trends**
Coverage	Statistics and analysis of the usage and installed base of operating systems for companies spending more than £15,000 on data processing. Based on research by the company.
Frequency	Annual
Web Facilities	
Cost	£2,600
Comments	
Address	34 Duncan Road, Richmond-upon-Thames TW9 2JD
Tel./e-mail	0208 940 4300
Fax / Web site	0208 948 1531

686	PEDDER ASSOCIATES
Title	**Applications Usage by Industry Sector**
Coverage	Statistics and analysis of applications usage by companies spending £15,000 or more on data processing. Usage is broken down into 31 areas. Based on research by the company.
Frequency	Annual
Web Facilities	
Cost	£2,600
Comments	
Address	34 Duncan Road, Richmond-upon-Thames TW9 2JD
Tel./e-mail	0208 940 4300
Fax / Web site	0208 948 1531

687	PEDDER ASSOCIATES
Title	**Software Package Trends**
Coverage	Statistics and analysis of expenditure on software by companies spending £15,000 or more on data processing. Based on research by the company.
Frequency	Annual
Web Facilities	
Cost	£2,600
Comments	
Address	34 Duncan Road, Richmond-upon-Thames TW9 2JD
Tel./e-mail	0208 940 4300
Fax / Web site	0208 948 1531

688	PEDDER ASSOCIATES
Title	**DP Expenditure by Industry Sector**
Coverage	Statistics and analysis covering expenditure on hardware, software, and services for 20 industry sectors. Based on research by the company.
Frequency	Annual
Web Facilities	
Cost	£2,600
Comments	
Address	34 Duncan Road, Richmond-upon-Thames TW9 2JD
Tel./e-mail	0208 940 4300
Fax / Web site	0208 948 1531

689	PEDDER ASSOCIATES
Title	**General Purpose Computer Systems**
Coverage	A report detailing the ten-year installed base of computers and shipments history, broken down model by model. Also includes five-year projections of the installed base. Based on research by the company.
Frequency	Annual
Web Facilities	
Cost	£7,500
Comments	
Address	34 Duncan Road, Richmond-upon-Thames TW9 2JD
Tel./e-mail	0208 940 4300
Fax / Web site	0208 948 1531

690	PEDDER ASSOCIATES
Title	**Computer Usage by Industry Sector**
Coverage	Statistics and analysis of the use of computers by companies spending over £15,000 on data processing per year. Covers 20 SIC sectors and based on research by the company.
Frequency	Annual
Web Facilities	
Cost	£2,600
Comments	
Address	34 Duncan Road, Richmond-upon-Thames TW9 2JD
Tel./e-mail	0208 940 4300
Fax / Web site	0208 94 8 1531

691	PEDDER ASSOCIATES
Title	**Computer Usage by Geographical Region**
Coverage	Statistics and analysis of the use of computers in companies spending £15,000 or over on data processing, broken down by region. Based on research by the company.
Frequency	Annual
Web Facilities	
Cost	£2,600
Comments	
Address	34 Duncan Road, Richmond-upon-Thames TW9 2JD
Tel./e-mail	0208 940 4300
Fax / Web site	0208 948 1531

692	PERIODICAL PUBLISHERS ASSOCIATION
Title	**The Magazine Handbook 20--**
Coverage	A compilation of data on the journal sector based on various sources. Statistics on the industry, circulation, advertising, readership, profitability, new media, and exports. Sections on both the consumer and business press.
Frequency	Annual
Web Facilities	
Cost	£25, £15 to members
Comments	Also publishes various research reports on the magazine sector.
Address	28 Kingsway, London WC2B 6JR
Tel./e-mail	0207 404 4166 info1@ppa.co.uk
Fax / Web site	0207 404 4167 www.ppa.co.uk

693	PERIODICAL PUBLISHERS ASSOCIATION
Title	**PPA/Wyatt Salary Survey**
Coverage	Survey of pay and benefits in the management, advertising, and editorial functions of magazine and directory publishing and telepublishing.
Frequency	Annual
Web Facilities	
Cost	On request
Comments	Results only available to those participating in the survey.
Address	28 Kingsway, London WC2B 6JR
Tel./e-mail	0207 404 4166 info1@ppa.co.uk
Fax / Web site	0207 404 4167 www.ppa.co.uk

694	PET FOOD MANUFACTURERS' ASSOCIATION
Title	**Pet Ownership**
Coverage	Statistics on pet ownership broken down by type of pet, and demographics of owners.
Frequency	Regular
Web Facilities	The data is published on the site and is available free.
Cost	Free
Comments	Also some basic market data available free on the site.
Address	20 Bedford Street, Covent Garden, London WC2E 9HP
Tel./e-mail	0207 379 9009 info@pfma.org.uk
Fax / Web site	0207 379 8008 www.pfma.com

695	PETROLEUM ARGUS LPG WORLD
Title	**Petroleum Argus Fundamentals**
Coverage	Statistical analysis of the petroleum sector with data on prices, output, trade, consumption.
Frequency	Monthly
Web Facilities	
Cost	On request
Comments	
Address	93 Shepperton Road, London N1 3DF
Tel./e-mail	0207 359 8792 lpgw@petroleumargus.com
Fax / Web site	0207 359 6661 www.petroleumargus.com

696	PETROLEUM ECONOMIST
Title	**Markets**
Coverage	Tables covering oil prices, world production, and tanker freight rates based on various sources.
Frequency	Monthly in a monthly journal
Web Facilities	
Cost	£365
Comments	Also publishes regular statistics on world oil trends.
Address	PO Box 105, Baird House, 15-17 St Cross Street, London EC1N 8VW
Tel./e-mail	0207 831 5588 petecon@easynet.co.uk
Fax / Web site	0207 831 4567 www.petroleum-economist.com

697	PETROLEUM ECONOMIST
Title	**UK North Sea Survey**
Coverage	Statistics on North Sea oil fields with data on reserves, ownership, production etc. Compiled from a variety of sources.
Frequency	Annual in a monthly journal
Web Facilities	
Cost	£365
Comments	Also contains regular statistics on world oil trends.
Address	PO Box 105, Baird House, 15-17 St Cross Street, London EC1N 8VW
Tel./e-mail	0207 831 5588 petecon@easynet.co.uk
Fax / Web site	0207 831 4567 www.petroleum-economist.com

698	PETROLEUM TIMES
Title	**Petroleum Times Energy Report**
Coverage	Provides pump prices for petrol in various towns and cities in the UK. Based on the journal's own survey with some supporting text.
Frequency	Twice monthly
Web Facilities	
Cost	£195 per annum
Comments	
Address	Nexus Media Ltd, Nexus House, Azalea Drive, Swanley BR8 8HY
Tel./e-mail	01322 660070
Fax / Web site	01322 667633 www.atelier.net/energyreport

699	PHARMACEUTICAL JOURNAL
Title	**Retail Sales Index for Chemists**
Coverage	General figures on the sales trends in total and for specific products sold in chemists. Based on Central Government data.
Frequency	Weekly
Web Facilities	
Cost	£99
Comments	Other statistics published occasionally.
Address	1 Lambeth High Street, London SE1 7JN
Tel./e-mail	0207 735 9141 pharmpress@rpsgb.org.uk
Fax / Web site	0207 735 5085 www.pharmpress.com

700	PHOTO MARKETING ASSOCIATION INTERNATIONAL (UK) LTD
Title	**UK Consumer Photographic Survey**
Coverage	A review of consumer and market trends in the sector based on original market research.
Frequency	Annual
Web Facilities	General details on site and members can download copies of report and extracts.
Cost	Free to members, £94 to others
Comments	
Address	Peel Place, 50 Carver Street, Hockley, Birmingham B1 3AS
Tel./e-mail	0121 212 0299 pmauk@pmai.org
Fax / Web site	0121 212 0298 www.pmai.org

701	PIRA INTERNATIONAL
Title	**Forecast Report - UK Packaging Markets to 2005**
Coverage	A detailed forecast for specific packaging markets with analysis and data.
Frequency	Regular
Web Facilities	Publication details and online ordering facilities on site.
Cost	£170
Comments	Also publishes reviews of the European printing and packaging sectors.
Address	Randalls Road, Leatherhead KT22 7RU
Tel./e-mail	01372 802000 publications@pira.co.uk
Fax / Web site	01372 802238 www.piranet.com

702	PIRA INTERNATIONAL
Title	**UK Printing**
Coverage	The report reviews trends in the key sectors such as book, periodicals, and newspaper publishing. The strategic issues facing the industry are examined and company profiles are also included.
Frequency	Annual
Web Facilities	Publication details and online ordering on site.
Cost	£332
Comments	Also publishes reviews of the European printing and packaging sectors.
Address	Randalls Road, Leatherhead KT22 7RU
Tel./e-mail	01372 802000 publications@pira.co.uk
Fax / Web site	01372 802238 www.piranet.com

703	PIRA INTERNATIONAL
Title	**Paper and Packaging Analyst**
Coverage	A review of trends in the paper and packaging sectors with articles and statistics.
Frequency	Quarterly
Web Facilities	Publication details and online ordering facilities on site.
Cost	£395
Comments	Also publishes reviews of the European printing and packaging sectors.
Address	Randalls Road, Leatherhead KT22 7RU
Tel./e-mail	01372 802000 publications@pira.co.uk
Fax / Web site	01372 802238 www.piranet.com

704	PKF
Title	**UK Trends**
Coverage	A review of the operating and financial characteristics of a sample of around 245 provincial hotels from AA five-star to two-star. Details of occupancy rates, revenues, costs and expenses with data for the latest year and the previous year. Some supporting text.
Frequency	Annual
Web Facilities	General details of publications and online ordering facilities on site.
Cost	£300
Comments	Published in August. Also publishes surveys on European and international trends. Company previously known as Pannell Kerr Foster.
Address	78 Hatton Garden, London EC1N 8JA
Tel./e-mail	0207 831 7393 hotels@uk.pkf.com
Fax / Web site	0207 404 8112 www.pkf.co.uk

705	PKF
Title	**London Trends**
Coverage	Summary of the performance of approximately 72 London hotels with details of occupancy levels, achieved room rate, sales, and the cost of sales of food and beverage departments. Some supporting text.
Frequency	Annual
Web Facilities	General details of publications plus online ordering facilities on site.
Cost	£200
Comments	Published in March. Also publishes surveys on European and international trends. Company previously known as Pannell Kerr Foster.
Address	78 Hatton Garden, London EC1N 8JA
Tel./e-mail	0207 831 7393 hotels@uk.pkf.com
Fax / Web site	0207 404 8112 www.pkf.co.uk

706	PMSI UK LTD
Title	**Medical Research Omnibus**
Coverage	A monthly omnibus survey of 400 general medical practitioners with face-to-face interviews in surgeries.
Frequency	Monthly
Web Facilities	
Cost	On request
Comments	Also carries out media advertising recall surveys and specialist omnibus surveys in the health care area.
Address	Mallard House, Peregrine Business Park, Gomm Road, High Wycombe HP13 7DL
Tel./e-mail	01494 893600
Fax / Web site	01494 893655

707	POSTAR
Title	**Postar**
Coverage	Postar audience research measures the effectiveness of outdoor advertising through travel and other surveys.
Frequency	Regular
Web Facilities	General details plus some basic data on site.
Cost	On request
Comments	
Address	Summit House, 27 Sale Place, London W2 1YR
Tel./e-mail	0207 479 7900 mail@postar.co.uk
Fax / Web site	0207 706 7143 www.postar.co.uk

708	PPL RESEARCH LTD
Title	**Board Market Digest**
Coverage	A monthly review of market trends for buyers and suppliers of packaging papers and boards.
Frequency	Monthly
Web Facilities	
Cost	£250
Comments	
Address	Suite 7, Apsley Mills Cottage, London Road, Hemel Hempstead HP3 9QU
Tel./e-mail	01442 232770 enquiries@pplresearch.co.uk
Fax / Web site	01442 232880

709	PPL RESEARCH LTD
Title	**UK Preview**
Coverage	The UK Preview includes demand and price forecasts for the UK paper and board market.
Frequency	Twice yearly
Web Facilities	
Cost	£650
Comments	
Address	Suite 7, Apsley Mills Cottage, London Road, Hemel Hempstead HP3 9QU
Tel./e-mail	01442 232770 enquiries@pplresearch.co.uk
Fax / Web site	01442 232880

710	PPL RESEARCH LTD
Title	**Paper Market Digest**
Coverage	Monthly digest which includes statistics on market trends and prices.
Frequency	Monthly
Web Facilities	
Cost	£250
Comments	
Address	Suite 7, Apsley Mills Cottage, London Road, Hemel Hempstead HP3 9QU
Tel./e-mail	01442 232770 enquiries@pplresearch.co.uk
Fax / Web site	01442 232880

711	**PRE-SCHOOL LEARNING ALLIANCE**
Title	**Facts and Figures**
Coverage	Facts and figures on pre-school play based on data collected by the association and published sources.
Frequency	Annual
Web Facilities	
Cost	On request
Comments	Also publishes an Annual Report. Previously known as the Pre-School Play Group Association.
Address	69 Kings Cross Road, London WC1X 9LL
Tel./e-mail	0207 833 0991
Fax / Web site	www.pre-school.org.uk

712	**PREMIER BRANDS**
Title	**Hot Beverages Handbook**
Coverage	A two-volume report on specific hot drinks segments, eg tea, coffee, milk-based drinks etc based mainly on commissioned research.
Frequency	Annual
Web Facilities	
Cost	Free
Comments	Monthly Hot Beverage Market Updates.
Address	PO Box 8, Moreton, Wirral CH46 8XF
Tel./e-mail	0151 522 4000
Fax / Web site	0151 522 4020 www.premierbrands.com

713	**PRICE WATERHOUSE COOPERS**
Title	**UK Economic Outlook**
Coverage	Analysis, commentary, and data on UK economic trends based on various sources.
Frequency	Three times a year
Web Facilities	Publication details and summary data on site.
Cost	Free
Comments	Publishes various other market and strategic reports.
Address	Southwark Towers, 32 London Bridge Street, London SE1 9SY
Tel./e-mail	0207 804 3000
Fax / Web site	0207 378 0647 www.pw.com/uk

714		PRICE WATERHOUSE COOPERS
	Title	**Financial Management in Law Firms**
	Coverage	Based on survey of firms with details of financial operations, staffing etc.
	Frequency	Regular
	Web Facilities	Publication details and summary data on site.
	Cost	On request
	Comments	Publishes various other market and strategic reports.
	Address	Southwark Towers, 32 London Bridge Street, London SE1 9SY
	Tel./e-mail	0207 804 3000
	Fax / Web site	0207 378 0647 www.pw.com/uk

715		PRICE WATERHOUSE COOPERS
	Title	**West and East Midlands Business Surveys**
	Coverage	An opinion survey of companies in the Midlands with expected trends for the next six months in orders, employment
	Frequency	Twice yearly
	Web Facilities	Publication details and summary data on site.
	Cost	On request
	Comments	Published in association with the business schools at Warwick, Wolverhampton, and Nottingham Trent University.
	Address	Cornwall Court, 19 Cornwall Street, Birmingham B3 2DT
	Tel./e-mail	0121 200 3000
	Fax / Web site	www.pw.com/uk

716		PRINTED CIRCUIT INTERCONNECTION FEDERATION (PCIF)
	Title	**UK PCB Report**
	Coverage	Statistics and analysis on production, imports, exports, UK market supply, employment, and a market breakdown. Based largely on original research supported by government import and export data.
	Frequency	Annual
	Web Facilities	Free market statistics on site.
	Cost	Free to members, £250 to others
	Comments	Merged with the Federation of the Electronics Industry in
	Address	Russell Square House, 10-12 Russell Square, London WC1B 5EE
	Tel./e-mail	0207 331 2035 enquiries@pcif.org.uk
	Fax / Web site	0207 331 2042 www.pcif.org.uk

717	PRINTED CIRCUIT INTERCONNECTION FEDERATION (PCIF)
Title	**Quarterly Monitor**
Coverage	Basic data on sales, orders, exports with percentage changes from the previous figures. Based largely on the federation's own research.
Frequency	Quarterly
Web Facilities	Free market statistics on site.
Cost	Free to members, £150 to others
Comments	Merged with the Federation of the Electronics Industry in
Address	Russell Square House, 10-12 Russell Square, London WC1B 5EE
Tel./e-mail	0207 331 2035 enquiries@pcif.org.uk
Fax / Web site	0207 331 2042 www.pcif.org.uk

718	PROCESSING AND PACKAGING MACHINERY ASSOCIATION (PPMA)
Title	**UK Imports and Exports of Packaging Machinery**
Coverage	Brief commentary and graphs showing exports and imports over a three-year period. The figures are produced from Customs and Excise sources and separate intra-EU and extra-EU trade.
Frequency	Annual
Web Facilities	
Cost	Free
Comments	
Address	New Progress House, 34 Stafford Road, Wallington SM6 9AA
Tel./e-mail	0208 773 8111 admin:ppma.co.uk
Fax / Web site	0208 773 0022 www.ppma.co.uk

719	PRODUCE STUDIES LTD
Title	**Omnifarm**
Coverage	An omnibus survey of 1,000 farmers in Great Britain with data on purchases, product awareness, general expenditure, readership etc.
Frequency	Three times a year
Web Facilities	
Cost	On request
Comments	Various other research projects and reports produced.
Address	Northcroft House, West Street, Newbury RG13 1HD
Tel./e-mail	01635 46112
Fax / Web site	01635 43945

720	**PROFESSIONAL PERSONNEL CONSULTANTS**
Title	**PPC High Technology Salary Survey**
Coverage	A survey of salaries and benefits for staff in small high technology companies based on data collected by the company.
Frequency	Annual
Web Facilities	
Cost	£65
Comments	
Address	Godwin House, George Street, Huntingdon PE18 6BU
Tel./e-mail	01480 411111
Fax / Web site	01480 411111

721	**PROFESSIONAL PERSONNEL CONSULTANTS**
Title	**PPC Wage and Salary Survey**
Coverage	A salary and wages survey covering around 60 managerial, administrative, and manual jobs. Based on data collected by the company.
Frequency	Twice yearly
Web Facilities	
Cost	£75
Comments	
Address	Godwin House, George Street, Huntingdon PE18 6BU
Tel./e-mail	01480 411111
Fax / Web site	01480 411111

722	**PROFESSIONAL PERSONNEL CONSULTANTS**
Title	**Review of Directors' Remuneration and Benefits**
Coverage	A survey of directors' salaries and benefits in small- and medium-sized companies employing up to 400 staff. Based on data collected by the company.
Frequency	Annual
Web Facilities	
Cost	£65
Comments	
Address	Godwin House, George Street, Huntingdon PE18 6BU
Tel./e-mail	01480 411111
Fax / Web site	01480 411111

723	PROFESSIONAL PERSONNEL CONSULTANTS
Title	**Salary Survey for Hospitals and Nursing Homes**
Coverage	A survey of salaries and benefits covering 31 job functions in hospitals and nursing homes. Based on data collected by the company.
Frequency	Annual
Web Facilities	
Cost	£145, £75 for participants
Comments	
Address	Godwin House, George Street, Huntingdon PE18 6BU
Tel./e-mail	01480 411111
Fax / Web site	01480 411111

724	PROPERTY INTELLIGENCE PLC
Title	**UK Town and County Focus**
Coverage	A database, available online or on disc, of over 700 UK towns and cities, plus counties. For each town there is a statistical profile including demographic data, projections, employment trends, socio-economic profiles, rents, and unemployment data. Additional information on local plans, major retailers, proximity to other towns, and recent articles on the town. Based on various sources including the population Census, geodemographic data, local information, and property consultants.
Frequency	Continuous
Web Facilities	General details plus paid-for access to service for members on site.
Cost	On request
Comments	Property Intelligence PLC offers various property, and related databases.
Address	Ingram House, 13-15 John Adam Street, London WC2N 6LD
Tel./e-mail	0207 839 7684 sales@focusnet.co.uk
Fax / Web site	0207 839 1060 www.focusnet.co.uk

725 PUBLISHERS' ASSOCIATION

Title	**Book Trade Yearbook**
Coverage	Commentary followed by a statistical section covering publishers' sales, consumer expenditure, prices, exports, export prices. Statistics in the latest issue cover seven or eight years in many tables.
Frequency	Annual
Web Facilities	Key statistics free on site under Key Facts and Figures pages.
Cost	£50, £10 to members
Comments	Also publishes various one-off reports.
Address	1 Kingsway, London WC2B 6XF
Tel./e-mail	0207 565 7474 mail@publishers.org.uk
Fax / Web site	0207 836 4543 www.publishers.org.uk

726 PURCON CONSULTANTS LTD

Title	**Purcon Index**
Coverage	A salary survey prepared from the Purcon Register which has records of over 10,000 candidates for jobs in purchasing.
Frequency	Twice yearly
Web Facilities	Online ordering facilities on site.
Cost	£50 per copy, £90 annual subscription
Comments	Published in March and September.
Address	Prospect House, Repton Place, Amersham HP7 9LP
Tel./e-mail	01494 737300 info@purcon.co.uk
Fax / Web site	01494 737333 www.purcon.co.uk

727 PURCON CONSULTANTS LTD

Title	**Purcon - IT Commodity Index**
Coverage	A regular salary survey for IT procurement professionals.
Frequency	Twice yearly
Web Facilities	Online ordering facilities on site.
Cost	£25 each, £45 annual subscription
Comments	Published in January and July.
Address	Prospect House, Repton Place, Amersham HP7 9LP
Tel./e-mail	01494 737300 info@purcon.co.uk
Fax / Web site	01494 737333 www.purcon.co.uk

728	QUANTIME LTD
Title	**UK Labour Force Surveys**
Coverage	Quantime is an agent for the UK government's labour force statistics and it can provide data for specific requests or produce regular packages for clients. The original data is based on a sample survey of 65,000 households.
Frequency	Regular
Web Facilities	General details of services and statistics available on site.
Cost	Varies according to information required
Comments	Available in various formats including a dial-up database, information sheets, discs, hard copy reports etc.
Address	Maygrove House, 67 Maygrove Road, London NW6 2EG
Tel./e-mail	0207 625 7111
Fax / Web site	0207 624 5293 www.quantime.co.uk

729	QUARRY PRODUCTS' ASSOCIATION
Title	**Quarterly Construction Materials Trends**
Coverage	Statistics on the production and use of core products, crushed rock, sand and gravel, asphalt, and ready mixed concrete.
Frequency	Quarterly
Web Facilities	Basic data and commentary every quarter free on site.
Cost	On request
Comments	More detailed statistics are available to members.
Address	156 Buckingham Palace Road, London SW1 9TR
Tel./e-mail	0207 730 8194 info@qpa.org
Fax / Web site	0207 730 4355 www.qpa.org

730	RADIO ADVERTISING BUREAU
Title	**Quarterly Marketplace Report**
Coverage	Audience and revenue results for the commercial radio sector based on research by RAB.
Frequency	Quarterly
Web Facilities	Free access to data and analysis on site, plus news and charts on the market bringing together data from various sources.
Cost	Free
Comments	
Address	The Radiocentre, 72 Shaftesbury Avenue, London W1D 5DU
Tel./e-mail	0207 306 2500 websupport@rab.co.uk
Fax / Web site	www.rab.co.uk

731	**RADIO JOINT AUDIENCE RESEARCH (RAJAR)**
Title	**Radio Audience Listening**
Coverage	Audience figures for BBC radio and national and local commercial radio.
Frequency	Quarterly
Web Facilities	Free summary data from the quarterly surveys on the site. Also paid-for access to detailed data for subscribers.
Cost	£1,100
Comments	
Address	Gainsborough House, 81 Oxford Street, London W1D 2EU
Tel./e-mail	0207 903 5350 info@rajar.co.uk
Fax / Web site	0207 903 5351 www.rajar.co.uk

732	**RECRUITMENT & EMPLOYMENT CONFEDERATION**
Title	**Recruitment Industry Survey**
Coverage	UK sales by the recruitment industry and total industry turnover. Also data broken down by temporary/permament workers. Based on a survey by the federation.
Frequency	Annual
Web Facilities	Online ordering facilities for statistics on the Web site.
Cost	£90 (survey participants receive a free copy)
Comments	Recent name change of organisation from Federation of Recruitment & Employment Services.
Address	36-38 Mortimer Street, London W1N 7RG
Tel./e-mail	0207 462 3260 info@rec.uk.com
Fax / Web site	0207 255 2878 www.rec.uk.com

733	**REED PERSONNEL SERVICES**
Title	**Reed Employment Index**
Coverage	A review of trends in the jobs market with separate indices for temporary employment and permanent employment. Based on information obtained by the company.
Frequency	Monthly
Web Facilities	
Cost	On request
Comments	
Address	6th Floor, Tolworth Tower, Ewell Road, Tolworth KT6 7EL
Tel./e-mail	0208 399 5221
Fax / Web site	0208 399 4930

734	**RESEARCH AND AUDITING SERVICES LTD**
Title	**National Business Omnibus**
Coverage	A regular omnibus survey of 2,000 businesses stratified by SIC code, UK region, and company size.
Frequency	Monthly
Web Facilities	
Cost	On request
Comments	
Address	Monarch House, Victoria Road, London NW3 6RZ
Tel./e-mail	0208 993 2220
Fax / Web site	0208 993 1114

735	**RESEARCH SURVEYS OF GREAT BRITAIN (RSGB)**
Title	**Mailmonitor**
Coverage	A panel of 1,350 households is used to obtain data on the receipt of mail, including direct mail.
Frequency	Quarterly
Web Facilities	
Cost	On request
Comments	Various other consumer surveys carried out.
Address	AGB House, West Gate, London W5 1EL
Tel./e-mail	0208 967 4201 pam.walker@tnagb.com
Fax / Web site	0208 967 4330 www.tnagb.com

736	**RESEARCH SURVEYS OF GREAT BRITAIN (RSGB)**
Title	**Baby Omnibus**
Coverage	Purchasing trends for baby products plus frequency of purchase, price paid, source of purchase, brand share. Also data on advertising awareness, and attitudes to new and existing products and images of products, services, and companies. Based on a sample of 700 mothers and analysis by age, social group, and incidence of birth.
Frequency	Quarterly
Web Facilities	
Cost	On request
Comments	Various other consumer surveys carried out.
Address	AGB House, West Gate, London W5 1EL
Tel./e-mail	0208 967 4201 pam.walker@tnagb.com
Fax / Web site	0208 967 4330 www.tnagb.com

737	RESEARCH SURVEYS OF GREAT BRITAIN (RSGB)
Title	**Omnibus Survey**
Coverage	A weekly omnibus survey based on face-to-face interviews with 2,000 adults. Demographic analysis and socio-economic analysis using the ACORN and MOSAIC classifications.
Frequency	Weekly
Web Facilities	
Cost	On request
Comments	Various other consumer surveys carried out.
Address	AGB House, West Gate, London W5 1EL
Tel./e-mail	0208 967 4201 pam.walker@tnagb.com
Fax / Web site	0208 967 4330 www.tnagb.com

738	RETAIL INTELLIGENCE
Title	**The Retail Rankings**
Coverage	Mainly financial and operating information on specific companies but it also has general statistics on retail sales, by sector, for the latest two years based on estimates produced by the company.
Frequency	Annual
Web Facilities	Details of publications and news on site
Cost	£675
Comments	Also publishes various other reports on UK retailing sectors and European retailing. Now part of Mintel.
Address	18-19 Long Lane, London EC1A 9PL
Tel./e-mail	0207 606 6000 sales@cior.com
Fax / Web site	0207 606 5932 www.cior.com

739	RETAIL INTELLIGENCE
Title	**UK Retail Report**
Coverage	Each report contains a number of surveys of specific retail sectors, with statistics, and most of these surveys are updated twice a year.
Frequency	Ten issues a year
Web Facilities	Details of publications and news on site.
Cost	£595
Comments	Also publishes various other reports on UK retailing sectors and European retailing. Now part of Mintel.
Address	18-19 Long Lane, London EC1A 9PL
Tel./e-mail	0207 606 6000 sales@cior.com
Fax / Web site	0207 606 5932 www.cior.com

740	REWARD GROUP
Title	**Marketing Rewards**
Coverage	Salary and benefits information for all levels of marketing staff and based on a survey of around 1,200 members of the Chartered Institute of Marketing (CIM).
Frequency	Annual
Web Facilities	General details of surveys, online ordering, and paid-for access to data on site.
Cost	£200
Comments	Produced in association with the Chartered Institute of Marketing (CIM) and discounts for members. Published in September. Specific inquiries answered from Reward's data bank.
Address	Reward House, Diamond Way, Stone Business Park, Stone ST15 0SD
Tel./e-mail	01785 813566 enquiries@reward-group.co.uk
Fax / Web site	01785 817007 www.reward-group.co.uk

741	REWARD GROUP
Title	**Clerical and Operative Rewards**
Coverage	A review of all clerical and operative positions analysed by size of company, sector, and geographical area. Based on research by the company.
Frequency	Twice yearly
Web Facilities	General details of surveys, online ordering, and paid-for access to data on site.
Cost	£450
Comments	Published in January and July. Specific inquiries answered from Reward's data bank.
Address	Reward House, Diamond Way, Stone Business Park, Stone ST15 0SD
Tel./e-mail	01785 813566 enquiries@reward-group.co.uk
Fax / Web site	01785 817007 www.reward-group.co.uk

742	REWARD GROUP
Title	**Engineering Rewards**
Coverage	Salary and benefits information for both salaried and hourly paid staff. Based on research by the company across 500 companies.
Frequency	Twice yearly
Web Facilities	General details of surveys, online ordering, and paid-for access to data on site.
Cost	£175
Comments	Published in April and October. Produced for the first time on 2000. Specific inquiries answered from Reward's data bank.
Address	Reward House, Diamond Way, Stone Business Park, Stone ST15 0SD
Tel./e-mail	01785 813566 enquiries@reward-group.co.uk
Fax / Web site	01785 817007 www.reward-group.co.uk

743	REWARD GROUP
Title	**Travel Industry Rewards**
Coverage	Salaries and benefits for a range of job functions in the travel industry. A new survey in 2000.
Frequency	Twice yearly
Web Facilities	General details of surveys, online ordering, and paid-for access to data on site.
Cost	£300
Comments	Published in association with ABTA and discounts for members. Published in November. Specific inquiries answered from Reward's data bank.
Address	Reward House, Diamond Way, Stone Business Park, Stone ST15 0SD
Tel./e-mail	01785 813566 enquiries@reward-group.co.uk
Fax / Web site	01785 817007 www.reward-group.co.uk

744	REWARD GROUP
Title	**Electronics Industry Rewards**
Coverage	Salary information on management, professional, technical, and commercial jobs in the software and electronics sector. Based on research by the company.
Frequency	Twice yearly
Web Facilities	General details of surveys, online ordering, and paid-for access to data on site.
Cost	£500
Comments	Published in March and September. Specific inquiries answered from Reward's data bank.
Address	Reward House, Diamond Way, Stone Business Park, Stone ST15 0SD
Tel./e-mail	01785 813566 enquiries@reward-group.co.uk
Fax / Web site	01785 817007 www.reward-group.co.uk

745	REWARD GROUP
Title	**Research and Development Rewards**
Coverage	An annual report covering basic salaries, total remuneration, and benefits in the R&D field. Based on research by the company.
Frequency	Annual
Web Facilities	General details of surveys, online ordering, and paid-for access to data on site
Cost	£280
Comments	Published in May. Specific inquiries answered from Reward's data bank.
Address	Reward House, Diamond Way, Stone Business Park, Stone ST15 0SD
Tel./e-mail	01785 813566 enquiries@reward-group.co.uk
Fax / Web site	01785 817007 www.reward-group.co.uk

746	REWARD GROUP
Title	**London Secretarial and Clerical Rewards**
Coverage	A salary survey of six types of secretarial jobs in the capital. Based on research by the company.
Frequency	Twice yearly
Web Facilities	General details of surveys, online ordering, and paid-for access to data on site.
Cost	£280
Comments	Published in February and August. Specific inquiries answered from Reward's data bank.
Address	Reward House, Diamond Way, Stone Business Park, Stone ST15 0SD
Tel./e-mail	01785 813566 enquiries@reward-group.co.uk
Fax / Web site	01785 817007 www.reward-group.co.uk

747	REWARD GROUP
Title	**Personnel Rewards**
Coverage	An annual report with details of basic and total pay, company cars and other benefits. Based on research by the company.
Frequency	Annual
Web Facilities	General details of surveys, online ordering, and paid-for access to data on site.
Cost	£295
Comments	Produced in association with the Chartered Institute of Personnel and Development (IPD) and discounts for members. Published in February. Specific inquiries answered from Reward's data bank.
Address	Reward House, Diamond Way, Stone Business Park, Stone ST15 0SD
Tel./e-mail	01785 813566 enquiries@reward-group.co.uk
Fax / Web site	01785 817007 www.reward-group.co.uk

748	REWARD GROUP
Title	**Sales Rewards**
Coverage	An annual review of salaries, bonuses, commission, company cars and other benefits. Based on research by the company.
Frequency	Annual
Web Facilities	General details of surveys, online ordering, and paid-for access to data on site.
Cost	£200
Comments	Produced in association with the Institute of Sales and Marketing Managers (ISSM) and discounts for members. Published in October. Specific inquiries answered from Reward's data bank.
Address	Reward House, Diamond Way, Stone Business Park, Stone ST15 0SD
Tel./e-mail	01785 813566 enquiries@reward-group.co.uk
Fax / Web site	01785 817007 www.reward-group.co.uk
749	REWARD GROUP
Title	**Directors Rewards**
Coverage	Detailed information of salaries and benefits for chairman, managing director, and a wide range of functional directors posts, analysed by company turnover and number of employees. Based on the company's own research.
Frequency	Annual
Web Facilities	General details of surveys, online ordering, and paid-for access to data on site.
Cost	£595
Comments	Produced in association with the Institute of Directors. Published in December. Specific inquiries answered from Reward's data bank.
Address	Reward House, Diamond Way, Stone Business Park, Stone ST15 0SD
Tel./e-mail	01785 813566 enquiries@reward-group.co.uk
Fax / Web site	01785 817007 www.reward-group.co.uk

750	REWARD GROUP
Title	**Management Rewards**
Coverage	A management salary report covering over 115 jobs and including advice, forecasts, and comments on salary movements. Based on the company's own research.
Frequency	Twice yearly
Web Facilities	General details of surveys, online ordering, and paid-for access to data on site.
Cost	£450
Comments	Published in March and September. Specific inquiries answered from Reward's data bank.
Address	Reward House, Diamond Way, Stone Business Park, Stone ST15 0SD
Tel./e-mail	01785 813566 enquiries@reward-group.co.uk
Fax / Web site	01785 817007 www.reward-group.co.uk

751	REWARD GROUP
Title	**Civil Service Rewards**
Coverage	An annual review of salaries and benefits based on data collected from civil service departments around the UK and relevant jobs selected from the company's database.
Frequency	Twice yearly
Web Facilities	General details of surveys, online ordering, and paid-for access to data on site.
Cost	£700
Comments	Published in February and June. Specific inquiries answered by Reward's data bank.
Address	Reward House, Diamond Way, Stone Business Park, Stone ST15 0SD
Tel./e-mail	01785 813566 enquiries@reward-group.co.uk
Fax / Web site	01785 817007 www.reward-group.co.uk

752	REWARD GROUP
Title	**Regional Surveys**
Coverage	Salaries and benefits in 17 regions of the UK. Based on Reward's own survey in key centres.
Frequency	Twice yearly
Web Facilities	General details of surveys, online ordering, and paid-for access to data on site.
Cost	£350 (2 surveys a year for each region)
Comments	Each regional survey is published twice a year. Specific inquiries answered from Reward's data bank.
Address	Reward House, Diamond Way, Stone Business Park, Stone ST15 0SD
Tel./e-mail	01785 813566 enquiries@reward-group.co.uk
Fax / Web site	01785 817007 www.reward-group.co.uk

753	REWARD GROUP
Title	**Charity Rewards**
Coverage	A survey of salaries in the charity sector with analysis by job and level of charity income for full-time employees. Based on research by the company.
Frequency	Annual
Web Facilities	General details of surveys, online ordering, and paid-for access to data on site.
Cost	£270
Comments	Published in September. Specific inquiries answered from Reward's data bank.
Address	Reward House, Diamond Way, Stone Business Park, Stone ST15 0SD
Tel./e-mail	01785 813566 enquiries@reward-group.co.uk
Fax / Web site	01785 817007 www.reward-group.co.uk

754	REWARD GROUP
Title	**IT Rewards**
Coverage	Pay market data for all IT and computing job functions ranging from computing directors to trainee computer operators. Based on research by the company.
Frequency	Twice yearly
Web Facilities	General details of surveys, online ordering, and paid-for access to data on site.
Cost	£175
Comments	Published in March and September. Specific inquiries answered from Reward's data bank.
Address	Reward House, Diamond Way, Stone Business Park, Stone ST15 0SD
Tel./e-mail	01785 813566 enquiries@reward-group.co.uk
Fax / Web site	01785 817007 www.reward-group.co.uk

755	REWARD GROUP
Title	**Distribution and Transport Rewards**
Coverage	Salary information on management, professional, technical, and commercial jobs in the distribution sector. Based on research by the company.
Frequency	Twice yearly
Web Facilities	General details of surveys, online ordering, and paid-for access to data on site.
Cost	£500
Comments	Produced in association with the Institute of Logistics and Transport and discounts for members. Specific inquiries answered by Reward's data bank.
Address	Reward House, Diamond Way, Stone Business Park, Stone ST15 0SD
Tel./e-mail	01785 813566 enquiries@reward-group.co.uk
Fax / Web site	01785 817007 www.reward-group.co.uk

756	REWARD GROUP
Title	**Finance Rewards**
Coverage	Salaries and benefits for financial positions across the UK. Based on research by the company.
Frequency	Annual
Web Facilities	General details of surveys, online ordering, and paid-for access to data on site.
Cost	On request
Comments	
Address	Reward House, Diamond Way, Stone Business Park, Stone ST15 0SD
Tel./e-mail	01785 813566 enquiries@reward-group.co.uk
Fax / Web site	01785 817007 www.reward-group.co.uk

757	RMIF LTD
Title	**New Car Sales by County**
Coverage	A regional and county breakdown of new car sales, in units, for the latest year with the percentage change over the previous year. Sales are broken down into total cars and company cars.
Frequency	Annual
Web Facilities	Free basic statistics on site.
Cost	Free
Comments	RMIF is the Retail Motor Industry Federation.
Address	201 Great Portland Street, London W1N 6AB
Tel./e-mail	0207 580 9122
Fax / Web site	0207 580 6376 www.rmif.co.uk

758	RMIF LTD
Title	**Monthly Statistics**
Coverage	Monthly figures for new car sales, in units, with a breakdown between total cars and company cars.
Frequency	Monthly
Web Facilities	Free basic statistics on site.
Cost	Free
Comments	RMIF is the Retail Motor Industry Federation.
Address	201 Great Portland Street, London W1N 6AB
Tel./e-mail	0207 580 9122
Fax / Web site	0207 580 6376 www.rmif.co.uk

759	ROYAL BANK OF SCOTLAND PLC
Title	**Scottish Retail Sales Monitor**
Coverage	A monthly review of retail sales in Scotland based on data collected by the Bank.
Frequency	Monthly
Web Facilities	Free access to data on the site.
Cost	Free
Comments	Also publishes some UK regional surveys.
Address	42 St Andrew Square, Edinburgh EH2 2YE
Tel./e-mail	0131 523 2393 economics@rbs.co.uk
Fax / Web site	0131 556 8555 www.royalbankscot.co.uk

760	ROYAL BANK OF SCOTLAND PLC
Title	**Monthly Economic Update**
Coverage	A review of general economic trends and analysis of key economic issues.
Frequency	Monthly
Web Facilities	Free access to data on site.
Cost	Free
Comments	Also publishes some UK regional surveys.
Address	42 St Andrew Square, Edinburgh EH2 2YE
Tel./e-mail	0131 523 2393 economics@rbs.co.uk
Fax / Web site	0131 556 8555 www.royalbankscot.co.uk

761	ROYAL BANK OF SCOTLAND PLC
Title	**Royal Bank of Scotland Oil and Gas Index**
Coverage	Data on production from North Sea oil fields and the average daily value of oil production based on a telephone survey of oil field operators. An analysis of the statistics is also included.
Frequency	Monthly
Web Facilities	Free access to data on site.
Cost	Free
Comments	Produced in association with BBC Radio Scotland. Also publishes some UK regional surveys.
Address	42 St Andrew Square, Edinburgh EH2 2YE
Tel./e-mail	0131 523 2393 economics@rbs.co.uk
Fax / Web site	0131 556 8555 www.royalbankscot.co.uk

762	ROYAL BANK OF SCOTLAND PLC
Title	**Update Scotland**
Coverage	A general survey of business and economic conditions in Scotland.
Frequency	Twice yearly
Web Facilities	Free access to data on site.
Cost	Free
Comments	Also publishes some UK regional surveys.
Address	42 St Andrew Square, Edinburgh EH2 2YE
Tel./e-mail	0131 523 2393 economics@rbs.co.uk
Fax / Web site	0131 556 8555 www.royalbankscot.co.uk

763	ROYAL BANK OF SCOTLAND PLC
Title	**Scottish Technology Industry Monitor**
Coverage	Regular survey of trends in the technology sector.
Frequency	Regular
Web Facilities	Free access to data on site.
Cost	Free
Comments	Also publishes some UK regional surveys.
Address	42 St Andrew Square, Edinburgh EH2 2YE
Tel./e-mail	0131 523 2393 economics@rbs.co.uk
Fax / Web site	0131 556 8555 www.royalbankscot.co.uk

764	ROYAL INSTITUTION OF CHARTERED SURVEYORS
Title	**Housing Market Survey**
Coverage	National figures and regional data each month for various types and ages of property. Shows the trends in prices over the previous three months and includes comments on the market situation from estate agents.
Frequency	Monthly
Web Facilities	
Cost	£10
Comments	
Address	12 Great George Street, Parliament Square, London SW1P 3AD
Tel./e-mail	0207 222 7000 publishing@rics.org.uk
Fax / Web site	0207 222 9430 www.rics.org.uk

765	RYDEN
Title	**Scottish Property Review**
Coverage	A review of economic trends in Scotland, with forecasts, is followed by a commentary on the Scottish property market covering Edinburgh, Glasgow, Aberdeen, and Dundee. Specific sections on shops, and industrial and warehouse property. Based primarily on data from the company.
Frequency	Twice yearly
Web Facilities	Free copies of reports can be downloaded from the site.
Cost	Free
Comments	
Address	46 Castle Street, Edinburgh EH2 3BN
Tel./e-mail	0131 225 6612
Fax / Web site	0131 225 5766 www.ryden.co.uk

766	RYDEN
Title	**North East of England Property Review**
Coverage	A review of economic and property trends in the North East. Sections on shops, and industrial and warehouse property.
Frequency	Regular
Web Facilities	Free copies of reports can be downloaded from the site.
Cost	Free
Comments	
Address	46 Castle Street, Edinburgh EH2 3BN
Tel./e-mail	0131 225 6612
Fax / Web site	0131 225 5766 www.ryden.co.uk

767	SALARY SURVEY PUBLICATIONS
Title	**Survey of Appointments' Data and Trends**
Coverage	A generic series title for various surveys of salaries and appointments in a range of sectors including IT, human resources personnel. Most surveys are based on an analysis of advertisements in the press and actual salary data.
Frequency	Regular
Web Facilities	
Cost	On request - typical prices are £295-£325 per survey
Comments	
Address	7 High Street, Lambourn RG17 8XL
Tel./e-mail	01488 72705 ssp@easynet.co.uk
Fax / Web site	

768

	SAMPLE SURVEYS LTD
Title	**Omnicar**
Coverage	A monthly motoring omnibus survey based on a sample of 1,000 motorists. Analysis of purchases, services, DIY, insurance, number of cars in household, engine size, make, model etc.
Frequency	Monthly
Web Facilities	General details of surveys on site.
Cost	On request
Comments	
Address	Mount Offham, Offham, West Malling ME19 5PG
Tel./e-mail	01732 874450 admin@sample-surveys.co.uk
Fax / Web site	01732 875100 www.sample-surveys.co.uk

769

	SCONUL
Title	**UK Higher Education Library Management Statistics**
Coverage	An annual review of management data based on sample returns from SCONUL members.
Frequency	Annual
Web Facilities	Member access to statistics and online ordering facilities on site.
Cost	£10
Comments	Usually published in September/October.
Address	102 Euston Street, London NW1 2HA
Tel./e-mail	0207 387 0317
Fax / Web site	0207 383 3197 www.sconul.ac.uk

770

	SCONUL
Title	**SCONUL Annual Library Statistics**
Coverage	Expenditure and operational trends based on the annual returns from SCONUL libraries. A small amount of text is included.
Frequency	Annual
Web Facilities	Member access to statistics and online ordering facilities on site.
Cost	£35
Comments	Usually published in September/October.
Address	102 Euston Street, London NW1 2HA
Tel./e-mail	0207 387 0317
Fax / Web site	0207 383 3197 www.sconul.ac.uk

771	SCOTCH WHISKY ASSOCIATION
Title	**Statistical Report**
Coverage	Figures on the activities of the industry including production, exports, stocks, and duty paid. Figures for some previous years also given. Based mainly on Central Government statistics with a small amount of original data.
Frequency	Annual
Web Facilities	General details of statistics, basic data, plus online ordering facilities on site.
Cost	£25
Comments	
Address	14 Cork Street, London W15 3NS
Tel./e-mail	0207 629 4384 contact@swa.org.uk
Fax / Web site	0207 493 1398 www.scotch-whisky.org.uk

772	SCOTCH WHISKY ASSOCIATION
Title	**Scotch at a Glance**
Coverage	A breakdown of the top export markets and UK markets for whisky.
Frequency	Annual
Web Facilities	General details, some basic data, and online ordering facilities on site.
Cost	Free
Comments	
Address	14 Cork Street, London W15 3NS
Tel./e-mail	0207 629 4384 contact@swa.org.uk
Fax / Web site	0207 493 1398 www.scotch-whisky.org.uk

773	SCOTTISH COUNCIL DEVELOPMENT AND INDUSTRY
Title	**Survey of Scottish Sales and Exports**
Coverage	Estimates of the value and volume of Scottish manufacturing and exports. Based on a sample of Scottish exporters with a commentary supporting the text.
Frequency	Annual
Web Facilities	General details and some free data on site.
Cost	£25, free to members
Comments	
Address	23 Chester Street, Edinburgh EH3 7AD
Tel./e-mail	0131 225 7911 enquiries@scdi.org.uk
Fax / Web site	0131 220 2116 www.scdi.org.uk

774		SCOTTISH COUNCIL DEVELOPMENT AND INDUSTRY
	Title	**Survey of Scottish Service Sector Exports**
	Coverage	A regular survey of service sector exports.
	Frequency	Annual
	Web Facilities	General details and some free data on site.
	Cost	Free
	Comments	
	Address	23 Chester Street, Edinburgh EH3 7AD
	Tel./e-mail	0131 225 7911 enquiries@scdi.org.uk
	Fax / Web site	0131 220 2116 www.scdi.org.uk

775		SCOTTISH COUNCIL DEVELOPMENT AND INDUSTRY
	Title	**Survey of Scottish Manufacturing Sector Exports**
	Coverage	A regular survey of manufacturing sector exports.
	Frequency	Annual
	Web Facilities	General details and some free data on site.
	Cost	Free
	Comments	
	Address	23 Chester Street, Edinburgh EH3 7AD
	Tel./e-mail	0131 225 7911 enquiries@scdi.org.uk
	Fax / Web site	0131 220 2116 www.scdi.org.uk

776		SCOTTISH COUNCIL DEVELOPMENT AND INDUSTRY
	Title	**Survey of Scottish Primary Sector Exports**
	Coverage	A regular survey of primary sector exports.
	Frequency	Annual
	Web Facilities	General details and some free data on site.
	Cost	Free
	Comments	
	Address	23 Chester Street, Edinburgh EH3 7AD
	Tel./e-mail	0131 225 7911 enquiries@scdi.org.uk
	Fax / Web site	0131 220 2116 www.scdi.org.uk

777	SCREEN PRINTING ASSOCIATION (UK) LTD
Title	**Survey of Trends**
Coverage	A survey of trends in the previous three months and likely trends in the coming three months based on returns from members. Includes data on costs, sales, orders, margins on sales, capital expenditure, employment, and prices.
Frequency	Quarterly
Web Facilities	
Cost	Free to participating members
Comments	
Address	7A West Street, Reigate RH2 9BL
Tel./e-mail	01737 240792
Fax / Web site	01737 240770

778	SEAFISH
Title	**Key Indicators**
Coverage	Key statistics on supplies, household consumption, prices, international trade etc. Based mainly on Central Government sources.
Frequency	Quarterly
Web Facilities	General details plus free summary data and online ordering facilities on site.
Cost	£35, £10 per issue
Comments	Also publishes a European Supplies Bulletin with statistics on specific European countries.
Address	18 Logie Mill, Logie Green Road, Edinburgh EH7 4HG
Tel./e-mail	0131 558 3331 seafish@seafish.co.uk
Fax / Web site	0131 558 1442 www.seafish.co.uk

779	SEAFISH
Title	**United Kingdom Fish Industry Annual Statistics**
Coverage	A compendium of data including landings and aquaculture production, fleet size, trade in fish and fish products, fish processing, household purchases of fish, catering sector. Historical data for at least six years is included in some tables.
Frequency	Annual
Web Facilities	General details plus free summary statistics and online ordering facilities on site.
Cost	£5
Comments	Also publishes a European Supplies Bulletin with statistics on specific European countries.
Address	18 Logie Mill, Logie Green Road, Edinburgh EH7 4HG
Tel./e-mail	0131 558 3331 seafish@seafish.co.uk
Fax / Web site	0131 558 1442 www.seafish.co.uk

780

	SEAFISH
Title	**UK Trade Bulletin**
Coverage	Quantity and value of imports and exports of fish intended for human consumption. The latest month's figures with the year to date and comparative figures for the previous year. Based on Central Government data.
Frequency	Monthly
Web Facilities	General details plus some free summary statistics and online ordering facilities on site.
Cost	£35, £5 per issue
Comments	Also publishes a European Supplies Bulletin with statistics on specific European countries.
Address	18 Logie Mill, Logie Green Road, Edinburgh EH7 4HG
Tel./e-mail	0131 558 3331 seafish@seafish.co.uk
Fax / Web site	0131 558 1442 www.seafish.co.uk

781

	SEAFISH
Title	**United Kingdom Fish Catering Sector Handbook**
Coverage	Published in the same format as the Fish Industry Annual Statistics, the booklet considers 10 sub-sectors of the catering market in detail. Data on total tonnage of fish, the most popular species, distribution channels, type of product.
Frequency	Regular
Web Facilities	General details plus free summary statistics and online ordering facilities on site.
Cost	£5
Comments	Also publishes a European Supplies Bulletin with statistics on specific European countries.
Address	18 Logie Mill, Logie Green Road, Edinburgh EH7 4HG
Tel./e-mail	0131 558 3331 seafish@seafish.co.uk
Fax / Web site	0131 558 1442 www.seafish.co.uk

782	SEAFISH
Title	**Household Fish Consumption in Great Britain**
Coverage	Analysis of sales by species for household consumption, split into fresh/chilled and frozen sales. The statistics are taken from a sample survey of households and comparable data for the previous year is given. Some text supports the data.
Frequency	Quarterly
Web Facilities	General details plus some free summary statistics and online ordering facilities on site.
Cost	£75, £20 per issue
Comments	Also publishes a European Supplies Bulletin with statistics on specific European countries.
Address	18 Logie Mill, Logie Green Road, Edinburgh EH7 4HG
Tel./e-mail	0131 558 3331 seafish@seafish.co.uk
Fax / Web site	0131 558 1442 www.seafish.co.uk

783	SEWELLS INTERNATIONAL
Title	**BCA Used Car Market Report**
Coverage	A regular review of the used car market with details of sales, prices, networks etc.
Frequency	Annual
Web Facilities	Publication details and online ordering facilities on site.
Cost	£99.95
Comments	
Address	Wentworth House, Wentworth Street, Peterborough PE1 1DS
Tel./e-mail	01733 467191
Fax / Web site	01733 467199 www.sewells.co.uk

784	SEWELLS INTERNATIONAL
Title	**Franchise Networks**
Coverage	Statistics on car distribution networks, commercial vehicle distribution networks, dealer groups, and petrol retailing.
Frequency	Annual
Web Facilities	Publication details and online ordering facilities on site.
Cost	£175
Comments	
Address	Wentworth House, Wentworth Street, Peterborough PE1 1DS
Tel./e-mail	01733 467191
Fax / Web site	01733 467199 www.sewells.co.uk

785	SEWELLS INTERNATIONAL
Title	**Retail Motor Industry Pay Guide**
Coverage	A survey of 15,000 dealers and garages with data for 26 franchise dealer jobs. Based on the company's own research.
Frequency	Annual
Web Facilities	Publication details and online ordering facilities on site.
Cost	£94.95
Comments	
Address	Wentworth House, Wentworth Street, Peterborough PE1 1DS
Tel./e-mail	01733 467191
Fax / Web site	01733 467199 www.sewells.co.uk

786	SHARWOOD & CO LTD
Title	**Ethnic Foods Market Review**
Coverage	An analysis of trends in the ethnic foods market with data on total sales, sales by market sector (eg Chinese, Indian etc), sales by type of product, household penetration, and brand shares. Based on research commissioned by the company.
Frequency	Annual
Web Facilities	
Cost	Free
Comments	
Address	J A Sharwood & Co Ltd, Egham TW20 9QG
Tel./e-mail	01784 473000
Fax / Web site	

787	SHAWS' PRICE GUIDES LTD
Title	**Shaws' Retail Price Guide**
Coverage	Fair selling prices, recommended by the manufacturers or by the editors, for 13,000 products divided into various categories, eg groceries, household, medicines, tobacco, etc. Based on regular surveys carried out by the company.
Frequency	Monthly
Web Facilities	
Cost	£18.50
Comments	
Address	Baden House, 7 St Peters Place, Brighton BN1 6TB
Tel./e-mail	01273 680041
Fax / Web site	01273 606588

788	SILK ASSOCIATION OF GREAT BRITAIN
Title	**Serica**
Coverage	Mainly news and comment on the silk industry but it includes some statistics, mainly imports and exports.
Frequency	Six issues per year
Web Facilities	Some free industry data on the site.
Cost	On request
Comments	
Address	5 Portland Place, London W1N 3AA
Tel./e-mail	0207 636 7788 sagb@dial.pipex.com
Fax / Web site	0207 636 7788 www.silk.org.uk
789	SMALL BUSINESS RESEARCH TRUST
Title	**NATWEST/SBRT Quarterly Survey of Small Businesses in Britain**
Coverage	A survey of small businesses in the UK, 95% of which employ less than 50 people. Information on turnover, employment, sales, exports, and business problems plus features on the sector.
Frequency	Quarterly
Web Facilities	General details of publications and online ordering facilities on site.
Cost	£75, £20 per issue
Comments	
Address	Small Business Research Trust, Open University Business School, Walton Hall, Milton Keynes MK7 6AA
Tel./e-mail	01908 655831 oubs-sbrt@open.ac.uk
Fax / Web site	01908 685898 www.sbrt.ac.uk
790	SMALL BUSINESS RESEARCH TRUST
Title	**Lloyds/TSB/SBRT Quarterly Small Business Management Report**
Coverage	A quarterly review of key management practices and problems in SMEs. Each issue includes an opinion survey covering a specific management topic.
Frequency	Quarterly
Web Facilities	General details of publications and online ordering facilities on site.
Cost	£75, £20 per issue
Comments	
Address	Open University, Walton Hall, Milton Keynes MK7 6AA
Tel./e-mail	01908 655831 oubs_sbrt@open.ac.uk
Fax / Web site	01908 685898 www.sbrt.co.uk

791

	SMART CARD CLUB
Title	**The Status of the UK Smart Card Marketplace**
Coverage	A review of the market broken down by applications plus a forecast of card penetration levels for the year 2000. Also includes details of suppliers, the history of the smart card, and technological issues. Mainly text with two main statistical tables.
Frequency	Regular
Web Facilities	Some news and industry data on site.
Cost	
Comments	The first report was produced in 1994 but there are plans for regular updates.
Address	St Andrews House, 59 St Andrews Street, Cambridge CB2 3BZ
Tel./e-mail	01223 329900 info@smartex.com
Fax / Web site	01223 358222 www.smartex.com

792

	SOCIETY OF BUSINESS ECONOMISTS
Title	**Business Economists' Salary Survey**
Coverage	Basic salaries and benefits by employment type, age, and sex. Based on a sample of society members. A commentary supports the data.
Frequency	Annual
Web Facilities	Free access to monthly survey (see other entry) on site.
Cost	£12.50
Comments	Published in the June issue of the Society's journal, 'The Business Economist'.
Address	11 Baytree Walk, Watford WD1 3RX
Tel./e-mail	01923 237287 www.sbe.co.uk
Fax / Web site	

793

	SOCIETY OF BUSINESS ECONOMISTS
Title	**SBE Monthly Economic Outlook and Interest Rate Survey**
Coverage	Based on an opinion survey of a sample of members.
Frequency	Monthly
Web Facilities	Free access to the survey on the site.
Cost	Free
Comments	Emailed to members and others.
Address	11 Baytree Walk, Watford WD1 3RX
Tel./e-mail	01923 237287
Fax / Web site	www.sbe.co.uk

794	SOCIETY OF COUNTY TREASURERS
Title	**Standard Spending Indicators**
Coverage	Statistics on spending on particular services by local authorities in England. Based on returns from the local authorities.
Frequency	Annual
Web Facilities	Details of publications and some basic data freely available on site.
Cost	£40 to members, £50 to local authorities, libraries and universities
Comments	Produced in association with the Society of Municipal Treasurers. Published on behalf of the Society by Somerset County Council.
Address	Financial Planning, Somerset County Council, County Hall, Taunton TA1 4DY
Tel./e-mail	01823 355432 dbford@somerset.gov.uk
Fax / Web site	01823 355554 www.sctnet.org.uk

795	SOCIETY OF MOTOR MANUFACTURERS AND TRADERS (SMMT)
Title	**UK Economic and Market Report**
Coverage	UK economic trends, car industry/market trends, and the global context reviewed through commentary and statistics.
Frequency	Monthly
Web Facilities	General details of publications plus free downloadable UK Market Industry Facts on site.
Cost	On request
Comments	The web site also has free summary information from UK Economic and Market Report.
Address	Automotive Data Services, Forbes House, Halkin Street, London SW1X 7DS
Tel./e-mail	0207 235 7000
Fax / Web site	0207 235 7112 www.smmt.co.uk

796	SOCIETY OF MOTOR MANUFACTURERS' AND TRADERS (SMMT)
Title	**MVRIS - Motor Vehicle Registration Information System**
Coverage	Monthly statistics plus individual tailored reports on vehicle registrations. Data available by model, manufacturer, location etc.
Frequency	Regular
Web Facilities	General details of publications plus free downloadable UK Motor Industry Facts on site.
Cost	Price depends on the nature of the information required
Comments	Also publishes monthly and annual statistics for other European countries and the world market.
Address	Automotive Data Services, Forbes House, Halkin Street, London SW1X 7DS
Tel./e-mail	0207 235 7000
Fax / Web site	0207 235 7112 www.smmt.co.uk

797	SOCIETY OF MOTOR MANUFACTURERS' AND TRADERS (SMMT)
Title	**SMMT Monthly Statistical Review**
Coverage	Production and registrations of motor vehicles by manufacturer and model plus imports and exports of products of the motor industry. Less frequent special tables such as forecasts and the annual motor vehicle census. Based on a combination of Central Government data and the society's own survey.
Frequency	Monthly
Web Facilities	General details of publications plus free downloadable UK Motor Industry Facts on site.
Cost	£150, £115 for members.
Comments	Also publishes monthly and annual statistics for European countries and the world market.
Address	Automotive Data Services, Forbes House, Halkin Street, London SW1X 7DS
Tel./e-mail	0207 235 7000
Fax / Web site	0207 235 7112 www.smmt.co.uk

798	SOCIETY OF MOTOR MANUFACTURERS' AND TRADERS (SMMT)
Title	**MPSS - Motorparc Statistics Service**
Coverage	A service based on the annual census of motor vehicles carried out by the government agency, DVLA.
Frequency	Regular
Web Facilities	General details of publications plus free downloadable UK Motor Industry Facts on site.
Cost	Price depends on the nature of the information required
Comments	Also publishes monthly and annual statistics for other European countries and the world market.
Address	Automotive Data Services, Forbes House, Halkin Street, London SW1X 7DS
Tel./e-mail	0207 235 7000
Fax / Web site	0207 235 7112 www.smmt.co.uk

799	SODEXHO
Title	**Sodexho Survey of Children's Eating Habits**
Coverage	A survey of eating habits of children including eating at school, snacks etc. Based on commissioned research.
Frequency	Regular
Web Facilities	
Cost	£75
Comments	Previously known as Gardner Merchant Survey but name changed to Sodexho.
Address	Kenley House, Kenley Lane, Kenley CR8 5ED
Tel./e-mail	01793 512112
Fax / Web site	01793 615075 www.sodexho.co.uk

800	SOIL ASSOCIATION
Title	**Organic Facts and Figures**
Coverage	General data on organic food sales and consumption including some European data.
Frequency	Annual
Web Facilities	Free access to data on the site.
Cost	Free
Comments	Other reports produced and details on Web site.
Address	Bristol House, 40-56 Victoria Street, Bristol BS1 6BY
Tel./e-mail	0117 929 0661 info@soilassociation.org
Fax / Web site	0117 925 2504 www.soilassociation.org

801	SOIL ASSOCIATION
Title	**Organic Food and Farm report**
Coverage	Data and analysis of organic food and farming trends based on data from the association.
Frequency	Regular
Web Facilities	Free access to some data on site.
Cost	On request
Comments	Other reports produced and details on Web site.
Address	Bristol House, 40-56 Victoria Street, Bristol BS1 6BY
Tel./e-mail	0117 929 0661 info@soilassociation.org
Fax / Web site	0117 925 2504 www.soilassociation.org

802	SPON PRESS
Title	**Spon's Landscape and External Works Price Book**
Coverage	Prices and costs covering hard and soft landscapes and external works generally. Based on Spon's own surveys and some other non-official data.
Frequency	Annual
Web Facilities	General details and online ordering facilities on site.
Cost	£80
Comments	Usually published in August.
Address	New Fetter Lane, London EC4P 4EE
Tel./e-mail	0207 583 9855 info.sponpress@sponpress.com
Fax / Web site	0207 842 2300 www.pricebooks.co.uk

803	SPON PRESS
Title	**Spon's Railway Construction Price Book**
Coverage	Annual rail cost information based on Spon's own surveys.
Frequency	Annual
Web Facilities	General details and online ordering facilities on site.
Cost	£125
Comments	Usually published in September.
Address	New Fetter Lane, London EC4P 4EE
Tel./e-mail	0207 583 9855 info.sponpress@sponpress.com
Fax / Web site	0207 842 2300 www.pricebooks.co.uk

804	SPON PRESS
Title	**Spon's Architects' and Builders' Price Book**
Coverage	Prices of materials, prices for measured work and rates of wages. Based mainly on Spon's own surveys with additional data from other non-official sources.
Frequency	Annual
Web Facilities	General details and online ordering facilities on site.
Cost	£110
Comments	Usually published in August.
Address	New Fetter Lane, London EC4P 4EE
Tel./e-mail	0207 583 9855 info.sponpress@sponpress.com
Fax / Web site	0207 842 2300 www.pricebooks.co.uk

805	SPON PRESS
Title	**Spon's House Improvements Price Book**
Coverage	Prices of house improvement services and materials. Based on Spon's own surveys.
Frequency	Annual
Web Facilities	General details and online ordering facilities on site.
Cost	£42.50
Comments	
Address	New Fetter Lane, London EC4P 4EE
Tel./e-mail	0207 583 9855 info.sponpress@sponpress.com
Fax / Web site	0207 842 2300 www.pricebooks.co.uk

806	SPON PRESS
Title	**Spon's Mechanical and Electrical Services Price Book**
Coverage	Prices and costs of heating, lighting, ventilation, air conditioning, and other service items in industrial and commercial property. Based on Spon's own surveys plus other non-official sources.
Frequency	Annual
Web Facilities	General details and online ordering facilities on site.
Cost	£110
Comments	Usually published in August.
Address	New Fetter Lane, London EC4P 4EE
Tel./e-mail	0207 583 9855 info.sponpress@sponpress.com
Fax / Web site	0207 842 2300 www.pricebooks.co.uk

807	SPON PRESS
Title	**Spon's Civil Engineering and Highway Works Price Book**
Coverage	Prices and costs of building, services, engineering, external work, landscaping etc. Based on Spon's own surveys and other non-official sources.
Frequency	Annual
Web Facilities	General details and online ordering facilities on site.
Cost	£120
Comments	Usually published in March.
Address	New Fetter Lane, London EC4P 4EE
Tel./e-mail	0207 583 9855 info.sponpress@sponpress.com
Fax / Web site	0207 842 2300 www.pricebooks.co.uk

808	SPORTS MARKETING SURVEYS
Title	**Sports Syndicated Surveys**
Coverage	Various syndicated surveys on a range of sports including running, football, golf, racing, fitness.
Frequency	Regular
Web Facilities	General details of services and some summary data on site.
Cost	On request
Comments	
Address	The Courtyard, Wisley GU23 6QL
Tel./e-mail	01932 350600 info@sportsmarketingsurveys.com
Fax / Web site	01932 350375 www.sportsmarketingsurveys.com

809	STATIONERY TRADE REVIEW
Title	**Reference Book and Buyers' Guide**
Coverage	The annual handbook for the stationery industry which includes an overview of the market and trends in the previous year. Includes market information on business machines, social stationery, and office products. Based on the journal's regular survey of manufacturers.
Frequency	Annual
Web Facilities	
Cost	£45
Comments	
Address	Nexus Media Ltd, Nexus House, Azalea Drive, Swanley BR8 8HY
Tel./e-mail	01322 660070 alison.bowles@nexusmedia.com
Fax / Web site	01322 667633 www.nexusmedia.com

810	SURVEY RESEARCH ASSOCIATES
Title	**SRA Omnibus Survey**
Coverage	A multi-client survey covering various topics and based on a sample size of 1,500 adults. Interviews are carried out in the home.
Frequency	Fortnightly
Web Facilities	
Cost	On request
Comments	
Address	Tower House, Southampton Street, London WC2E 7HN
Tel./e-mail	0207 612 0369
Fax / Web site	0207 612 0361

811	SYSTEM THREE SCOTLAND
Title	**Scottish Opinion Survey**
Coverage	A regular survey monitoring opinion, marketing, and advertising activity in Scotland. Based on a sample of 1,000 adults.
Frequency	Monthly
Web Facilities	
Cost	On request
Comments	
Address	6 Hill Street, Edinburgh EH2 3JZ
Tel./e-mail	0131 220 1178
Fax / Web site	0131 220 1181

812	TAS PUBLICATIONS AND EVENTS LTD
Title	**Bus Industry Monitor**
Coverage	A four-volume report with individual volumes on the market, public spending and invetsment on transport, vehicles and equipment, industry resources.
Frequency	Annual with quarterly updates
Web Facilities	General details of publications, and online ordering facilities, on site.
Cost	£249
Comments	
Address	Ross Holme, West End, Long Preston, Skipton BD23 4QL
Tel./e-mail	01729 840756 info@tas-passtrans.co.uk
Fax / Web site	01729 840705 www.tas-passtrans.co.uk

813	TAS PUBLICATIONS AND EVENTS LTD
Title	**Rail Finance Monitor**
Coverage	A review of financial trends in, and the financial position of, the rail sector.
Frequency	Annual
Web Facilities	General details of publications, and online ordering facilities on site.
Cost	£99
Comments	
Address	Ross Holme, West End, Long Preston, Skipton BD23 4QL
Tel./e-mail	01729 840756 info@tas-passtrans.co.uk
Fax / Web site	01729 840705 www.tas-passtrans.co.uk

814	TAS PUBLICATIONS AND EVENTS LTD
Title	**Rail Industry Monitor**
Coverage	A review of rail industry trends including the market, public spending and investment, vehicles and equipment, and industry performance.
Frequency	Annual
Web Facilities	General details of publications, and online ordering facilities, on site.
Cost	£199
Comments	
Address	Ross Holme, West End, Long Preston, Skipton BD23 4QL
Tel./e-mail	01729 840756 info@tas-passtrans.co.uk
Fax / Web site	01729 840705 www.tas-passtrans.co.uk

815	TATE & LYLE SPECIALITY SWEETENERS
Title	**Sucralose Soft Drinks Report**
Coverage	Data and commentary on drinks by type, packaging trends, industrial structure, market outlook. Ten years data in some tables.
Frequency	Annual
Web Facilities	Free copy can be downloaded from the site.
Cost	Free to trade.
Comments	
Address	The Science & Technology Centre, Earley Gate, Whiteknights, Reading RG6 6BZ
Tel./e-mail	0118 925 2929 sucralose@tateandlyle.com
Fax / Web site	0118 926 8008 www.sucralose.co.uk

816	TAYLOR NELSON SOFRES
Title	**Personal Care Panel**
Coverage	A twice-yearly consumer panel covering purchases of cosmetics and toiletries based on a sample of 4,000.
Frequency	Twice yearly
Web Facilities	Services details and some summary data on site.
Cost	On request
Comments	Various other research services available.
Address	Westgate, London W5 1VA
Tel./e-mail	0208 967 0007 research@tnsofres.com
Fax / Web site	0208 967 4060 www.tnsofres.com

817	TAYLOR NELSON SOFRES
Title	**Omnimas**
Coverage	Omnibus survey based on a sample of 2,000 adults every week. Face-to-face interviews in the home.
Frequency	Weekly
Web Facilities	Services details and some summary data on site.
Cost	On request
Comments	Various other research services available.
Address	Westgate, London W5 1VA
Tel./e-mail	0208 967 0007 research@tnsofres.com
Fax / Web site	0208 967 4060 www.tnsofres.com

818	TAYLOR NELSON SOFRES
Title	**SuperPanel**
Coverage	Weekly omnibus survey based on a sample of 10,000 homes and covering product areas in the packaged groceries, fresh foods, and toiletries markets.
Frequency	Weekly
Web Facilities	Services details and some summary data on site.
Cost	On request
Comments	Various other research services available.
Address	Westgate, London W5 1VA
Tel./e-mail	0208 967 0007 research@tnsofres.com
Fax / Web site	0208 967 4060 www.tnsofres.com

819	**TAYLOR NELSON SOFRES**
Title	**Family Food Panel**
Coverage	Monthly omnibus survey of 4,200 homes monitoring food and drink consumption.
Frequency	Monthly
Web Facilities	Services details and some summary data on site.
Cost	On request
Comments	Various other research services available.
Address	Westgate, London W5 1VA
Tel./e-mail	0208 967 0007 research@tnsofres.com
Fax / Web site	0208 967 4060 www.tnsofres.com

820	**TAYLOR NELSON SOFRES**
Title	**Impulse**
Coverage	Monthly omnibus survey based on a sample of 4,300 individuals and covering impulse buying and casual purchases.
Frequency	Monthly
Web Facilities	Services details and some summary data on site.
Cost	On request
Comments	Various other research services available.
Address	Westgate, London W5 1VA
Tel./e-mail	0208 967 0007 research@tnsofres.com
Fax / Web site	0208 967 4060 www.tnsofres.com

821	**TELECOMMUNICATIONS INDUSTRY ASSOCIATION**
Title	**Telecommunication Yearbook**
Coverage	Statistics on the industry based primarily on research by the association.
Frequency	Regular
Web Facilities	General details of publications, news, and online ordering facilities on site.
Cost	£70
Comments	Usually only available to members but requests from others considered. Price refers to non-member price.
Address	Douglas House, 32-34 Simpson Road, Fenny Stratford, Milton Keynes MK1 1BQ
Tel./e-mail	01908 645000 info@tia.org.uk
Fax / Web site	01908 632263 www.tia.org.uk

822	**TELMAR COMMUNICATIONS LTD**
Title	**Telmar Databases**
Coverage	Telmar has access to various media and consumer databases containing statistics, including the British Business Survey (see other entry).
Frequency	Continuous
Web Facilities	
Cost	On request, and depending on the nature and range of information required
Comments	
Address	21 Ivor Place, London NW1
Tel./e-mail	0207 224 9992
Fax / Web site	0207 723 5265

823	**THE GROCER**
Title	**Grocer Price List**
Coverage	A supplement usually produced on the first Saturday of each month giving detailed prices for various foods and grocery products.
Frequency	Monthly supplement to a weekly journal
Web Facilities	
Cost	£45, £1.30 per issue
Comments	'The Grocer' also has regular market surveys of the main food and non-food markets.
Address	William Reed Publishing Ltd, Broadfield Park, Crawley RH11 9RT
Tel./e-mail	01293 610259 grocer.editorial@william-reed.co.uk
Fax / Web site	01293 610333 www.william-reed.co.uk

824

	THE GROCER
Title	**Market Figures**
Coverage	Prices of various foods including vegetables, meat, salad, cheese, egg, butter, lard etc. Based on various non-official sources with some supporting text.
Frequency	Weekly in a weekly journal
Web Facilities	
Cost	£45, £1.30 per issue
Comments	'The Grocer' also has regular market surveys of the main food and non-food markets.
Address	William Reed Publishing Ltd, Broadfield Park, Crawley RH11 9RT
Tel./e-mail	01293 610259 grocer.editorial@william-reed.co.uk
Fax / Web site	01293 610333 www.william-reed.co.uk

825

	THE HBC LTD
Title	**Home Facts & Fotos: Consumer Lifestyle**
Coverage	Data and a photographic report on home design, decorating, and colour.
Frequency	Annual
Web Facilities	
Cost	£1,750
Comments	
Address	45 Parkfield Road, Coleshill, Birmingham B46 3LD
Tel./e-mail	01675 464216 hbc@easynet.co.uk
Fax / Web site	01675 467524

826

	THE HBC LTD
Title	**UK Housewares Datapack**
Coverage	Market information on 85 product sectors classified as non-electrical housewares used in the kitchen. Over 900 pages of analysis and data based on research by the company.
Frequency	Annual
Web Facilities	
Cost	£2,950
Comments	Also undertakes commissioned research on the housewares sector. Previously known as the Housewares Business Centre.
Address	45 Parkfield Road, Coleshill, Birmingham B46 3LD
Tel./e-mail	01675 464216 hbc@easynet.co.uk
Fax / Web site	01675 467524

827	**TIMBER TRADES JOURNAL**
Title	**Markets**
Coverage	Various statistics on timber and wood consumption, trade, prices etc. Different statistics appear each week and based on various sources.
Frequency	Weekly in a weekly journal
Web Facilities	Free access to market reports and news on site.
Cost	£129
Comments	
Address	Polygon Media Ltd, Tubs Hill House, London Road, Sevenoaks TN13 1BY
Tel./e-mail	01732 470042
Fax / Web site	01732 470049 www.worldwidewood.com

828	**TIN INTERNATIONAL**
Title	**LME Prices/Stocks/Turnover**
Coverage	Prices, stocks, and turnover of tin on the London Metal Exchange plus a general market report.
Frequency	Monthly in a monthly journal
Web Facilities	
Cost	£120
Comments	
Address	Tin Magazines Ltd, Kingston Lane, Uxbridge UB8 3PJ
Tel./e-mail	01895 272406 info@tininternational.com
Fax / Web site	01895 251841 www.tininternational.com

829	**TOBACCO MANUFACTURERS' ASSOCIATION**
Title	**Factbook of UK/EU Statistics on Tobacco**
Coverage	Statistics and commentary on the tobacco industry with tables covering the market, taxes, employment, sponsorship, and advertising. Based on various sources.
Frequency	Regular
Web Facilities	Free access to data on site.
Cost	Free
Comments	
Address	55 Tufton Street, London SW1P 3QL
Tel./e-mail	0207 544 0108 information@the-tma.org.uk
Fax / Web site	0207 544 0117 www.the-tma.org.uk

830	TOP PAY RESEARCH GROUP
Title	**Independent Chairman and Non-Executive Directors' Survey**
Coverage	Based on over 1,400 interviews per year, a survey of pay for board chairs and non-executive directors.
Frequency	Annual
Web Facilities	Free summary data on site and details of other services.
Cost	£60
Comments	Other surveys and services available.
Address	9 Savoy Street, London WC2R 0BA
Tel./e-mail	0207 836 5831 pbrown@toppay.co.uk
Fax / Web site	0207 379 3230 www.toppay.co.uk
831	TRAVEL AND TOURISM RESEARCH LTD
Title	**UK Airlines Travel Trade Image Survey**
Coverage	Examines travel agents' images of the main international airlines. Annual report compares latest annual results with some previous years.
Frequency	Annual
Web Facilities	News and report details on site.
Cost	£5,000
Comments	Now part of the Mintel Group.
Address	18-19 Long Lane, London EC1A 9HE
Tel./e-mail	0207 606 6000 sales@t-ti.com
Fax / Web site	0207 606 5932 www.t-ti.com
832	TRAVEL AND TOURISM RESEARCH LTD
Title	**Travel Agents' Omnibus Survey**
Coverage	A survey of travel agency staff with a sample of approximately 200 for each survey.
Frequency	Six issues a year
Web Facilities	News and report details on site.
Cost	On request
Comments	Now part of the Mintel Group.
Address	18-19 Long Lane, London EC1A 9HE
Tel./e-mail	0207 606 6000 sales@t-ti.com
Fax / Web site	0207 606 5932 www.t-ti.com

833	TREBOR BASSETT LTD
Title	**20-- Confectionery Review**
Coverage	Figures for recent years on the confectionery market with data on specific sectors, eg chocolate, sugar, seasonal sales etc. Data on key brands, trade sector performance, advertising, retailing, the consumer. Includes a supporting commentary.
Frequency	Annual
Web Facilities	
Cost	Free to the trade, £10 to others
Comments	
Address	Hertford Place, Denham Way, Maple Cross WD3 2XB
Tel./e-mail	01923 896565
Fax / Web site	www.cadburyschweppes.com

834	ULSTER MARKETING SURVEYS
Title	**Northern Ireland Omnibus**
Coverage	A regular survey of 1,100 adults in Northern Ireland based on face-to-face interviews in the home. Covers consumer markets for both products and services.
Frequency	Twice monthly
Web Facilities	General details on the site.
Cost	On request
Comments	
Address	115 University Street, Belfast BT7 1HP
Tel./e-mail	02890 231060 vmoore@ums-research.com
Fax / Web site	02890 243887 www.ums-research.com

835	ULSTER MARKETING SURVEYS
Title	**Internet Usage in Northern Ireland**
Coverage	A review of Internet usage and penetration in Northern Ireland based on original research.
Frequency	Annual
Web Facilities	General details on the site.
Cost	£80
Comments	
Address	115 University Street, Belfast BT7 1HP
Tel./e-mail	02890 231060 vmoore@ums-research.com
Fax / Web site	02890 243887 www.ums-research.com

836

	ULSTER MARKETING SURVEYS
Title	**Northern Ireland Car Market**
Coverage	A review of the car market in Northern Ireland based on original research.
Frequency	Annual
Web Facilities	General details on the site.
Cost	£160
Comments	
Address	115 University Street, Belfast BT7 1HP
Tel./e-mail	02890 231060 vmoore@ums-research.com
Fax / Web site	02890 243887 www.ums-research.com

837

	UNITED KINGDOM AGRICULTURAL SUPPLY TRADE ASSOCIATION LTD (UKASTA)
Title	**Annual Report**
Coverage	Includes some data on use of raw materials, feedstuffs, and compounds.
Frequency	Annual
Web Facilities	
Cost	Free
Comments	
Address	3 Whitehall Court, London SW1A 2EQ
Tel./e-mail	0207 930 3611 enquiries@ukasta.org.uk
Fax / Web site	0207 930 3952 www.ukasta.org.uk

838

	UNIVERSITY OF DURHAM BUSINESS SCHOOL
Title	**Small Business Trends**
Coverage	Detailed analysis and statistics on SMEs with sections on general trends, SMEs by industrial and service sector, and future trends. Based on an analysis of various sources.
Frequency	Every two years
Web Facilities	
Cost	On request
Comments	
Address	Mill Hill Lane, Durham DH1 3LB
Tel./e-mail	0191 374 2211
Fax / Web site	0191 374 3748

839

UNIVERSITY OF NOTTINGHAM BUSINESS SCHOOL, CENTRE FOR MANAGEMENT BUY-OUT RESEARCH

Title	**Management Buy-Out Quarterly Review**
Coverage	A market overview and commentary on recent market trends with some statistics on buy-outs.
Frequency	Quarterly
Web Facilities	
Cost	£350, £100 per issue
Comments	The centre was founded by Deloitte & Touche and Barclays Private Equity Ltd.
Address	University of Nottingham, Jubilee Campus, Wollaton Road, Nottingham NG8 1BB
Tel./e-mail	0115 9515493 Mike.Wright/Andrew.Burrows@nottingham.a
Fax / Web site	0115 9515204 www.nottingham.ac.uk/unbs/cmbor.html

840

UNIVERSITY OF READING, DEPARTMENT OF AGRICULTURAL ECONOMICS AND MANAGEMENT

Title	**Horticultural Business Data**
Coverage	Analysis and statistics for three business groups - glasshouse holdings, vegetable and mixed horticultural holdings, and fruit holdings. Based largely on the university's survey supplemented by some Central Government data.
Frequency	Annual
Web Facilities	
Cost	£14
Comments	
Address	4 Earley Gate, Whiteknights Road, Reading RG6 6AR
Tel./e-mail	0118 987 5123 aedept@reading.ac.uk
Fax / Web site	0118 975 6467

841

UNIVERSITY OF READING, DEPARTMENT OF AGRICULTURAL ECONOMICS AND MANAGEMENT

Title	**Farm Managers in 20-- - Their Jobs and Their Pay**
Coverage	A regular analysis of the work of farm staff and wages trends.
Frequency	Regular
Web Facilities	
Cost	£18
Comments	Published in 1995 followed by another issue in 1999.
Address	4 Earley Gate, Whiteknights Road, Reading RG6 6AR
Tel./e-mail	01734 875 5123 aedept@reading.ac.uk
Fax / Web site	01734 975 6467

842	UNIVERSITY OF READING, DEPARTMENT OF AGRICULTURAL ECONOMICS AND MANAGEMENT
Title	**Farm Business Data**
Coverage	Based partly on a survey carried out by the university and summaries of other surveys, the report analyses performance trends in the farming sector.
Frequency	Annual
Web Facilities	
Cost	£14
Comments	
Address	4 Earley Gate, Whiteknights Road, Reading RG6 6AR
Tel./e-mail	0118 9875123 aedept@reading.ac.uk
Fax / Web site	0118 9756467
843	UNIVERSITY OF WARWICK, CENTRE FOR RESEARCH IN ETHNIC RELATIONS
Title	**National Ethnic Minority Data Archive**
Coverage	A database of statistics on the UK's ethnic minority population, largely based on the 1991 population Census. Various reports are published from the database on specific topics, eg economic activity, age/sex characteristics, households, demographic distribution etc.
Frequency	Continuous
Web Facilities	Online ordering facilities for various publications on Web site.
Cost	On request
Comments	
Address	University of Warwick, Gibbett Hill Road, Coventry CV4 7AL
Tel./e-mail	02476 524869 crer@warwick.ac.uk
Fax / Web site	02476 524324 www.warwick.ac.uk/CRER

844	**UNIVERSITY OF WARWICK, INSTITUTE FOR EMPLOYMENT RESEARCH**
Title	**IER Bulletin**
Coverage	Contains regular data and analysis on labour market trends and general economic trends with features on specific aspects of the labour market. Includes regional, sector data and some forecasts of employment trends.
Frequency	Six times a year
Web Facilities	Free access to some statistics, plus online ordering facilities for publications, on site.
Cost	£30, £6 per issue
Comments	
Address	University of Warwick, Gibbett Hill Road, Coventry CV4 7AL
Tel./e-mail	02476 524127 ier@warwick.ac.uk
Fax / Web site	02476 524241 www.warwick.ac.uk/ier
845	**UNIVERSITY OF YORK, CENTRE FOR HOUSING POLICY**
Title	**University of York Index of Private Rents and Yields**
Coverage	Statistics on average rents and yields with regional data and data for local authority areas. There is also a Valuations Index and a Transactions Index.
Frequency	Quarterly
Web Facilities	General details of statistics on site.
Cost	£200
Comments	Published in partnership with the Association of Residential Letting Agents and other agents, Halifax, and the Rent Officer Service.
Address	University of York, York YO10 5DD
Tel./e-mail	01904 433691 jd19@york.ac.uk
Fax / Web site	01904 432318 www.york.ac.uk/inst/chp/
846	**VENTURE CAPITAL REPORTS**
Title	**The Venture Capital Report Guide to Venture Capital in the UK and Europe**
Coverage	General review of the venture capital sector with statistics on total trends and details of specific companies.
Frequency	Annual
Web Facilities	
Cost	£106
Comments	
Address	Boston Road, Henley-on-Thames RG9 1DY
Tel./e-mail	01491 579999
Fax / Web site	01491 579825

847	VERDICT RESEARCH LTD
Title	**Verdict on Clothing Discounters**
Coverage	Analysis and statistics on market trends and value, consumer spending, key players, and the issues affecting the sector. Based on a combination of published data and original research.
Frequency	Annual
Web Facilities	General details of all publications, paid for online access to data and reports.
Cost	£990
Comments	Also publishes monthly newsletters on retailing in the UK, USA, and Europe.
Address	Newlands House, 40 Berners Street, London W1P 4DX
Tel./e-mail	0207 255 6400 retail@verdict.co.uk
Fax / Web site	0207 637 5951 www.verdict.co.uk

848	VERDICT RESEARCH LTD
Title	**Verdict on Childrens Retailing**
Coverage	Analysis and statistics on market trends and value, consumer spending, key players, and the issues affecting the sector. Based on a combination of published data and original research.
Frequency	Annual
Web Facilities	General details of all publications, paid for online access to research, and free executive summaries.
Cost	£990
Comments	Also publishes monthly newsletters on retailing in the UK, USA, and Europe.
Address	Newlands House, 40 Berners Street, London W1P 4DX
Tel./e-mail	0207 255 6400 retail@verdict.co.uk
Fax / Web site	0207 637 5951 www.verdict.co.uk

849	VERDICT RESEARCH LTD
Title	**Verdict on Womenswear Retailing**
Coverage	Analysis and statistics on market trends and value, consumer spending, key players, and the issues affecting the sector. Based on a combination of published data and original research.
Frequency	Annual
Web Facilities	General details of all publications, paid for online access to research, and free executive summaries on site.
Cost	£990
Comments	Also publishes monthly newsletters on retailing in the UK, USA, and Europe.
Address	Newlands House, 40 Berners Street, London W1P 4DX
Tel./e-mail	0207 255 6400 retail@verdict.co.uk
Fax / Web site	0207 637 5951 www.verdict.co.uk

850	VERDICT RESEARCH LTD
Title	**Retail Demographics**
Coverage	Analysis and statistics on consumer trends, consumer spending, and the issues affecting retail demographics. Based on a combination of published data and original research.
Frequency	Annual
Web Facilities	General details of all publications, paid for online access to research, and free executive summaries on site.
Cost	£990
Comments	Also publishes monthly newsletters on retailing in the UK, USA, and Europe.
Address	Newlands House, 40 Berners Street, London W1P 4DX
Tel./e-mail	0207 255 6400 retail@verdict.co.uk
Fax / Web site	0207 637 5951 www.verdict.co.uk
851	VERDICT RESEARCH LTD
Title	**Verdict on Grocers and Supermarkets**
Coverage	Analysis and statistics on market trends and value, consumer spending, key players, and the issues affecting the sector. Based on a combination of published data and original research.
Frequency	Annual
Web Facilities	General details of all publications, paid for online access to research, and free executive summaries.
Cost	£990
Comments	Also publishes monthly newsletters on retailing trends in the UK, USA, and Europe.
Address	Newlands House, 40 Berners Street, London W1P 4DX
Tel./e-mail	0207 255 6400 retail@verdict.co.uk
Fax / Web site	0207 637 5951 www.verdict.co.uk
852	VERDICT RESEARCH LTD
Title	**Verdict on Housewares Retailers**
Coverage	Analysis and statistics on market trends and value, consumer spending, key players, and the issues affecting the sector. Based on a combination of published data and original research.
Frequency	Annual
Web Facilities	General details of all publications, paid for online access to research, and free executive summaries on site.
Cost	£990
Comments	Also publishes monthly newsletters on retailing trends in the UK, USA, and Europe.
Address	Newlands House, 40 Berners Street, London W1P 4DX
Tel./e-mail	0207 255 6400 retail@verdict.co.uk
Fax / Web site	0207 637 5951 www.verdict.co.uk

853	VERDICT RESEARCH LTD
Title	**Verdict on the Internet**
Coverage	Analysis and statistics on market trends and value, consumer spending, key players, and the issues affecting the sector. Based on a combination of published data and original research.
Frequency	Annual
Web Facilities	General details of all research, paid for online access to research, and free executive summaries on site.
Cost	£990
Comments	Also publishes monthly newsletters on retailing in the UK, USA, and Europe.
Address	Newlands House, 40 Berners Street, London W1P 4DX
Tel./e-mail	0207 255 6400 retail@verdict.co.uk
Fax / Web site	0207 637 5951 www.verdict.co.uk
854	VERDICT RESEARCH LTD
Title	**Verdict on Footwear Retailers**
Coverage	Analysis and statistics on market trends and value, consumer spending, key players, and the issues affecting the sector. Based on a combination of published data and original research.
Frequency	Annual
Web Facilities	General details of all publications, paid for online access to research, and free executive summaries on site.
Cost	£990
Comments	Also publishes monthly newsletters on retailing in the UK, USA, and Europe.
Address	Newlands House, 40 Berners Street, London W1P 4DX
Tel./e-mail	0207 255 6400 retail@verdict.co.uk
Fax / Web site	0207 637 5951 www.verdict.co.uk
855	VERDICT RESEARCH LTD
Title	**Verdict on Home Deliveries and Fulfilment**
Coverage	Analysis and statistics on market trends and value, consumer spending, key players, and the issues affecting the sector. Based on a combination of published data and original research.
Frequency	Annual
Web Facilities	General details of all publications, paid for online access to research, and free executive summaries on site.
Cost	£990
Comments	Also publishes monthly newsletters on retailing in the UK, USA, and Europe.
Address	Newlands House, 40 Berners Street, London W1P 4DX
Tel./e-mail	0207 255 6400 retail@verdict.co.uk
Fax / Web site	0207 637 5951 www.verdict.co.uk

856	VERDICT RESEARCH LTD
Title	**Verdict on Electrical Retailers**
Coverage	Analysis and statistics on market trends and value, consumer spending, key players, and the issues affecting the sector. Based on a combination of published data and original research.
Frequency	Annual
Web Facilities	General details of all publications, paid for online access to research, and free executive summaries on site.
Cost	£990
Comments	Also publishes monthly newsletters on retailing in the UK, USA, and Europe.
Address	Newlands House, 40 Berners Street, London W1P 4DX
Tel./e-mail	0207 255 6400 retail@verdict.co.uk
Fax / Web site	0207 637 5951 www.verdict.co.uk
857	VERDICT RESEARCH LTD
Title	**Verdict on DIY Retailers**
Coverage	Analysis and statistics on market trends and value, consumer spending, key players, and the issues affecting the sector. Based on a combination of published data and original research.
Frequency	Annual
Web Facilities	General details of all publications, paid for online access to research, and free executive summaries on site.
Cost	£990
Comments	Also publishes monthly newsletters on retailing in the UK, USA, and Europe.
Address	Newlands House, 40 Berners Street, London W1P 4DX
Tel./e-mail	0207 255 6400 retail@verdict.co.uk
Fax / Web site	0207 637 5951 www.verdict.co.uk
858	VERDICT RESEARCH LTD
Title	**Verdict on Furniture and Floor Coverings Retailers**
Coverage	Analysis and statistics on market trends and value, consumer spending, key players, and the issues affecting the sector. Based on a combination of published data and original research.
Frequency	Annual
Web Facilities	General details of all publications, paid for online access to research, and free executive summaries on site.
Cost	£990
Comments	Also publishes monthly newsletters on retailing in the UK, USA, and Europe.
Address	Newlands House, 40 Berners Street, London W1P 4DX
Tel./e-mail	0207 255 6400 retail@verdict.co.uk
Fax / Web site	0207 637 5951 www.verdict.co.uk

859	VERDICT RESEARCH LTD
Title	**Verdict on Out of Town Retailing**
Coverage	Analysis and statistics on sector trends and value, consumer spending, key players, and the issues affecting the sector. Based on a combination of published data and original research.
Frequency	Annual
Web Facilities	General details of all publications, paid for online access to research, and free executive summaries on site.
Cost	£990
Comments	Also publishes monthly newsletters on retailing in the UK, USA, and Europe.
Address	Newlands House, 40 Berners Street, London W1P 4DX
Tel./e-mail	0207 255 6400 retail@verdict.co.uk
Fax / Web site	0207 637 5951 www.verdict.co.uk

860	VERDICT RESEARCH LTD
Title	**Verdict on Department Stores**
Coverage	Analysis and statistics on market trends and value, consumer spending, key players and the issues affecting the sector. Based on a combination of published data and original research.
Frequency	Annual
Web Facilities	General details of all publications, paid for online access to research, and free executive summaries on site.
Cost	£990
Comments	Also publishes monthly newsletters on retailing in the UK, USA, and Europe.
Address	Newlands House, 40 Berners Street, London W1P 4DX
Tel./e-mail	0207 255 6400 retail@verdict.co.uk
Fax / Web site	0207 637 5951 www.verdict.co.uk

861	VERDICT RESEARCH LTD
Title	**Verdict on CTNs**
Coverage	Analysis and statistics on market trends and value, consumer spending, key players, and the issues affecting the sector. Based on a combination of published data and original research.
Frequency	Annual
Web Facilities	General details of all publications, paid for online access to research, and free executive summaries on site.
Cost	£990
Comments	Also publishes monthly newsletters on retailing in the UK, USA, and Europe.
Address	Newlands House, 40 Berners Street, London W1P 4DX
Tel./e-mail	0207 255 6400 retail@verdict.co.uk
Fax / Web site	0207 637 5951 www.verdict.co.uk

862	VERDICT RESEARCH LTD
Title	**Retailing 20--**
Coverage	Forecasts of retailing trends with overviews and details of prospects for specific sectors.
Frequency	Annual
Web Facilities	General details of all publications, paid for online access to research, and free executive summaries on site.
Cost	£1,250
Comments	Also publishes monthly newsletters on retailing in the UK, USA, and Europe.
Address	Newlands House, 40 Berners Street, London W1P 4DX
Tel./e-mail	0207 255 6400 retail@verdict.co.uk
Fax / Web site	0207 637 5951 www.verdict.co.uk

863	VERDICT RESEARCH LTD
Title	**Verdict on Book Retailers**
Coverage	Analysis and statistics on market trends and value, consumer spending, key players, and the issues affecting the sector. Based on a combination of published data and original research.
Frequency	Annual
Web Facilities	General details of all publications, paid for online access to research, and free executive summaries on site.
Cost	£990
Comments	Also publishes monthly newsletters on retailing in the UK, USA, and Europe.
Address	Newlands House, 40 Berners Street, London W1P 4DX
Tel./e-mail	0207 255 6400 retail@verdict.co.uk
Fax / Web site	0207 637 5951 www.verdict.co.uk

864	VERDICT RESEARCH LTD
Title	**Verdict on Menswear Retailing**
Coverage	Analysis and statistics on market trends and value, consumer spending, key players, and the key issues affecting the sector. Based on a combination of published data and original research.
Frequency	Annual
Web Facilities	General details of all publications, paid for online access to data and reports.
Cost	£990
Comments	Also publishes monthly newsletters on retailing in the UK, USA, and Europe.
Address	Newlands House, 40 Berners Street, London W1P 4DX
Tel./e-mail	0207 255 6400 retail@verdict.co.uk
Fax / Web site	0207 637 5951 www.verdict.co.uk

865	**WALLCOVERING MANUFACTURERS' ASSOCIATION OF GREAT BRITAIN**
Title	**Annual Statistics**
Coverage	Data on the UK wallcoverings sector based on an analysis of returns from member companies.
Frequency	Annual
Web Facilities	
Cost	Free
Comments	Usually only available to members but plans to offer a summary version to the public for a fee.
Address	James House, Bridge Street, Leatherhead KT22 7EP
Tel./e-mail	01372 360660 alison.brown@bcf.co.uk
Fax / Web site	01372 376069
866	**WATSON WYATT WORLDWIDE**
Title	**Employment and Salary Surveys**
Coverage	Various surveys of employment and earnings in sectors such as corporate services, architecture, IT etc.
Frequency	Regular
Web Facilities	
Cost	On request
Comments	
Address	Watson House, London Road, Reigate RH2 9PP
Tel./e-mail	01737 241144
Fax / Web site	01737 241496 www.watsonwyatt.com
867	**WEATHERALL GREEN AND SMITH**
Title	**London Office Market**
Coverage	Details of rates for premium offices in areas of London. Based on data collected by the company.
Frequency	Twice yearly
Web Facilities	Free access to reports on site.
Cost	Free
Comments	Various ad-hoc and international reports also available.
Address	22 Chancery Lane, London WC2A 1LT
Tel./e-mail	0207 738 4000 info@weatheralls.co.uk
Fax / Web site	0207 831 2564 www.weatheralls.co.uk

868	WEATHERALL GREEN AND SMITH
Title	**Office Rent Survey**
Coverage	Details of rates for prime offices in the main regional town centres and business parks. Based on data collected by the company.
Frequency	Twice yearly
Web Facilities	Free access to reports on site.
Cost	Free
Comments	Various ad-hoc and international reports also available.
Address	22 Chancery Lane, London WC2A 1LT
Tel./e-mail	0207 738 4000 info@weatheralls.co.uk
Fax / Web site	0207 831 2564 www.weatheralls.co.uk
869	WEATHERALL GREEN AND SMITH
Title	**Industrial Rents Survey**
Coverage	Details of rates for industrial premises in the UK with regional data. Based on data collected by the company.
Frequency	Regular
Web Facilities	Free access to all reports on site.
Cost	Free
Comments	
Address	22 Chancery Lane, London WC2A 1LT
Tel./e-mail	0207 338 4000 info@weatheralls.co.uk
Fax / Web site	0207 831 2564 www.weatheralls.co.uk
870	WHITBREAD BEER COMPANY
Title	**Whitbread Take-Home Market Report**
Coverage	Commentary and statistics on the take-home market for alcoholic drinks with data on market size, brands, outlets, and current trends. Based primarily on commissioned research.
Frequency	Annual
Web Facilities	
Cost	Free
Comments	
Address	Porter Tun House, Capability Green, Luton LU1 3LW
Tel./e-mail	01582 391166
Fax / Web site	01582 397397 www.whitbread.co.uk

871	WHITBREAD BEER COMPANY
Title	**Whitbread On-Trade Market Report**
Coverage	Commentary and statistics on the on-trade market for alcoholic drinks. Based primarily on commissioned research.
Frequency	Annual
Web Facilities	
Cost	Free
Comments	
Address	Porter Tun House, Capability Green, Luton LU1 3LW
Tel./e-mail	01582 391166
Fax / Web site	01582 397397 www.whitbread.co.uk

872	WILLIAMS DE BROE
Title	**Weekly Economic Indicators**
Coverage	Weekly data on UK economic trends with regular forecasts for the main economic indicators.
Frequency	Weekly
Web Facilities	
Cost	Free
Comments	
Address	6 Broadgate, London EC2M 2RP
Tel./e-mail	0207 898 2402 david.smith@wdebroe.com
Fax / Web site	0207 410 9932

873	WILLIAMS DE BROE
Title	**Quarterly Interest Rate Outlook**
Coverage	Detailed review of interest rates and the UK economic and financial outlook.
Frequency	Quarterly
Web Facilities	
Cost	Free
Comments	
Address	6 Broadgate, London EC2M 2RP
Tel./e-mail	0207 898 2402 david.smith@wdebroe.com
Fax / Web site	0207 410 9932

874	WOOL DEVELOPMENT INTERNATIONAL LTD
Title	**Wool Figures**
Coverage	Statistics covering raw fibres, net domestic availability, the manufacturing process, end products, and consumption. Historical data in most tables and based on various sources.
Frequency	Annual
Web Facilities	
Cost	£20
Comments	
Address	Development Centre, Valley Drive, Ilkley LS29 8PB
Tel./e-mail	01943 603376
Fax / Web site	

875	WORLD TEXTILE PUBLICATIONS
Title	**The Wool Market**
Coverage	Statistics on the prices of wool based on data collected by the journal.
Frequency	Monthly in a monthly journal
Web Facilities	Details of publications and online ordering facilities on site.
Cost	£80
Comments	
Address	World Textile Publications Ltd, Perkin House, 1 Longlands Street, Bradford BD1 2TP
Tel./e-mail	01274 378800 info@world-textile.net
Fax / Web site	01274 378811 www.world-textile.net

876	WORLD TEXTILE PUBLICATIONS
Title	**Weekly Market Report**
Coverage	A weekly summary of prices and news relating to the wool market.
Frequency	Weekly
Web Facilities	Details of publications and online ordering facilities on site.
Cost	£175
Comments	Published every Thursday.
Address	World Textile Publications Ltd, Perkin House, 1 Longlands Street, Bradford BD1 2TP
Tel./e-mail	01274 378800 info@world-textile.net
Fax / Web site	01274 378811 www.world-textile.net

877	YOUTH RESEARCH GROUP
Title	**YORG Survey**
Coverage	A survey of 6 to 16 year-olds in the UK and other European countries. Based on a sample of around 8,000, and the survey is conducted by the company.
Frequency	Annual
Web Facilities	General details and some summary data on site.
Cost	On request
Comments	
Address	4 Pinetrees, Portsmouth Road, Esher KT10 9LF
Tel./e-mail	01372 468554 yorg@supanet.com
Fax / Web site	01372 469788 www.yorg.com

Part II

Title Index

315

Part III

Subject Index

A

Accidents – Packaging   301
Accountants – Salaries   430, 417
Actuaries – Salaries   262
Adhesives   67
Advertising   6, 9, 468, 491, 492, 655
Advertising – Complaints   11
Advertising – Costs   344
Advertising – Employment   490
Advertising – Expenditure   4, 7, 10
Advertising – Forecasts   8, 10
Advertising – Media   344
Advertising – Outdoor   502, 660, 707
Advertising – Poster   502, 660, 707
Aerosols   68, 576
Aggregates   729
Agricultural Machinery   12, 69
Agriculture   213, 719, 842,
Agriculture – Feed   837
Agriculture – Land   372
Agriculture – Omnibus   504
Agriculture – Organic   801
Agriculture – Salaries   841
Agrochemicals   311
Airlines   252, 831
Airports   46, 47, 48, 193, 251
Alcoholic Drinks   65, 408, 476, 771, 772, 870, 871
Alternative Investment   532, 562
Aluminium   18
Architects   21, 22, 639
Archives   216
Arts – Sponsorship   3

Assets – Local Government   205
Audio Equipment   122
Audio Software   122
Automatic Vending   45
Automotives   757, 758
Automotives – Company   599
Automotives – Prices   255

B

Baby Foods   310
Baby Products – Omnibus   736
Bakery Products   376
Banking Staff – Salaries   430
Bankruptcies   32, 336
Banks   49, 50, 77, 78
Banks – Clearings   24, 25, 26, 27, 556
Banks – Lending   76, 394
Banks – Mortgages   79
Barley   66
Beer   65
Benefits   16
Benefits – Housing   238
Biscuits   59, 58
Board   148, 671, 672, 676, 677, 680, 681, 708
Board – Energy Use   674
Board – Forecasts   709
Board – Overseas Trade   678
Boating   109, 110, 111
Books   60, 61, 62, 85, 86, 725
Books – Prices   61, 550
Books – Retailing   63, 863
Bottled Water   138, 254
Bottles – Glass   105
Bread   387

Dictionary of Social and Market Research

Wolfgang J Koschnick

Anyone working in the worlds of social or market research is faced with a daunting plethora of special terms, techniques and jargon covering everything from statistical methods through to specialised advertising and social science terminology.

The *Dictionary of Social and Market Research* has been compiled to provide academics, researchers and professionals with an exhaustive reference work containing definitions for, and explanations of, terms, techniques and concepts from all areas of social and market research. Entries have been selected on the basis of their value in answering questions arising from both the theory and practice of social and market research.

The 2,500 entries in *Dictionary of Social and Market Research* therefore provide an invaluable reference to the terminology that is increasingly encountered in these complex and specialised fields.

Gower

Effective Document Management

Unlocking Corporate Knowledge

Bob Wiggins

Document management is a key to business success. It has a major contribution to play in delivering effective enterprise knowledge management.

This book suggests how this can be achieved in the context of knowledge management and improvement approaches such as business process re-engineering, quality management and Investors in People. The author explains how different technologies can support the life-cycle from creation, indexing, retrieval and communication to disposal or storage. Both strategic and project-level issues are addressed, from developing an information systems strategy, to day-to-day records and document management practice and establishing user requirements for new systems, tendering procedures, system selection and implementation. Contributed case studies in the last chapter relate the real-life benefits of introducing document management and related technologies.

Effective Document Management also provides a useful reference point for information technology terminology and standards, the potential of the Internet and Web-based technologies, and details of major suppliers and products. Sources of further information are provided to help the reader keep up-to-date in this fast changing world.

The book should benefit a range of business management and staff from those senior managers who need to develop coherent and consistent business and IT strategies; to information professionals, such as records managers and librarians who will gain an appreciation of the impact of the technology and of how their particular areas of expertise can best be applied; to system designers, developers and implementers who will better understand the approach to a document management project and the information and knowledge management context in which it has to operate; and finally to users who should be suitably involved at all stages so they can fully exploit the benefits of the delivered systems.

Gower

Global Sourcebook of Address Data Management

A Guide to Address Formats and Data in 194 Countries

Graham Rhind

Which part of this Asian address is the street? What is this accent and is it correct? Which one of these numbers is the postcode? In which language should I be corresponding? How do I salute this person? In which order should I output this name?

For every individual entered on to a world-wide address database, these questions, and others, need to be answered accurately and correctly. This one-stop reference work covering 194 countries will enable you to have the most accurate international marketing database around - one that makes optimal use of the direct marketing activity generated in your company and ensures that your post is delivered to the correct destination and recipient.

Global Sourcebook of Address Data Management provides, for each country, such information as address and postcode formats, postbox names, salutations, personal name patterns, information about languages, diacritical marks, job titles, casing rules, street types and much more. It will make the management and development of any marketing database more efficient, less expensive and will result in fewer errors and, most importantly, will present the best first impression of the company to its potential customers.

No other book can claim to offer such a comprehensive source of essential information for any manager of an international database, from data quality, direct marketers, market researchers through to telemarketing managers.

Gower

Practical International Data Management

A Guide to Working with Global Names and Addresses

Graham Rhind

New data collection methods (such as the Internet), the globalization of economies and improving computer hardware and software are allowing companies to collect information about their customers and prospects in ever greater numbers and from increasingly further afield. Managing this data brings with it a whole raft of practical issues of which most companies are unaware and which, if ignored, are expensive and time-consuming to correct.

This book details the problems that a company is likely to encounter and suggests, where available, solutions and ways of preventing the problems arising. Unlike other books on the subject it tackles data management from the point of view of the data and the reason for creating the database, rather than approaching it as a technical issue. Topics covered include database structure and data format, data cleaning and standardization, language issues, personal name and address component management and de-duplication.

Gower

Sources of Non-Official UK Statistics

Fifth Edition

Compiled by
DAVID MORT
IRN Services Ltd

Gower

First edition published 1985

Published by
Gower Publishing Limited
Gower House
Croft Road
Aldershot
Hampshire GU11 3HR
England

Gower Publishing Company
131 Main Street
Burlington, VT 05401-5600 USA

Gower website: http://www.gowerpub.com

British Library Cataloguing in Publication Data
Sources of non-official UK statistics. - 5th ed.
    1. Great Britain - Statistical services - Directories
    I. Mort, D. (David), 1952- II. Wilkins, Wendy III. Sources of
    unofficial UK statistics
    016.3'141

Library of Congress Control Number: 2001099785

ISBN 0 566 08449 X

Printed and bound in Great Britain by MPG Books Ltd, Bodmin, Cornwall